AF846592

# Legal Mechanisms for Film Financing and Support in China

Jun Wu

# Legal Mechanisms for Film Financing and Support in China

SSAP

Springer

Jun Wu
Institute of Law
Chinese Academy of Social Science
Institute of Law
Beijing, China

ISBN 978-981-95-0921-8 ISBN 978-981-95-0922-5 (eBook)
https://doi.org/10.1007/978-981-95-0922-5

Jointly published with Social Sciences Academic Press
The print edition is not for sale in China (Mainland). Customers from China (Mainland) please order the print book from: Social Sciences Academic Press.
ISBN of the Co-Publisher's edition: 978-7-5097-5173-2

Published with financial support of the Innovation Program of the Chinese Academy of Social Sciences.

Translation from the Chinese language edition: "寻找庇护的艺术?: 电影融资与扶持法律制度" by Jun Wu, © Social Sciences Academic Press 2013. Published by Social Sciences Academic Press. All Rights Reserved.

© Social Sciences Academic Press 2026

This work is subject to copyright. All rights are solely and exclusively licensed by the Publisher, whether the whole or part of the material is concerned, specifically the rights of reprinting, reuse of illustrations, recitation, broadcasting, reproduction on microfilms or in any other physical way, and transmission or information storage and retrieval, electronic adaptation, computer software, or by similar or dissimilar methodology now known or hereafter developed.
The use of general descriptive names, registered names, trademarks, service marks, etc. in this publication does not imply, even in the absence of a specific statement, that such names are exempt from the relevant protective laws and regulations and therefore free for general use.
The publishers, the authors, and the editors are safe to assume that the advice and information in this book are believed to be true and accurate at the date of publication. Neither the publishers nor the authors or the editors give a warranty, express or implied, with respect to the material contained herein or for any errors or omissions that may have been made. The publishers remain neutral with regard to jurisdictional claims in published maps and institutional affiliations.

This Springer imprint is published by the registered company Springer Nature Singapore Pte Ltd.
The registered company address is: 152 Beach Road, #21-01/04 Gateway East, Singapore 189721, Singapore

If disposing of this product, please recycle the paper.

# Preface

Film Industry Promotion Law has been adopted for nearly 9 years. With more regulatory measures adopted to build up a legal framework for a more growth-oriented film industry, one observation is that the industry under the heavy compliance burden is becoming more careful to present its products to the public when facing unnecessary controversy. On the other hand, audience released from the pandemic are longing to see more favourite films in the theatre. The encouraging market potential in this regard reveals the resilience of China's film industry after the COVID-19 pandemic. This complicated landscape of China's film industry cannot be explained without analysing the law and its implementation in the first place. In this sense, with the necessary introduction of the legal background, this book focuses on the relations between the directors, producers, distributors and exhibitors, which is also the issues targeted by Film Industry Promotion Law.

As a huge film market, China's film law and its corresponding regulatory system is always evolving. The whole legal mechanism applied to the film industry can also be found in its deep roots in Chinese cultural tradition, which evolves also during the transit from the past to present. Therefore, the analysis of the film law in China shall not overlook the context of a specific statutory stipulation.

Every law is an answer to the issue in reality. Film law in China is not an exception. With the dominance of Hollywood films on the global market, China has to keep a balance between promoting a dynamic film industry while maintaining its culture reflected in the cinema sector. As we can see in the book, culture pluralism principle inherent in the film import mechanism reveals China's mentality in this regards. In a sense, a confident film culture embraces pluralism, which will oversee a film market to nourish a prosperous and balanced film industry. Actually, culture itself denies homogeneity. A healthy culture system reserves its pluralism via general competition rules and value of tolerance inherent in the legal system. Only when some sub-culture sector feels menacing crisis, can the culture pluralism be raised as an urgent topic for an established patron for its rescue.

Film is a quite unique art. The striking characteristic is that a film production needs huge budget in comparison with the other forms of art. The individuality seems to be so fragile in present mechanism. Since the film at present also needs cinema, a public place, to release its full beauty, it is also an intellectual creation exploited best via commercial use, instead of the private or fair use channel offered for individuals by copyright law. Therefore, film is a most expensive art, even an industrialised one. Hollywood dominance both in EU countries and China may be an issue of the globalisation, which means opportunity as well as crisis.

How has the competition law been tailored for a film? Could individuality override the capital element in a film? This book is trying to find the answer.

I am deeply indebted to Prof. Rolf H. Weber, who encouraged me to take this interesting topic and has offered me the valuable guidance for this writing continuously.

Beijing, China
February 2025

Jun Wu

# Table of Statutes and Documents

## PRC Law

Authors' Rights Law of PRC, adopted by the Standing Committee of People's Congress on 7 September, 1990 and amended by the Standing Committee of People's Congress on 7 October 2001, further amended in 27 October 2010 and 11 November 2020 ("Authors' Rights Law of China" or "Copyright Law of China")

The Film Industry Promotion Law, adopted at the 24th meeting of the Standing Committee of the National People's Congress on 7 November 2016

## PRC Regulations

Regulations on Film Administration of the People's Republic of China adopted by the State Council on 19 June 1996 and amended on 12 December 2001 ("Film Regulations")

Regulations on the Administration of Publishing in the People's Republic of China adopted on 12 December 2001 and amended later on 19 March 2011, 18 July 2013, 29 July 2014, 6 February 2016 and 29 November 2020 by the State Council ("Publishing Regulations")

Regulations on the Administration of Audio-Visual Products in the People's Republic of China adopted on 12 December 2001 and amended later on 19 March 2011, 7 December 2013, 29 November 2020 and 22 November 2024 by the State Council ("Audio-Visual Products Regulations")

Regulations on the Administration of Commercial Performances adopted by the State Council on 7 July 2005 and amended on 22 July 2008 (State Council Order No. 439)

Regulations on the Protection of Information Network Dissemination Rights adopted by the State Council on 18 May 2006 ("Internet Dissemination Regulations")

## PRC Departmental Rules

Interim Measures for the Examination of Film Screenplays and Films, issued and implemented by the Ministry of Culture on 15 December 1974

Measures for the Administration of Imported Films issued by the Ministry of Culture and the General Administration of Customs in 1981 and abolished in 1991

Notice on Implementing a Review and Screening Rating System for Some Films (Guangfa Yingzi [1989] No. 201) issued by the MBRT on 25 March 1989 (hereinafter referred to as the "Rating Notice")

Notice on Clarifying the Management Authority of Film Ticket Prices and Establishing a Special Fund for the Development of the National Film Industry jointly issued by the MRFT, the Ministry of Finance, the State Price Bureau, the State Taxation administration and the Industrial and Commercial Bank of China on 9 January 1991 ("Ticket Price Notice")

Opinions on Deepening the Reform of the Film Industry by the MRFT (Guangfa Film No. [1993] 3) issued in January 1993 ("Decree No. 3")

Interim Provisions on Film Censorship issued by the MRFT on 4 June 1993

Rules on Reforming Feature Film Production Work issued by the MRFT on 5 January 1995

Notice on the Relevant Provisions for Establishing Special Funds to Support the '9550' Project of Film Masterpieces issued by the MRFT and the Ministry of Finance on 18 March 1996 ("Notice on Special Fund for Film Masterpieces")

Administrative Measures for Special Funds for the Development of the National Film Industry issued in 1996 and revised in 2006 by the Ministry of Finance and the SARFT through Document No. 115 of CAI Jiao [2006]

Notice for Film Channel issued by the BRFR on 14 June 1996

Provisions on the Main Creative Personnel of Domestic Feature Films and Co-produced Film issued by the MRFT on 4 November 1996

Provisions on Film Censorship issued by the MRFT on 16 January 1997

Implementation Detailed Rules for Reforming the Film Distribution and Screening Mechanism (Trial) by the National Radio and Television Administration and the Ministry of Culture issued on 18 December 2001

Implementing Rules for the Qualification Certification System of Obtaining the "Film Production License (Single Film)" (Trial) issued by the SARFT on 20 December 2001 ("Single Film Rules")

Interim Provisions on the Administration of Digital Film issued by the SARFT on 7 August 2002

Interim Provisions on the Project Approval of Film Scripts (Synopses) and the Review of Film Productions issued by the SARFT on 28 September 2003, re-issued by the SARFT on 6 July 2004

Provisions on the Administration of Sino-Foreign Cooperative Film Production issued by the SARFT on 8 October 2003 ("Order No. 19")

Provisional Regulations on Access to Qualifications for Film Production, Distribution and Exhibition Operations issued by the SARFT on 29 October 2003 ("Decree No. 20")

Notice on the Issuance of the Detailed Rules for the Implementation of the 'Provisions on the Administration of Films from Sino-Foreign Cooperative Production Sites' (Interim) issued by the SARFT on 27 November 2003

Opinions on Promoting the Development of Radio, Film and Television Industry issued by the SARFT on 8 January 2004

Interim Provisions on Access to Film Business Qualifications jointly issued by the SARFT and the MOFCOM on 10 October 2004, as amended by the SAPPRFT on 28 August 2015 ("Film Business Qualification Provisions")

Provisions on Sino-Foreign Cooperative Film Production issued by the SARFT on 6 July 2004 ("Order No. 31" or "Joint Production Rules")

Administrative Measures on Agents issued by the State Administration for Industry and Commerce on 28 August 2004 and abolished on 29 April 2016

Interim Provisions on Access to Film Business Qualifications jointly issued by the SARFT and the MOFCOM on 10 October 2004, as amended by the SAPPRFT on 28 August 2015 ("Film Business Qualification Provisions")

Interim Measures for the Administration of Sino-Foreign Joint Venture and Cooperative Production and Operation of Broadcasting and Television Programs jointly issued by the SARFT and the MOFCOM on 28 October 2004 ("Order No. 44")

Catalogue for the Guidance of Foreign Investment Industries (Revised in 2004) jointly issued by the NDRC and the MOFCOM on 30 October 2004

Accounting Rules for Film Enterprises issued by the Ministry of Finance on 9 December 2004

Supplementary Regulations on Interim Regulations on Film Business Qualification Provisions by the SARFT and the Ministry of Culture on 7 March 2005

Interim Provisions on the Project Approval of Film Scripts (Synopses) and the Several Opinions on Introducing Foreign Investment in the Cultural Field issued jointly by Ministry of Culture, the SARFT, the General Administration of Press and Publication, the NDRA and the MOFCOM on 6 July 2005

Provisions on the Filing of Film Scripts (Synopses) and the Administration of Film Productions issued by the SARFT on 22 May 2006 ("Provisions on Scripts and Film Productions")

Provisions on the Administration of Internet Audio-Visual Program Services issued by the SARFT in 2007 and amended by the SAPPRFT in 2015

Notice on Reiterating Film Censorship Standards issued by the SARFT on 3 March 2008

Guidance on Box Receipt Split of National Films issued by the SARFT on 19 December 2008 (Document No. 866)

Implementation Regulations for the Administration of Commercial Performances issued by the Ministry of Culture on 28 August 2009 (Ministry of Culture Order No. 47)

Notice of the SARFT on Improving and Perfecting the Filing of Film Scripts (Synopses) and the Examination of Film Works issued by the SARFT on 4 February 2010 ("Notice for Better Examination")

Announcement on the Comprehensive Implementation of the "One Filing and Two Reviews System" for Films issued by the SARFT on 10 May 2010

Provisions of the Ministry of Commerce on the Implementation of the Security Review System for the Merger and Acquisition of Domestic Enterprises by Foreign Investors issued by the MOFCOM on 25 August 2011 (the "M&A Security Review Provisions")

Guiding Opinions on Promoting Coordinated Development of Film Distribution and Screening issued by the SARFT on 29 November 2011 (Document No. 992)

Transitional Policies for the Pilot Reform of Business Tax to Value-Added Tax in the Transportation Industry and Certain Modern Service Industries" in Document Cai Shui [2013] No. 37

Interim Regulations on Foreign Investment in Cinemas issued by the SAPPARFT on 28 August 2015

Notice on Strengthening the Planning, Development and Management of Online Original Audio-Visual Programs by the SAPPRFT in December 2016

Notice on Further Strengthening the Management of Radio, Television and Online Audio-Visual Programs issued by the NRTA in October 2018

Further Strengthening the Management of Radio, Television, and Online Audio-visual Arts Programs issued by the NRTA on 31 October 2018

Opinions on Accelerating Cinema Construction to Promote the Prosperity and Development of the Film Market issued by the CFA on 11 December 2018

Further Strengthening the Management of Creative Production in TV Dramas and Web Dramas issued by the NRTA on 6 February 2020

Promoting the Strengthening and Improvement of Broadcasting Institutions in the New Era issued by the NRTA on 15 October 2020

Notice on Matters Concerning the Administration of Licensing Services for the Distribution of Domestic Online Dramas and Films" (Guangdian Ban Fa [2022] No. 128) by the NRTA in October 2022

Notice on Continuing the Implementation of Value-Added Tax Policies to Support the Development of Cultural Enterprises issued by the Ministry of Finance and State Administration of Taxation (Announcement No. 61 of 2023)

## Other PRC Documents

Instruction on Film Work to the Publicity Department of the Northeast Bureau issued by the Publicity Department of the Central Committee of the Communist Party of China in October 1948

Decision on Strengthening the Film Business to the Central Bureau and the Political Departments of various military groups issued by the Publicity Department of the Central Committee of the Communist Party of China on 14 August 1949

Decision on Strengthening Film Production Work issued and implemented by the former Government Administration Council on 1 December 1954

The report "Reforming the Management System of Film Distribution and Screening" forwarded by the State Council from the Ministry of Culture and the Ministry of Finance in 1979

Decision of the Standing Committee of the National People's Congress on Transforming the Ministry of Radio and Television into the Ministry of Radio, Film and Television (Adopted on 20 January 1986)

Notice on Several Economic Policies to Support the Development of Cultural Undertakings issued by the State Council on 18 December 2000 ("Document No. 41")

Document No. 17 issued by the General Office of the CPC Central Committee and the General Office of the State Council in 2001, forwarding the "Several Opinions of the Central Publicity Department, State Administration of Radio, Film and Television, and General Administration of Press and Publication on Deepening the Reform of the Press, Publishing, Radio, Film and Television Industries" ("Document No. 17")

Provisions on the Administration of Foreign-invested Telecommunications Enterprises (No. 333) issued by the State Council on 11 December 2001

Mainland and Hong Kong Closer Economic Partnership Arrangement signed by the Financial Secretary of the Hong Kong Special Administrative Region and the MOFCOM on 29 June 2003 ("Closer Economic Partnership Arrangement" or "CEPA")

Several Opinions on Promoting the Development of the Animation Industry issued by the State Council on 25 April 2006.

Guidance Opinions on Promoting the Prosperity and Development of the Film Industry (Guo Ban Fa [2010] No. 9) issued by General Office of the State Council on 21 January 2010 ("Film Promotion Opinion").

Guidance on Financial Support for the Revitalization, Development and Prosperity of the Cultural Industry jointly issued by nine ministries and commissions, including the Ministry of Publicity of CPC, the People's Bank of China, the Ministry of Finance, the Ministry of Culture, the SARFT, and the General Administration of Press and Publication on 9 April 2010 ("Cultural Industry Financial Support Guidance")

Notice of the General Office of the State Council on Printing and Distributing the Two Provisions on the Transformation of Operating Cultural Institutions into Enterprises and Further Supporting the Development of Cultural Enterprises (Guobanfa [2014] No. 15)

Decision of the First Session of the Thirteenth National People's Congress on the State Council Institutional Reform Proposal (Adopted at the First Session of the Thirteenth National People's Congress on 17 March 2018)

Programme for Deepening the Reform of Party and State Institutions, issued by The Central Committee of the Communist Party of China (CPC) on 21March 2018.

Further Supporting the Development of Cultural Enterprises (Guo Ban Fa [2018] No. 124)

Notice of The General Office of the State Council on Fully Implementing the List Management of Administrative Licensing Matters" (Guo Ban Fa [2022] No. 2) issued in January 2022

## International Instruments

Universal Declaration on Cultural Diversity adopted by the General Conference of the UNESCO at its 31st Session on 2 November 2001

Convention on the Protection and Promotion of Diversity in Cultural Expressions adopted by the General Conference of the UNESCO at its 33st Session on 20 October 2005 ("Convention on Cultural Diversity")

## Referenced Instruments in Other Jurisdictions

The British Film Industry, Sixth Report of Session 2002–03, prepared by the Culture, Media and Sport Committee House of Commons in 2003 ("The British Film Industry").

Communication of the 26th, September, 2001, from the Commission to the Council, the European Parliament, the Economic and Social Committee and the Committee of the Regions on certain legal aspects relating to cinematographic and other audiovisual works, COM(2001) 534 final (the "COM(2001) 534 final").

Communication from the Commission to the Council, the European Parliament, the European Economic and Social Committee and the Committee of the Regions, the future of European regulatory audiovisual policy, COM(2003) 784 final, adopted on the 15th, December, 2003 (the "COM(2003) 784 final").

Commission adopts communication on future of cinema and audiovisual industry in Europe of the 17th, September, 2001, DN: IP/01/1326.

Commission renews UIP authorisation for five years of the 14th, September, 1999, DN: IP/99/681.

Communication from the Commission, Making citizenship Work: fostering European culture and diversity through programmes for Youth, Culture, Audiovisual and Civic Participation, COM (2004) 154 final, presented on the 9th, March, 2004 (the "COM (2004) 154 final").

Competition Policy and Film Distribution, OCDE/GD (96)60, OECD Paris 1996 ("OCDE/GD (96)60")

Convention on Human Rights and Fundamental Freedoms signed in Rome on the 4th, November, 1950.

Corrigendum to Council Decision 2000/821/EC of the 20th, December, 2000 on the implementation of a programme to encourage the development, distribution and promotion of European audiovisual works (MEDIA Plus — Development, Distribution and Promotion) (2001-2005) OJL 336 of the 30t, December 2000) (the "MEDIA Plus Decision").

Council Directive of the 3rd, October, 1989 on the coordination of certain provisions laid down by law, regulation or administrative action in Member States concerning the pursuit of television broadcasting activities, (89/552/EEC) (OJL 298, 17.10.1989, p. 23) and amended on the 30th, June, 1997 by the Directive 97/36/EC of the European Parliament and of the Council of 30th, June, 1997 (the "TV Directive").

Council Directive 92/100/EEC of the 19th, November, 1992 on rental right and on lending right and on certain rights related to copyright in the field of intellectual property, OJL 346, the 27th, November, 1992, 61 (the "Rental Directive").

Council Directive 93/98/EEC of the 29th, October, 1993 harmonising the term of protection of copyright and certain related rights, OJL 290, the 24th, November, 1993, 9 (the "Term Directive").

Directive 2001/29/EC of The European Parliament and of The Council of the 22nd, May, 2001 on the harmonisation of certain aspects of copyright and related rights in the information society, OJL 167, the 22nd, June, 2001, 10 (the "Copyright Directive").

Die Europäische Audiovisuelle Informationsstelle, Rückgang der Kinobesuche 2003 in der Europäischen Union um geschätzte 5 %, downloaded on the 13th, April, 2004 from the website http://www.obs.coe.int/about/oea/pr/admissions2003.html.

EIB Sector Paper, O. DEBANDE & G. CHETRIT, The European Audiovisual Industry: An Overview, September, 2001 (the "EIB Sector Paper").

European Parliament resolution (P5_TA-PROV(2002)0347) on the Commission communication to the European Parliament, the Council, the Economic and Social Committee and the Committee of the Regions on certain legal aspects relating to cinematographic and other audiovisual works (COM(2001) 534 – C5-0078/2002 – 2002/2035(COS)) (the "Parliament Film Resolution").

FOCUS 2003 World Film Market Trends, issued by European Audiovisual Observatory in 2003, downloaded from http://www.obs.coe.int ("FOCUS 2003").

Form 10-K Annual Report filed by MGM for 2003.

The Fragmented Universe of Film Distribution Companies in Europe, European Audiovisual Observatory, Contribution to the Workshop "Distribution of European Films", Venezia, 29 – 31 August, 2003, downloaded from http://www.obs.coe.int on 23rd, April, 2004.

Gesetz über Urheberrecht und verwandte Schutzrechte vom 9. September 1965 (BGBl. I S. 1273, zuletzt geändert durch Art. 1 Gesetz zur Regelung des Urheberrechts in der Informationsgesellschaft v. 10. September 2003, BGBl. I S. 1774) ("DUrG")

# Contents

# Abbreviations

| | |
|---|---|
| CEPA | Closer Economic Partnership Arrangement |
| CFA | China Film Administration |
| CFC | China Film Corporation |
| CSRC | China Securities Regulatory Commission |
| DSB | Dispute Settlement Body |
| DSU | Dispute Settlement Understanding |
| DVD | Digital Versatile Disc |
| EC | European Community |
| ECJ | European Court of Justice |
| e.g. | for example, for instance |
| EIB | European Investment Bank |
| EU | European Union |
| EUR | Euro |
| FBMC | Film Bureau under Ministry of Culture |
| FEE | Fund for Films of Excellence |
| FFI | Film Finances |
| FY | Fiscal Year |
| GATS | General Agreement on Trade in Service |
| GATT | General Agreement on Tariffs and Trade |
| GEM | Growth Enterprise Market |
| HDTV | High Definition Television |
| HK | Hong Kong |
| ibid. | *ibidem*, in the same place |
| i.e. | *id est*, which is to say, in other words |
| IMAX | Image Maximum |
| Inc. | Incorporated |
| IRIS | Legal Observations of the European Audiovisual Observatory |
| MEDIA | Measures to Encourage the Development of the European Audiovisual Industry |
| MFN | Most Favoured Nation Treatment |
| MGM | Metro-Goldwyn-Mayer Inc. |

| | |
|---|---|
| mm | millimetre |
| MOFCOM | Ministry of Commerce of China |
| MRFT | Ministry of Radio, Film and Television |
| NDRC | Natioinal Development and Reform Commission |
| NIICD | New International Instrument on Culture Diversity |
| NRTA | National Radio and Television Administration |
| PICC | The People's Insurance Co. (Group) of China |
| PRC | People's Republic of China |
| RMB | Ren Ming Bi, China's currency unit |
| SAPPRFT | State Administration of Press, Publication, Radio, Film and Television |
| SARFT | State Administration of Radio, Film and Television |
| SFDC | State Film Distribution Company |
| SFDF | State Film Development Fund |
| TV | Television |
| VAT | Value-Added Tax |
| VIE | Variable Interest Entity |
| UK | United Kingdom |
| US | United States of America |
| USD | US Dollar |
| WTO | World Trade Organisation |

# Chapter 1
# Movie Business: Industry or Culture?

To begin discussing the nature of film, it is pertinent to first consider copyright law. Typically, cinematographic or audiovisual works are recognized under copyright law and this includes films. However, such works are considered subordinate to literary and artistic works. As such, a roll of film lacking originality or individuality would not be protected by copyright law. Fortunately, the neighboring rights system allows for the producer to hold rights in the recording, even if the film merely consists of moving pictures. This system is present to varying degrees in EU countries and China within the broader copyright system.[1] Most movies shown in theaters are protected by copyright, which carries both cultural and financial significance. This suggests that film may be considered a cultural element, regardless of whether it is mainstream or experimental, as it provides access to specific spiritual expressions. This enables a group of individuals to gather in a dark room for roughly two hours to be entertained or to enjoy themselves. As a result, film serves as a form of beauty that is reliant on an established copyright system. However, this aesthetic requires a significant investment before it can be made available to the general public. Thus, the film industry must support itself and be profitable in order to thrive.

In addition, the production cost has experienced a significant increase since the 1980s. In 2002, an English film typically cost USD 8.81 million, which was the highest in the European Union. However, compared to the average budget per movie of major US studios, which was USD 58.8 million during the same period,[2] the British film industry could only lament its status as a cottage industry.[3] Films appear to be a trend that generates emotional consumption and guarantees substantial profit

[1] Author's Rights Law of China lists the items protected as works in Article 3, in which Item (6), "cinematographic works and works created by virtue of an analogous method of film" are included. It is more or less the same case in the EU. Article 2 of the Rental Directive specifies the authors' rights, which include the rights of film producers and principal directors on the film. See also Kamina Pascal, 54.

[2] FOCUS 2003, 7.

[3] The British Film Industry, 19.

© Social Sciences Academic Press 2026

J. Wu, *Legal Mechanisms for Film Financing and Support in China*,
https://doi.org/10.1007/978-981-95-0922-5_1

in subsequent rounds of production, distribution, and exhibition. It is fair to say that film is a symbol of a profit-driven industry. If a global market exists, as advocated by the WTO's worldwide industry liberation, big-budget films dominate the top 10 box office list globally. Capital-based voices are overwhelmingly significant. If capital investment truly determines a film's market success, which implies the number of viewers a film can attract in a globalized market, is film still a part of culture?

# 1 A Particular Item for WTO

## *1.1 Culture Exception?*

Certain nations, notably France, perceive the current worldwide film market configuration as a potential danger to a country's cultural identity if the industry is allowed to operate freely. In 1993, the European Union advocated for the concept of "cultural exception" during the Uruguay Round Multilateral Negotiations, with the support of countries such as Canada and Australia, and in opposition to the United States and a few other nations, including Japan. The notion of cultural exception primarily entailed that the cinema sector should not be subject to liberalization and should not be included in the list of products or services to be made available for free trade.[4]

Culture exception argument caused a stand-off between US group and EU-Canada Group. Both parties held on to the all-or-nothing mentality, which nearly led to the break-down of Uruguay Round Multilateral Negotiations.[5] Even now, the repercussions of the culture exception are still there.[6] For the next round of negotiations, US, Brazil, Switzerland, Canada and Japan have respectively submitted their proposals, which reflect, to some degree, some re-thinking of the culture exception concept from various respects and offer some prospective for the future development.[7] In which, the documents submitted by delegations of Switzerland and Brazil put emphasis on culture diversity instead of a mere culture exception, which reflects the latest development of international level regarding the culture policy.[8] However, Canada still champions a movement named NIICD,[9] aiming to create an instrument outside of WTO to cater for a culture exception.[10]

---

[4] As to the argument for or against the culture exception suggestion, please see Divina Frau-Meigs; Tanja Nadine Ertel, 315–317; Tyler Cowen.

[5] Christoph B. Graber, Handel und Kultur im Audiovisionsrecht der WTO, 138–140; Tanja Nadine Ertel 271–328.

[6] Christopher Maule; Anna Herold; Divina Frau-Meigs.

[7] Christoph B. Graber, Audiovisual Policy: The Stumbling Block of Trade Liberalisation? 2.

[8] Ibid.; Switzerland has formed an essential film supply diversity principle in her Law of Film Production and Film Culture. See Weber/Unternährer/Zulauf, 114. Roland Unternährer, 223–226.

[9] Christopher Maule.

[10] Christopher Maule; Christoph B. Graber has expressed his doubts and opposition to this mentality. See Christoph B. Graber, Handel und Kultur im Audiovisionsrecht der WTO, 140–144.

Is culture exception trade protectionism disguised with noble reasons like culture reservation? Speaking of the target audience for the cinema market, which seemed to be supported mainly by the adolescence,[11] one has reason to ask, if this trend continues, why are those who were ever mad about the Hollywood dominated cinema have withdrawn from the cinemas when they grow up? If the reason is that they are tired of the shallow pictures stuffed by American majors, the conclusion may be that film actually has only limited influence to shake out the audiences' original culture elements. However, this conclusion finds no empiric proof available to support it. At least, nobody can comfortably say that the withdrawing grow-ups left cinema because they just have seen through the "shallow" films instead of following the advice given by the popular films.

Here exist two different legal mentalities, free choice and protection for the adolescence. Considering the subtle function culture can be of, it shall have exceeded the legal area to argue which mentality is more effective. However, film industry means tremendous money movement, on which the culture oriented film policy will touch inevitably. Therefore, without making a white-or-black choice between these two mentalities, legislators, practitioners or regulators have to take painful efforts to find the balance between capital and culture therein, which is almost a mission impossible.

## *1.2 Goods or Service?*

Traditionally, film was regarded as goods in GATT system. Or, film is the only service touched upon by GATT. Article IV of GATT provides a unique exception for cinematic films[12] to national treatment rules and duty concessions have been made in relation to films. Moreover, screen quotas,[13] which serves as an essential measure covered by Article IV, still plays an important role for domestic film industry protection, although it is subject to the further liberalisation and negotiations. However, the technologic development has broadened the exhibition means and TV has been an important way to show a movie, i.e. it is not easy to draw a clear-cut line between film and TV programmes. Therefore, it is easy to understand why EU extended this screen

---

[11] FOCUS 2003, 6.

[12] There are three markets for the films according to the exhibition media and budget level. The A-level market includes higher budget pictures intended principally and initially for theatrical release with video and television rights providing security for acquisition costs and print and advertising cost shortfalls, plus profits. The B-level market principally includes lower budgeted genre pictures directed toward initial video and television distribution in most markets, but with the possibility of selected theatrical release. The C-level market consists of even lower budgeted fare, directed solely to the video and non-prime time television markets. See Jeffrey S. Konvitz, Independent Wealth, in Los Angeles Lawyer, Issue of May, 2004, Vol. 27, 44. Here, cinematic films should refer to the films for A- and B-level market.

[13] Richard Senti, 60; Christoph B. Graber, Handel und Kultur im Audiovisionsrecht der WTO, 175–176.

quotas system to TV sector via TV Directive,[14] which led to a stand-off although luckily solved later. Although audiovisual sector (including film sector) was agreed to be part of GATS' area,[15] it still leaves something uncertainty of the applicable treaty in some cases.[16] Nevertheless, since Article IV of GATT appears to confine to the cinematic film regarding culture policy and GATS offers more flexibility in market access, national treatment and MFN treatment,[17] GATS may offer more protection of film industry than GATT does.

## 2 China's Cinema in Transition—For Culture as Well as for Market

For China with a planned system regarding film production, before defining a film as a service or a good, a film market had to be liberalised to make such definitions relevant. In addition, with a strict film content review system in place, China has to decide whether to apply the same content review system to films not for theatres before reform the content review system substantively.

### *2.1 Evolution of China's Film Industry and Legal Environment*

From 1949 to the mid-1980s, China's film industry was operated and owned by the State, with producers creating films according to the state's production plan. Before the film industry's reform, the ideological function of films was emphasized and managed as a means for publicity since the established of New China. Even before the founding of New China, the Publicity Department of the Central Committee of the Communist Party of China (CPC) issued an Instruction on Film Work to the

---

[14] Article 5, the TV Directive.

[15] Aerico Beviglia Zampetti, 3.

[16] For example, Turkey imposed a tax on the film imported. US argued that this tax violated Article III of GATT, the national treatment. See Christoph B. Graber, Handel und Kultur im Audiovisionsrecht der WTO, 264.

[17] GATS takes so called "positive list" approach in relation to the service supply and sectors. Accordingly, all WTO members have established specific commitments in the respective schedules under GATS. Without specifications to the contrary, members of WTO guarantee both the right of market access (Article XVI) and the right to national treatment (Article XVII) in scheduled sectors. However, as to MFN treatment, which provides the best treatment given to the supply of service from any nation, whether the nation is a WTO member or not, must be given to all WTO members. Any exception will be strictly conditioned as "carve-outs" and permitted under "Annex on Article II Exemptions", which are not supposed to exceed 10 years without considering the "grandfather" situations. EC and a few other countries have film co-production agreement. See Aerico Beviglia Zampetti, 8.

Publicity Department of the Northeast Bureau in October 1948, highlighting that film exhibition in a class society should be a tool for class struggle. The Publicity Department of the Central Committee of the CPC issued a "Decision on Strengthening the Film Business" to the Central Bureau and the Political Departments of various military groups on 14 August 1949, which proposed that film art was the most popular entertainment to the public and therefore had the most extensive publicity effect. It was suggested that this business must be strengthened for the benefit of the publicity work of the Party to construct a new democracy on a national scale.[18] In the early years of the founding of New China, the law preserved the ideological function of films as the highest value. This might be explained as the policy consideration behind the planned industrial structure and a strict censorship mechanism built in alongside.

Between 20 November to 24 December 1949, the Film Bureau under the Ministry of Culture convened an administrative meeting where two major objectives were established for 1950. Firstly, on the cultural front, progressive films were to be elevated from a disadvantaged to a superior position in the film market. Secondly, on the economic front, state-run units were put on trial with entrepreneurship. To achieve these goals, a large number of films depicting the revolutionary struggle of the Chinese people and the various aspects of construction of society during the new democratic period was systematically planned. Additionally, a significant number of Soviet film translations and progressive films from other countries were to be introduced to gain a competitive edge in the film market. This production model was implemented in China until 1980s, with a film studio coordinating its film production according to the plan set by the regulator. State funds were allocated each year, and bank loans were made available when necessary.[19] The Soviet film management system served as the basis for this model, characterised by the unity of government and enterprise, with film production and distribution carried out in strict accordance with the State administrative directives.[20]

In 1956, a proposal for a major reform of feature film studios was made during the "SheFanSi Conference" (舍饭寺会议) by directors of said studios. This proposal was based on a study trip to Western Europe and Yugoslavia by Cai Chusheng, Situ Huimin, and others, against the anxiety caused by the inherent limitations of the centralised and closed system. The conference introduced the concept of "three freedoms and one domination," which was later incorporated into the Report on Certain Issues Concerning the Promotion of Film Production. This report clarified that a director-dominated structure could be installed for film production, and an independent project team could be established upon self-financing means, with autonomy to produce scripts, select actors and make its own project development plan. The multi-layered censorship system was suggested to be overhauled to respect the autonomy of the studios, which should enjoy the independence to make and distribute a film

[18] Shen Yun, 'The Beginning and End of the Creation of the New Chinese Film Industry (1949–1957)', in Contemporary Film, No. 4, 2005, pp. 35–38.

[19] Yu Li (ed.), Studies in the Professional History of Chinese Cinema: Film Production, Distribution and Projection, China Film Press, 2006, p. 89.

[20] op. cit., pp. 92–93.

and leave the artistic treatment or judgement entirely to the discretion and responsibility of the creative team. Additionally, a film could be distributed based on sale splitting mode or copyright acquisition according to the film's quality and price. The reform of the remuneration of artistic creators and other matters were also clarified. Unfortunately, the "Anti-Rightist" campaign of 1957 dampened the enthusiasm of many film creators and negated the impact of the "SheFanSi Conference," resulting in the failure of the proposed film reform.

In the meanwhile, film companies in private hands were gradually nationalised from 1949 to 1953. At the beginning of the founding of New China, both the Central Committee of the CPC and the front-line personnel in the film industry advocated the establishment of State-run studios. Under these circumstances, by the end of 1949, three major State-run film enterprises, the Northeast Film Studio, the Beiping Film Studio and the Shanghai Film Studio, had been established. There were then still eight private film companies. But in February 1953, the nearly half-century history of the private sector in China's film industry came to an halt when the Shanghai United Film Studio, formed by the merger of the private studios, was incorporated into the Shanghai Film Studio.[21] In the 1950s, there were thus only three State-run film studios in China.[22] Those companies thus became the mainstay of China's film industry.

Following a decade of turmoil, the Chinese film industry experienced a rapid recovery as the nation's audience regained enthusiasm for cinema. However, due to the industry's adherence to the Soviet model, there was a significant mismatch between film production, distribution, and exhibition. As a result, market demand and film production were not compatible at all. This distorted situation could not nurture a healthy film industry to prosper in China. In this circumstances, the government redefined the film industry as a "culture industry" rather than a "publicity institution." As part of the reform, then MRFT decentralized its monopoly on distribution, pushing filmmakers further into the market. However, this abrupt liberalisation measure led inadvertently to a crisis for Chinese filmmakers to overcome. As the State withdrew its support from the State owned studios, which immediately experienced inferior management and less funding, without substantial market players enter to fill the vacuum left by the State. Additionally, the outdated regulatory system regarding production license and quotas, distribution aimed at enterprises established for film planning era further hindered development of the film industry in China.

It was the western film maker whose access to China's audiovisual market exposed the potential of the film industry in China. In the earlier 1980s, 20th Century Fox, one of Hollywood major studios, entered into the Chinese television market by by providing a weekly film to the State owned national TV channel. This agreement lasted nearly two years and introduced a plethora of Western audiovisual programmes

[21] Shen Yun, "The Beginning and End of the New Chinese Film Industry (1949–1957)", in Contemporary Cinema, Vol. 4, No. 4, 2005, pp. 35–38.

[22] Lv Xiaoming, "An Important Issue in Film Reform: Assumptions on Transforming Government Functions", in Zhang Zhenqin and Yang Yuanying, eds, WTO and Chinese Cinema, Beijing: China Film Press, October 2002.

to the Chinese audience. As a result, the film importation shifted from the USSR or other Eastern European countries to the United States and other Western countries. Despite government regulations, the influx of the imported blockbusters overshadowed the domestic film industry's output. Meanwhile, China's television market began to captive a significant portion of the movie-going audience throughout the country.[23]

To accelerate the reform in the film industry, China began its process of establishing the modern enterprises in the film industry. In May 1984, the Ministry of Culture proposed the establishment of China Film Corporation. In January 1985, the Film Bureau held a symposium on the reform of the film system in Guangzhou, proposing the simplification and decentralization of film regulation system, the separation of governmental control from enterprises, and the expansion of the autonomy of the production and distribution enterprises to operate in the film sector.

However, it was not always the case when come to the regulatory approach to the market demand of the film production. Under the planed system for film industry, production of a film was governed by the quota allocation system under the planned economy model, with only the State-run film enterprises allowed to produce feature films. In March 1986, the MRFT issued a Notice to strictly implement certain provisions on production management, which reiterate the quotas system to be followed by the film studios. The quotas system was therefore lingered on for another 10 years. Under the quotas system reiterated, the annual production was around 100 films.

In the end, the quotas system had to be reformed to make the film production match the real demand in the market. In January 1993, the MRFT released "Opinions on Deepening the Reform of the Film Industry" (Guangfa Film No. [1993] 3) (hereinafter referred to as "Decree No. 3"), which emphasized the need for films to be produced with a market-oriented approach. According to Decree No. 3, "Film production, distribution, and exhibition enterprises must conform to the socialist market economy system established by the 14th Party Congress. As a cultural product, the audience (including cinemas, rural projection teams, and audiences for film and video screenings of films) forms the corner stone of the film's market. The development of the film market relies on both social and economic benefits."[24] Moreover, Decree No. 3 dismantled the monopoly of the China Film Corporation over the distribution of domestic feature films by allowing production units to sell regional distribution rights, contract for individual films, receive a share of box office receipts, or act as distribution agents.[25] This marked the beginning of China's film market opening up and its transition towards marketization. By 1995, 16 studios had been licensed to produce feature films.[26] In October 1994, the MRFT authorized the screening of ten

[23] In just one year, between 1984 and 1985, the number of film goers fell by 5.2 billion. See Yu Li (ed.), Studies in the Professional History of Chinese Cinema: A Volume on Film Production, Distribution and Exhibition, China Film Press, 2006, p. 125.

[24] Decree No. 3, Article 1.

[25] Decree No. 3, Article 3.

[26] "A major reform of the film mechanism, with provincial studios having the right to produce films", in Film Literature, 1995, Issue 3, p. 57.

imported blockbusters each year, and required the distribution and screening of films that "basically reflect the achievements of the world's best civilization and contemporary cinema" on a box receipt split basis in China. Additionally, in March 1996, the Publicity Department of the CPC organised a national conference on film work in Changsha, which proposed the production of more high-quality films, the implementation of the so-called 9550 project, the establishment of special State funds to support films, and the introduction of a single-film production license for individual feature film making. Despite various challenges, the Chinese film industry eventually moved towards industrialization and marketization.

From the early 1990s, China had been proposing to draft a law regarding film promotion while encouraging development of a resilient film production industry. Film Industry Promotion Law was adopted in 2016 and has become effective since 2017. Since the implementation of the Film Industry Promotion Law, Chinese films have continued to thrive. 2017 saw the production of 970 films of all types, a box office of RMB 55.9 billion and 1.622 billion cinema visits, with year-on-year growth in all indicators above double digits. The first three quarters of 2018 were also in good shape, with the first and second quarters in particular showing strong growth momentum. As of 4 October 2018, the box office exceeded RMB 50 billion, one and a half months ahead of its record 2017.

## 2.2 *Evolution of China's Film Regulatory System*

Initially, in 1949, the Ministry of Culture held jurisdiction over the sector, with the Film Bureau operating under its umbrella, in charge of the specific regulation of the film industry. With an evolving acknowledgement of the film industry in the market, the film regulatory system in China has also undergone significant changes over time.

In April 1983, the Investigative Panel for Reform of Film and Television Regulatory System was established jointly by the Publicity Department of CPC and Ministry of Culture. This led to a motion being submitted in January 1986 to the Standing Committee of the National People's Congress, calling for the Ministry of Radio and Television to be transformed into the Ministry of Radio, Film and Television. The aim was to regulate the closely related film and television industries in a more unified manner, and thus promote their joint development and prosperity.[27] The motion was adopted at the 14th meeting of the Standing Committee of the Sixth National People's Congress, leading to the establishment of the Ministry of Radio, Film and Television (MRFT) as the governing body for the film industry in China.[28] Later, in accordance with the State Council's institutional reform programme approved at the First Session

[27] Xinhua News Agency, The 14th Session of the Standing Committee of the Sixth National People's Congress held a Plenary Session, in Guangming Daily (Tuesday, 14 January 1986, page 04).

[28] Decision of the Standing Committee of the National People's Congress on Transforming the Ministry of Radio and Television into the Ministry of Radio, Film and Television (Adopted on 20 January 1986).

of the Ninth National People's Congress and the Notice of the State Council on the Establishment of Institutions (Guo Fa [1998] No. 5), the MRFT was reorganized as the State Administration of Radio, Film and Television (at the level of a full ministry, hereinafter referred to as the SARFT). The SARFT was an agency directly under the State Council as the regulator for radio, film and television industries.

To further the advancement of the cultural regulatory system and streamline the resources of the press, publishing, broadcasting, film, and television industries, the State Administration of Press and Publication merged with the SARFT in March 2013 to form the State Administration of Press, Publication, Radio, Film and Television (SAPPRFT). The main objective of SAPPRFT was to coordinate and facilitate the growth of the press, publishing, broadcasting, film, and television industries while supervising and regulating the respective institutions and businesses. Additionally, SAPPRFT was responsible for ensuring the quality and content of publications, broadcasting, film and television programming, and managing copyright.

In 2018, the audiovisual regulatory framework underwent a complete overhaul, resulting in the dismantling of the unified mechanism put in place in 1986. The previous regulatory mechanism that was in place before 1986 was reinstated in a sense. As part of the 2018 governmental restructure scheme, the Publicity Department of CPC has taken on the responsibility of comprehensive film regulation in China. This move was made to enhance the role of films in public media and cultural entertainment, and to foster growth in the film industry. The SAPPRFT's film management duties have been thus transferred to the Publicity Department of CPC and specifically delegated to the China Film Administration (CFA) as an external portfolio. Following the adjustment, the CFA's primary responsibilities include the regulation of the film sector, supervision of film production, distribution and exhibition, censorship of film content, coordination of major national film events, and management of international cooperation and exchange of foreign co-productions, imported and exported films, among others.[29] Additionally, the National Radio and Television Administration (NRTA) has been established as a direct agency under the State Council, taking over the radio and television regulatory duties of the SAPPRFT.[30] Under the new regulatory regime, the film sector has thus been singled out from the general audiovisual sector and is subject to special regulatory treatment.

## *2.3 China's Film Industry Promotion Law*

The growth of China's film industry and the opening of its market have resulted in a pressing need for effective legal measures to acknowledge the reform of the industry

[29] Item 12, Programme for Deepening the Reform of Party and State Institutions, issued by The Central Committee of the Communist Party of China (CPC) on 21 March 2018.

[30] Section II (2), Decision of the First Session of the Thirteenth National People's Congress on the State Council Institutional Reform Proposal (Adopted at the First Session of the Thirteenth National People's Congress on 17 March 2018).

while keeping up the momentum for film promotion. A law in this regard can also define the power and jurisdiction of the regulatory agency while safeguarding the legitimate expectations of the film industry in the process. In response, the State Council issued Decree No. 342 on 25 December 2001, which amended and reissued the Film Regulations. Over the past two decades, Film Regulations had served as the legal foundation for China's film industry, and have been instrumental in its recovery from a period of stagnation to the era of rapid growth. Such governmental efforts to establish a legal environment for the film industry seems having been paid well. China's film industry has recently experienced a significant resurgence and has become a vital component of the country's economy.

The Film Industry Promotion Law, adopted at the 24th meeting of the Standing Committee of the National People's Congress on 7 November 2016, marks a significant milestone in the Chinese film industry. It is the first law adopted in the field of culture and art since the founding of the People's Republic of China. This law highlights the leading position of Chinese film in the cultural and artistic fields and officially ushers in a new era of rule of law. Additionally, this law calls for the development of the film industry to be included in the national economic and social development plan and for policies related to the film industry to be formulated by the State to promote the prosperous development of films. Furthermore, the Film Industry Promotion Law has absorbed valuable experience from the reform process and has incarcerated it in the stipulations of the law. This includes the decentralization of the final review of films and the devolution of the censorship system to the competent authorities of the provinces, autonomous regions, and municipalities directly under the Central Government, where a films is actually filmed and completed. The law encourages citizens, legal persons, and other organizations to develop derivative products such as film image commodities in accordance with the law. Additionally, it requires the promulgation of laws and regulations for film industry organizations, which emphasizes the adherence to moral and artistic principles, laws and regulations, respect for social morality, professional ethics, self-discipline, and the establishment of a good social image for actors, directors, and other film professionals.

The Film Industry Promotion Law comprises six chapters and a total of 60 Articles. It covers various aspects such as the value to be preserved, the purpose and requirements of the law, film creation and production, distribution, exhibition, industry support, and legal responsibilities. The Law has played a significant role in promoting the steady, sustained, and healthy growth of the film industry by providing an effective legal framework. In less than a month after the implementation of the Law, the National Office of Film Market Supervision and Consolidation conducted a crackdown on 326 cinemas that had illegally evaded and concealed box office receipts. Consequently, the offenders were punished with suspensions, fines, and reports of criticism in varying degrees according to the Film Industry Promotion Law.

To establish a culture industry in the global market, China must find a subtle balance between market liberalization and cultural identity. Regulators are now considering mechanisms to promote a diversified culture environment, such as lighter regulations and subsidies while still emphasizing the role of the market in modernizing the film industry.[31] With the adoption of the Film Industry Promotion Law, China has begun its exploration in this regard. This book will try to unfold China's efforts in establishing the legal mechanisms regarding film production, distribution and exhibition sector, with the hope that some fresh experience could be abstracted to facilitate the study in the related area.

## 3 Theatre Matters

Similar to the other jurisdictions, China's film legal system has been focused on the film produced for the theatrical release, or theatrical film, which have, however, been subject to a strict regulatory system for many years.

### *3.1 Dual Regulatory Structure*

According to Article 2 of the Film Industry Promotion Law, a film refers to a work that is produced by using audio-visual technology and artistic means, recorded on film or digital carriers, composed of continuous sound or silent images expressing certain content, meets the technical standards prescribed by the state, and is publicly screened in fixed screening venues such as cinemas or by mobile screening equipment. In this way, an audiovisual work not made for theatrical release is not a film promoted by the law, and thus saves the need of itself being subject to the intensified regulatory regime. Please be noted that the so-called mobile screening equipment refers to the facilities used in the interim film screening events, especially in the rural area without a fixed screening venue like cinema or theatre. It was once quite popular in the less-developing parts of China. With the rapid development of cinema screening business, mobile screen of a film is now rare, only being organised occasionally as a social event.

Therefore, the Film Industry Promotion Law definitely excludes other audio-visual products such as TV series and online films. On the other hand, film can also be exhibited by non-theatrical means. Non-theatrical sectors could also have their impact felt in a film production. According to Paragraph 2, Article 2 of the Film Industry Promotion Law, "the dissemination of films through information networks

---

[31] For a review of the reform of the film industry before 1993, see Tang Rong, 'The reform of the film system in the 30 years of reform and opening up and its impact on Chinese cinema', in Film Bureau of the State Administration of Radio, Film and Television, China Film Art Research Centre, Film Channel Programme Centre (eds.), Reform and Opening Up and 30 Years of Chinese Cinema, China Film Publishing House, 2008, pp. 474–75; Yu Li (ed.), Studies in the History of Chinese Film Profession: Film Production, Distribution and Projection, China Film Publishing House, 2006, pp. 126–127. (2008), pp. 474–475; Yu Li (ed.), Studies in the Professional History of Chinese Cinema: Film Production, Distribution and Screening, China Film Press, 2006, pp. 126–127.

such as the Internet, telecommunications networks, radio and television networks, etc., shall also abide by the provisions of laws and administrative regulations on the management of information networks such as the Internet, telecommunications networks, radio and television networks, etc." This way, the Film Industry Promotion Law covers the entire theatrical film screening process and applicable to the activities of production, distribution and screening of a theatrical film, as stipulated in the first paragraph of Article 2.

Although the Film Industry Promotion Law is a promotion law in name, it also inherits, summarizes and updates China's film regulatory regime effective for a long times, maintaining a strict regulatory framework for films made for theatrical release. On the other, for audio-visual works not for theatrical release, or non-theatrical films, the regulatory system is more flexible.

There exists therefore a dual regulatory framework for the whole audiovisual industry: a strict regulatory system for theatrical films industry and a flexible regulatory system for other audio-visual industries. In the past, this dual regulatory structure was mainly reflected in the distinction between the regulatory systems of the film industry and those of the radio and television industry. However, with the rapid development of the Internet industry, the Internet has become one of the main exhibition channels for audio-visual works. Online audio-visual service has becoming more and more influential in the audiovisual market. The waxing and waning of the business models driven by the new technologies in the audiovisual market have also posed a certain degree of impact on China's dual regulatory structure for the audiovisual market.

## *3.2 Development of Online Films and the Relevant Regulatory System*

The ten-year evolving process of online films in China, as the result of the combined effect of regulatory impact and market development, revealing the legal implications of the definition of films in the legal system.

Before 2010, the vast majority of TV dramas and films distributed online in China were films that had already been shown in cinemas or TV series and animated films that had been aired on TV stations, rather than those specifically produced for online streaming. Network service providers rarely produced their own videos, and the duration and influence of audio-visual works created and uploaded by users were not prominent. Although the SAPPRFT incorporated the production and broadcasting services of online dramas (films) in catalogue of the Internet audio-visual program services in 2010, dissemination of online video information was treated part of the business of online information service providers.

Since 2010, major Internet video service providers have built up their strength in a intensified competition. The platform's self-produced dramas have thus developed rapidly, giving rise to dramas such as "Old Boys" (2010), "Poor Men" (2012), and

"Unexpectedly, I Never Thought" (2013) by Kuaizi Brothers, which were only exhibited online. In 2014, iQIYI proposed the concept of "online feature films", and the online film model was thus launched. In 2015, the number of online films launched on iQIYI alone exceeded that of theatrical film market. This has drawn the attention of relevant regulatory authorities.

Under the dual regulatory system of cinema films and online audio-visual products, capital naturally flows into the online audio-visual field where regulation is more flexible. To counter this trend, the SAPPRFT revised in 2015 the "Provisions on the Administration of Internet Audio-Visual Program Services" its predecessor issued earlier in 2007, stipulating that online dramas (films) should be covered under the "online audio-visual programs" and requiring filing of the online dramas (films) to be uploaded on the Internet. It has since also been required that an Internet service provider could not provide online dramas (films) without the License for the Dissemination of Audio-Visual Programs via Information Network. Since online films are self-reviewed by online service providers and do not require prior censoring, they are still favored by capital and the market. In 2019, the total revenue sharing of nearly 40 online films exceeded 10 million yuan. The influence and commercial value of online dramas and films have thus become increasingly prominent.

To maintain the effectiveness of the current supervision over cinema films, with the rapid development of non-cinema audiovisual products, especially online films, the regulatory authorities have tightened the supervision over non-cinema audiovisual products to a certain extent. On the one hand, the regulatory authorities hope to review the content of some non-cinema audio-visual products. In February 2016, at the National TV Drama Industry Annual Conference, the official of the SAPPRFT revealed its intention to establish the review standards for online films and TV series and implement unified review both online and offline. In October 2016, the Film Industry Promotion Law was submitted for deliberation for the third time at the 24th meeting of the Standing Committee of the National People's Congress. At the meeting, Sun Zhijun, the vice minister of the Publicity Department of the Communist Party of China Central Committee, proposed that online films should be covered by the law reviewed. This is the first time that the government tried to regulate online films. In October 2018, issued the Notice on Further Strengthening the Management of Radio, Television and Online Audio-Visual Programs, implementing a "uniform standard and uniform scale" management for online films from several aspects such as content orientation, click rate and high remuneration for act staff. On the other hand, drawing on the regulatory system for cinema films, the NRTA has gradually established an administrative licensing mechanism for the distribution of online films. In December 2016, the NRTA issued Document No. 198, "Notice on Strengthening the Planning, Development and Management of Online Original Audio-Visual Programs", requiring overall regulation of online audio-visual programs. For key online film and television programs such as online dramas, online feature films and online variety shows, a dual-review and filing registration system should be implemented, and the online video platforms should uniformly affix their seals and submit them to the provincial bureau for filing. The document clearly stipulates that "all audio-visual program websites should proactively file the names of key online original programs, production institutions, themes, durations, as well as content descriptions of no less than 1500 words and explanations of ideological connotations of no less than 300 words through the 'Online Drama, Micro Film and Other Online Audio-Visual Program Information Filing System' during the inception stage." In addition, it is prohibited to shoot major and special theme film and television works without authorization. In 2019, the filing system was launched. Since then, online films have adopted a dual filing system, which has been adjusted from unified filing by video platforms to independent filing by film producers, from "planning filing" before production to "online filing" before the final product is released, with two filings and two public announcements.

In accordance with the Notice of The General Office of the State Council on Fully Implementing the List Management of Administrative Licensing Matters (Guo Ban Fa [2022] No. 2) issued in January 2022, the General Office of the NRTA has officially incorporated the review of domestic online dramas and films as one of the administrative licensing matters. The Notice on Matters Concerning the Administration of Licensing Services for the Distribution of Domestic Online Dramas and Films (Guangdian Ban Fa [2022] No. 128) was thus issued, implementing a licensing system for the distribution of key domestic online dramas and films. Under the new regime, only those key domestic online dramas and films with "Online Drama and Film Distribution License" can be put online. Since then, for key online dramas and films, the dual filing system has been transformed into a filing before production and licensing before online system. For non-key online dramas and films, online audiovisual program service provider should implement a review system for the audiovisual works to be uploaded online. For which a so called chief editor's content responsibility system should be installed for an effective review and control of the audiovisual works to be put online. Furthermore, The NRTA may conduct random review of the audiovisual works online to see whether a Internet audiovisual service provider has fulfilled its responsibilities as an editor. After the filing and licensing system was established by the NRTA, "Leaves on the Golden Mountain", launched on iQIYI, Youku and Tencent Video on 18th May 2022, became the first online drama to obtain the distribution license with the registration number "(General Administration) Net Film Review Word (2022) No. 001".

Introduction of licence regime in the internet dramas (films) has actually led to the approximation of legal measures adopted under the dual regulatory structure for the whole audiovisual regime. This regulatory move, having intensified the regulation on the non-theatrical drama (films), definitely has repercussions on the market with the output of online dramas (films) significantly reduced. The number of online series has sharply declined from 2463 in 2016 to 241 in 2023, and the number of films with revenue sharing exceeding 10 million yuan has dropped from 68 in 2021 to 36 in 2023.

## 3.3 Conclusion

Online dramas and films are now treated as the audiovisual works similar to TV dramas at least. The producer has to obtain qualification from the NRTA before starting an online drama project. This de facto incorporation of online dramas into the TV drama regulatory system has created a new administrative license, which could not made simply by the decree from the NRTA according to China's Administration License Law. In other words, the licence regime for online dramas needs to find a solid legal basis before it could withhold possible legal challenge. Even the licence regime could finally find its legal basis, given the enormous number of dramas with various duration on the Internet, the licence regime has to pick up the so-called "key" drama to licence. Too many key online dramas with a broad construction may overburden the licence regime while too few selected key online drama may impair the significance of the licence regime. The ambiguous criteria, listed in by the NRTA to select the key drama for licence regime, have led to an uncertain environment and caused anxiety to the audiovisual investors. This may be the logic explanation of the falling amount of the online dramas after the licence regime was installed.

Economically speaking, success of a theatrical release determine the economic returns for the film producers or right owners. It is undeniable that production of a theatrical film is much more complicated and demanding than a non-theatrical audiovisual work. But a successful theatrical release of a film can bring more economic benefits to the film right holder than those non-theatrical audiovisual works without being screened in theatre. In this sense, when a film is produced for theatre, its theatrical release have to meet the high expectation for its success. To reform the current regulatory content review system or let the current system spill over the other non-theatrical audiovisual sector, the further reform should make a choice.

# Chapter 2
# Film Production: Legal Framework Regarding Film Production

The creation of a film marks the beginning stage for the whole industry chain to operate. While copyright is the main issue for a film production team to deal with, among the other things, the rising production cost required for a film further complicates the legal mechanisms at this stage. Considering the substantial capital investment in a film, the daunting production threshold for a film creation has definitely a significant impact on competition within the film market. In the global film market, currently dominated by Hollywood majors, the preservation of culture value inherent in a film is naturally a concern for EU countries and China when designing or recognizing a legal framework, under which a film industry is expected to flourish. A feasible option is to provide subsidies for film production to lower down the threshold for film production investment while free the creative team from the capital pressure when trying to producing a film; however, it is important to consider how far government intervention in the form of subsidies should go before it becomes merely a convenient tool for protectionism. In this sense, it is highly important to implement a subsidy system in a way that does not harm the market's function or distort the competition therein.

The perspective of film makers regarding the legal framework that applies to film production is primarily concerned with copyright matters. Nonetheless, in China, this framework also encompasses production regulations.

## 1 Copyright Issue

China has experienced lots of copyright issues in the dramatically arising film market. As a leading stipulation of the Film Industry Promotion Law, Article 7 relates film copyright in twofold approach, protecting while exploiting. Given the copyright issues are dealt with by the author's right law and civil law, Article 7 simply reiterate the importance to strictly protect and effectively exploit the intellectual property

© Social Sciences Academic Press 2026

J. Wu, *Legal Mechanisms for Film Financing and Support in China*,
https://doi.org/10.1007/978-981-95-0922-5_2

rights related to a film, without a published case specifically referred thereto. Therefore, we have turn to China's Author's Right Law to clarify the specific relationship between stakeholders regarding the copyright of a film.

## 1.1 Two Models

As we know, the production of a film can be complicated by numerous copyright issues. A significant number of entertainment professionals are typically involved in the process, including producer, screenwriter, director, music composer, actors, actresses, editors, directors of photography, to name a few. It is however generally more efficient to recognise fewer initial copyright owners in the production process. The key figures responsible for the smooth operation of a production are typically the director and producer. The director is responsible for ensuring the artistic completion of the film, while the producer invests large sums of money into the project with no guaranteed success.

When it comes to the relationship between the producer and director, there are typically two options to consider.

- The production of a film involves various copyright issues due to the large working team required. In the US, the "Work made for hire" doctrine is mainly adopted,[1] where the initial ownership of the film vests in the producer if the director is regarded as an employee of the producer.[2]
- In *droit d'auteur* countries, primarily continental Europe, the creative authors, who must be natural persons and make real creative contributions to the film, are considered the initial copyright owners. The producer is not typically the author of a film and does not enjoy initial copyright in a film. However, the producer can still benefit from the heavily invested film through copyright transfer from the author or initial copyright owner, by contract or by statutory assumption. In droit d'auteur countries, the producer of a film generally has no right to decide the significant issues of art in a film without obtaining the consent of the directors or other relevant authors in the first place,[3] allowing for the emergence of cinéma d'auteur in France and enabling some directors to call their films author's films.[4]

Determining the initial copyright owner or author of a film involves a delicate balance of power between creative artists and producers.[5] Applying the employer-employee relationship to designate the producer as the sole copyright owner may undervalue or even ignore the creativity of artists, particularly the directors. In countries with

---

[1] Nikolaus Reber, 10. In UK, before the Copyright and Related Rights Regulations took effect in 1996, the producer of a film was the sole initial owner of the film. See Pascal Kamina, 164.

[2] Nikolaus Reber, 10.

[3] Tanja Nadine Ertel, 46, 47.

[4] Serge Toubiana.

[5] Nikolaus Reber, 2.

limited film investment, the cultural value of a film may need to be altered or even distorted to meet the market demands which could negatively impact the artistic integrity of a film. Conversely, if the law assigns all copyright ownership to the director, investors may have to shoulder significant financial risks for a film made by a director with a limited market influence. Without a dedicated investor, it may be unrealistic to expect a director to produce a successful film.

## *1.2 China's Statutory Designation System*

Before Authors' Rights Law of China was firstly adopted in 1990, the initial ownership of the authors' rights was a contentious issue.[6] After some broad discussion, the version of compromise survived. Article 15 Paragraph 1 of Authors' Rights Law of China, amended in 2010, read as follows,

> The copyright in a cinematographic work and any work created by an analogous method of film production shall be enjoyed by the producer of the work, but the scriptwriter, director, cameraman, lyricist, composer, and other authors thereof shall enjoy the right of authorship in the work, and have the right to receive remuneration pursuant to the contract concluded with the producer.

Apparently, as a country with civil law tradition, China sticks to the authors' rights system like the continental Europe. However, from Article 15 Paragraph 1 we read an incomplete "work made for hire" doctrine, which was qualified with the rights to be identified of the artists including a director, who is also named authors (to what?). Here, both "work made for hire" and *droit d'auteur* theory had made awkward peace with each other.

Article 15 Paragraph 1 of Authors' Rights Law of China (2010) was based on the following considerations:

- According to the drafters of China's Authors' Rights Law, the full ownership of authorship is deemed crucial for the successful creation and distribution of a film.[7]
- In the past, under China's State-owned and centralised studio system, every studio was responsible for maintaining a full team of professionals, including performers, writers, directors, cinematographers, technicians, and other supporting staff.[8] Films produced by these studios were created according to their internal job assignments. As a result, these stipulations served somehow as an acknowledgement of a common practice in the Chinese film industry until recently.

Since the implementation of the Copyright Law of China in 1990, China's film industry has undergone significant transformation. With the development of economic reforms and the introduction of the concept of culture industry, State-owned studios have increasingly adopted a profit-oriented mindset and now operate

---

[6] Wei Zhi, 47.

[7] Ibid.

[8] Ibid.

more like conventional enterprises. Film production teams are no longer strictly limited to employees of a single studio, and artists such as directors and cinematographers now have greater flexibility to choose which projects they are willing to participate in, be it their own studios or not. The traditional studio unit system has become outdated and State control in production, distribution, and exhibition has been gradually withdrawn, opening the gate for other types of capital to invest in the film business. Although China amended its Copyright Law in anticipation of joining the WTO on 27 October 2001, the previous Article 15 Paragraph 1 remained largely intact.

However, China's Copyright Law underwent significant changes when it was amended and adopted by the Standing Committee of the National People's Congress on 11 November 2020, after nine years of extensive work. The new law, which came into effect on 1 June 2021, divides audiovisual works into two categories: "cinematographic and television series works" and "other audiovisual works". Article 17 Paragraphs 1 and 2 of the amended Copyright Law provide for the ownership of copyright in these two categories of audiovisual works, respectively. While Article 17 Paragraph 1 on the attribution of copyright in "works of cinema and television dramas" are similar to those of Article 15 Paragraph 1 of the 2010 Copyright Law, the term "producer" has been replaced by "maker". This change in terminology is due to the fact that the amended Copyright Law makes a clear distinction between "film and television series works" and "other audiovisual works", with the legislator considering that there is a "producer" for a film and a television series but not for a short video. The copyright owner to "other audiovisual works" is determined by a prior agreement, with different norms in operation depending on the specific type of audiovisual work.

The present wording of Article 17 Paragraph 1 implies that the director shall be one of the authors. However, what works has the director created? Is there any other works besides an cinematographic work exist in a film? As to the later question, Article 17 Paragraph 3 reads like follows,

> The authors of the screenplay, musical works and other works that are incorporated in an audiovisual work and can be exploited separately shall be entitled to exercise their copyright independently.

Article 17 Paragraph 3 dose not provide any answer to the first question. This is due to the fact that the producer of a film has been identified as the exclusive author, suggesting that a director's contribution is limited to labor and not considered a work. The conclusion drawn from the collective interpretation of Article 17 Paragraphs 1 and 3 contradicts the notion of a director's authorship as suggested in Article 17 Paragraph 1. This may pose only a technical challenge if it does not have any adverse implications in practice. However, it is worth noting that the aforementioned legislative provision fails to recognize the pivotal role of a director, who is widely regarded as the most significant creative contributor in the film making process, under our current copyright law system at least. As a result, the director's contributions are not accorded the same level of importance as those of a scriptwriter or the author of a soundtrack, given that the works of the latter two are explicitly acknowledged in the third paragraph of Article 17.

The initial section of Article 17 has further bolstered the already influential position of film producers. Specifically, in regard to a team solely focused on domestic film production,[9] the current state of affairs has resulted in a diminished bargaining power for artists, rendering their unique talents and innovative contributions as mere expenses on the balance sheet for producers. This unfortunate reality underscores the inextricable link between art and capital, prompting some directors to take on the role of producers themselves.[10] Assessing the impact of the film industry on cultural diversity in China is a complex matter. It is widely acknowledged that producers wield significant influence in the film production process, particularly when the director lacks the necessary clout to push back against purely market-driven demands. In the case of projects with foreign investment, the current legal framework stipulates that the foreign party may provide capital, while the Chinese party may contribute labor, equipment, and/or location, among other resources.[11] The Article 17 Paragraph 3's allocation system for author rights could potentially have adverse effects on the Chinese film industry. In 2010, Kung Fu Dreams, a US-Chinese co-production, garnered the highest number of viewers among the top 20 grossing films in the EU. This achievement was unparalleled by any other film produced solely by EU member countries in the same year. The film also exhibited strong market dynamics in major global markets, amassing a worldwide gross of $3.95. However, Kung Fu Dreams did not fare as well in Chinese mainland where it grossed significantly less than expected. Under the general principles of co-production distribution, the film was financed by the US, and although China provided the main cast and crew, the copyright of the film belongs to the US financier. As a result, the Chinese was partner was only licensed the release rights in the Chinese mainland market, while the American financier took away all rights outside the mainland Chinese market. Therefore, despite its success in the global film market, the Chinese partner did not benefit much from it. Additionally, the film did not resonate with mainstream audiences in Chinese mainland, and its unique Chinese cultural elements did not seem to have garnered much overseas appeal. The success of Kung Fu Dreams in foreign markets underscores the weakness of overseas distribution of Chinese films, which have had to cede overseas markets in order to secure investment. Furthermore, the bias towards capitalist control in Article 17(1) of the Copyright Law has left Chinese collaborators without a strong bargaining position in the co-production system, and therefore unable to achieve satisfactory returns from it.[12] Despite having a wealth of cultural

---

[9] Domestic production team here means that no capital from overseas involved in the film production.

[10] For a commercial film to be finished in 2004, the wife of Chen Kaige, Chen Hong, acts as the producer for the film of his husband. See Wu Ji missed Cannes, http://www.netandtv.com/newspage/htm2004-5/20045141743325358 79.shtml.

[11] Article 5(2) The Joint Production Rules.

[12] Ironically, the film *Bicycle* was shot without any qualification certificate or exhibition certificate issued by the regulators of China. According to the practices adopted by the regulators, Bicycle should have no chance to attend and international film festival or be exhibited anywhere. However, since the producer is from Taiwan, not from Main Land, Bicycle was luckily regarded as a Taiwan

talent, China's lack of specialised film capital places it at a disadvantage compared to the United States. The implementation of Article 17 Paragraph 3 may nullify China's advantages in the film industry, while bolstering the position of Hollywood majors. This could result in increased barriers to entry for new players who have to secure significant capital investment for the project proposed in the first place. Consequently, the cultural diversity of China's film industry may be compromised.

## 2 Film Financing Practices in China

A film is a legally acknowledged commodity or service that requires significant capital investment for its production and distribution. Its creation involves not only the artistic efforts undertaken by the creator, but also the financial supports from investors and distributors to ensure its market success. The legal framework governing the financing of the film industry is crucial in securing the necessary investment and establishing support measures for the industry. It is only through this framework that a structure of subsidies and support measures can be established.

Film financing is thus a key issue to be dealt with in the Film Industry Promotion Law, according to which China encourages financial institutions to provide financing services to film business[13] while trying to channel relevant cultural industry specific special funds to invest in the film industry.[14] Under the general framework established by the Film Industry Promotion Law, it is the State Council and its subordinated departments who adopt specific measure to establish a legal environment beneficial for film financing. Such efforts date back to 2010.

The General Office of the State Council issued the Guidance Opinions on Promoting the Prosperity and Development of the Film Industry (Guo Ban Fa [2010] No. 9) (hereafter referred as "Film Promotion Opinion") on 21 January 2010. Article

film and took the box office in Europe with USD 1500. See Xianming Zhang. Later, Bicycle was released on the exhibition round in China as a Chinese film.

[13] "The state encourages financial institutions to provide financing services for film-related activities and the improvement of film infrastructure, to carry out intellectual property pledge financing business related to films in accordance with the law, and to support the development of the film industry through credit and other means. The state encourages insurance institutions to develop insurance products that meet the needs of the development of the film industry in accordance with the law. The state encourages financing guarantee institutions to provide financing guarantees to the film industry in accordance with the law, and to diversify risks through re-guarantees, joint guarantees, and a combination of guarantees and insurance. For the production of films announced by the film administrative department of the State Council in accordance with the provisions of this Law, the loan term and interest rate shall be reasonably determined in accordance with the relevant provisions of the state." Article 40, the Film Industry Promotion Law.

[14] "The State guides relevant cultural industry special funds and funds to increase their investment in the film industry. Based on the development of the film industry at different stages and periods, combined with financial conditions and the needs of economic and social development, it comprehensively considers and makes overall arrangements for the support of fiscal funds to the film industry, and strengthens the auditing of the use of relevant funds and funds." Article 37, the Film Industry Promotion Law.

5 there in highlights the importance of "encouraging greater support for investment and financing policies" as a major measure. It specifically encourages financial institutions to provide more financial support to film enterprises and to develop financing measures and supporting financial services suitable to facilitate development of the film industry. Under the Film Promotion Opinion, while financial institutions may determine loan terms and interest rates reasonably for film enterprises that meet the credit conditions, they should improve the quality and efficiency of their services in this regard. The document also supports eligible film enterprises in expanding their financing channels, increasing their scale, and enhancing their strength through the issuance of corporate bonds, short-term financing bills, medium-term notes, apart from bank loans. It promotes the restructuring and listing of State-owned and State-controlled film enterprises that meet the requirements and suggests the more advanced financial measures, including encouraging venture capital or other equity investment means, to support the film industry. Local governments are encouraged to utilize investment funds for small and medium-sized enterprise entrepreneurship to support operation of a film venture capital. They should also encourage large enterprises to invest in films through equity participation and holding, and promote the formation of various film investment companies. The Film Promotion Opinion also stresses to nurture strategic investors in the film industry.

Furthermore, on 9 April 2010, a joint announcement was made by nine ministries and commissions, including the Ministry of Publicity of CPC, the People's Bank of China, the Ministry of Finance, the Ministry of Culture, the SARFT, and the General Administration of Press and Publication. The announcement, titled "Guidance on Financial Support for the Revitalization, Development and Prosperity of the Cultural Industry" (Cultural Industry Financial Support Guidance) has outlined three distinct financial measures aimed at providing support to the film industry, among the other culture industries. Firstly, financial institutions are urged to actively create credit products that cater to the specific characteristics of cultural enterprises. They should increase their credit investments and establish a framework to promote the listing and financing of eligible cultural enterprises. Additionally, diversified funds are encouraged to play a role in supporting the development of the cultural industry. This directive provides valuable assistance to the media industry, as it receives a substantial support from the financial sector. The financial measures mentioned are inherently applicable to the China film industry as well.

## *2.1 Bank Credit and Loans and Completion Guarantee*

Given that China adopts a highly regulated financial system, in which banks hold a primary position to provide financial services. Maybe the emerging equity investment vehicles have diversified the channels for a start-up enterprise in other industries to obtain the fund. However, banks credits are still the basic means for a film company to build up financially.

### 2.1.1 Bank Credit and Loans in General

Bank credit and loans have long been the conventional means to finance a film production in China. According to Article 40 Paragraph 1 of Film Industry Promotion Law, the State shall encourage financial institutions to provide financial services for film business operation and the enhancement of film exhibition infrastructure. It shall also facilitate financing through the collateralization of intellectual property rights associated with films. Additionally, the State will adopt various measures to promote the film industry.

Development of Bank Credit Services for the Film Industry

The financing method of bank loans can be traced back to as early as 2002, when the film "Hero", directed by Zhang Yimou, successfully secured a loan from an international financial institution.[15] This was a significant milestone for the Chinese film industry, as it demonstrated the potential for international financing in domestic film production. The success of "Hero" in terms of financing and production set a precedent for future films.

Huayi Brothers obtained a 100 million yuan loan from Shenzhen Development Bank (now Ping An Bank) for the production of the film "The Banquet" released in 2006.[16] As the first film project in China to complete its fundraising through Chinese bank loans, this marked a significant development for the Chinese film industry, as it showed the growing acceptance and utilization of traditional financial institutions in supporting the creation and production processes of film making.

With the explosive growth of the Chinese film market and the continuous business expansion of film companies, several leading private film companies in China have started to obtain bank credit and loans with the concerned copyrights pledged. In 2007 and 2008, Huayi Brothers, Enlight Media, Polybona, and other film companies received loans worth tens of billions of yuan from Beijing Bank, some of which were guaranteed by the Beijing Cultural and Creative Industry Promotion Center, while others obtained project loans solely through copyright pledged without professional guarantee companies.[17] The essence of ensuring a secure and seamless operation of bank credit and loans lies in the implementation of a meticulously crafted pledge or guarantee mechanism. So far, the vast majority of the deals has been done via traditional pledge or security arrangement as established practices provided under the realm of the civil law system.

---

[15] CCTV Economy Half Hour. "Hero" Smiles Triaphantly on the Market, Shen Bing Interview with Zhang Yimou (Economic Half Hour Reporters Li Weibing, Liu Yuchen, Yan Wenyu and Yan Jingfeng edited and reported on the 23 December 2002).

[16] See Capital Wings for the Film and Television Industry, Shanghai Financial News, A08 Edition, 4 August 2009.

[17] Tang Rong, 'Financial Innovation and Film Growth', in Cui Baoguo, ed. *Media Blue Book: 2010: Report on the Development of China's Media Industry*, Social Science Literature Press, 2010, pp. 299–311.

These examples highlight the evolution of financing strategies in the China film industry, from relying on international loans to the more conventional use of domestic bank loans. This trend reflects the increasing maturity and sophistication of the film market in China, as well as the confidence of financial institutions in the potential of the domestic film industry.

## Forms of Bank Credit Services for the Film Industry

Credit financing can be categorized into three types: mortgage financing, pledge financing, and credit guarantee financing.

In mortgage financing, a debtor uses its property as collateral for the loan, without possession of the property being transferred. If the debtor fails to repay the debt, the creditor has the right to be paid first through the sale of the property. Banks initially provided mortgage financing to a film project to avoid the volatile risk inherent in the film industry. Compared with TV series, the investment risk of a film is greater. After a TV series is purchased by a television station, there is basically not much pressure on repayment since the television station will manage to find the sponsorship from the advertising industry. That way, the main buyer of TV series is normally a business or businesses, not the audience. However, it is a different case for a film. A film released requires the audience to vote directly with individual film tickets. The business quality of a film determines its final box office performance and thus the economic returns. On one hand, when a bank tries to seek stable returns from a film project, it may find the high risks inherent in a film project make such an expectation quite a challenge to meet. Therefore, their overall attitude is relatively conservative. In this case, it is natural for a bank to require a mortgage before it agrees to release loans to a film project. On the other hand, mortgage loan is a general form of credit service, without any consideration specific to a film project. When a bank invests in a film project, it may lack sufficient understanding of the project, incapable of judging the business quality of the film to be made. Consequently, they focus more on the enterprise behind the project. That way, a bank still actually values strong guarantees such as real estate mortgages to control the risks associated with the film project. Since a film company may have limited assets to provide as mortgage, the film company owner or the other related individuals are normally required to provide mortgage with their personal assets for the loan to be released to the film company on the project. This is so-called mandatory joint and several guarantee requirement, which have been quite popular when Chinese banks try to provide credit services for film production. A bank can thus obtain the personal assets of the financed party if the project goes flop. This practice significantly limits the financing amount of a film project. In a way, the mandatory joint and several guarantee requirement is similar to the practice where a creditor requires the shareholder to assume unlimited joint and several liabilities when financing a one-person company. Mortgage financing reveals a bank's unfamiliarity with and distrust of film projects.

Pledge financing involves a debtor transferring movable property or rights to the creditor as security for the loan. If the debtor fails to repay the debt, the creditor can be compensated through the sale of the pledged property or rights. For a company majoring in film business, lack of tangible assets make it hard to obtain bank loans. To facilitate credit financing support to the film industry, Article 40, paragraph 1 of the Film Industry Promotion Law stipulates, "intellectual property pledge financing operations related to films shall be carried out in accordance with the law, and the development of the film industry shall be supported through means such as credit." This statutory calling helps to build up a positive legal environment for film financing. However, in reality, some issues need to be resolved before hand. On the one hand, for the copyright held by a film production company, its value is hard to be assessed. At the moment, China has not seen reliable mechanisms to provide credible assessment on the film to be pledged for the bank loans. The answer lies only in a steady development of a healthy industry to be fostered in a competitive film market. On the other, the purpose of a loan sought after by the film maker is to produce a film. In this sense, the film to be produced matters for the repayment of the bank loan. Therefore, some banks accept the expected box office receipt as the pledge for the company concerned to be granted the loan requested. This is a bank loan based on so-called expected copy right. Although this right of expectation is not a completed copyright and cannot be pledged, according to Article 66 of the "Minutes of the National Court Civil and Commercial Trial Work Conference", if a contract with a guarantee concluded by the parties does not lead to any legally invalid circumstances, it shall be recognized as valid. Article 388, paragraph 1 of the Civil Code stipulates that a guarantee contract includes a mortgage contract, a pledge contract, and other contracts with guarantee provisions, which means that an expected copyright pledge contract reached for film financing is legally valid, thus providing a legal basis for bank loans provided based on such expected copyrights. This way, a financing tool specific to the film industry has since developed in China.

Credit guarantee financing refers to the guarantee provided by a financial institution to a film company during the financing process. If the film company fails to fulfill its debt obligations, the institution providing financial guarantee may assume the responsibility of reimbursement as stated in the contract. Credit guarantee financing has gained popularity in the film industry while banks are gradually exploring credit guarantee loans as a more advanced form of financing compared to mortgages. Unlike mortgage loans, credit guarantee loans do not require collateral property be offered. Instead, the guarantee offering financial institution assesses the comprehensive capabilities of the film company regarding the film project, including factors relating to scripts, directors, actors, and schedules. This reflects the financial institution's growing understanding and trust in the film industry, as well as their belief in controlling credit risk through the profitability of film projects. In 2008, Huayi Brothers successfully obtained a loan for the film "The King of Kung Fu" using the credit guarantee loan model, with the guarantee provided by China Export and Credit Insurance Corporation.[18]

[18] Liu Yi, Mengjia Li, Research on the Financing Legal Issues of China's Film Industry—From the Perspective of the Article Fortieth of Film Industry Promotion Act of People's Republic of China, in Journal of Beijing Union University (Humanities and Social Sciences) Vol. 56, p. 106.

### 2.1.2 Completion Guarantee in China

For a film financing project, the duly completion of the film financed is the key for the financing parties to have their investment back with satisfactory returns. If a specialised party could step up and guarantee the duly completion of the film, it will be easier for a film company to have its film project financed in the market.

Furthermore, obtaining bank loans can be a challenge for a medium-sized or independent film maker, who usually has neither solid assets to provide as collateral nor trusted third parties to offer personal guarantee to secure a bank loan. In this case, the completion guarantee arrangement mechanism, as an established practice to facilitate financing for a film project in many jurisdictions, may offer a solution by providing a third party guarantee for an independent film maker to obtain bank loans before starting a film project.

Currently, the concept of completion guarantee is not widely used in China's film market, despite its unique ability to meet the investment needs of certain film production projects.

In 2015, Film Finances (FFI), the largest global film completion insurance company, initiated its entry into the market of China. By June 2017, FFI had announced a cooperative agreement with PICC Property and Casualty Insurance to jointly introduce film completion insurance. PICC Property and Casualty Insurance will issue policies for FFI's services in China, offering comprehensive risk solutions encompassing personal, property, and liability insurance to support domestic film projects. This collaboration aims to promote the localization of film and TV completion and production insurance. The first domestic film to utilize FFI's film completion guarantee service is Blood of the Machine, under the control of Unity Film.

In addition, Ping An Insurance has also ventured into providing similar services in China. In 2015, Ping An Insurance introduced film completion insurance products, primarily focusing on personal accident insurance and property insurance. The company, in partnership with Central New Film Group, conducts a thorough risk assessment before underwriting insurance policies. This assessment covers the overall situation of the film, budget rationality, filming plans, and more. After underwriting the insurance policy, Ping An Insurance may review the progress of filming and provide recommendations, although it does not monitor the entire film shooting process. Furthermore, the company offers a package service of "film completion + physical damage" to reduce the film completion risk.

Local film and television companies have also explored the film completion guarantee market. For instance, Huali Chenguang International Culture and Media, the production company behind the "Small Times" series, launched related products. In 2016, Huali Chenguang signed an exclusive cooperation agreement with Pacific Insurance Company and introduced various product models, including "film completion guarantee," "film completion guarantee + production," and "film completion guarantee + production + investment."[19]

[19] "Completion Guarantee: Can it become a "must-have" tool for film and television over-budget filming?," 21st Century Business Herald, 21 July 2018.

Despite these efforts, the utilization of film completion guarantees remains limited in China. Currently, only Jackie Chan's "Blood of the Machine" serves as an example of a Chinese film utilizing the film completion guarantee. Most related cases have been concentrated in Sino-foreign co-production projects such as The Great Wall and Crouching Tiger, Hidden Dragon 2. The film financing market still has a long way to go to provide mature film completion guarantee services, which is still in its initial stages of development in China.

## 2.2 *Financing in the Capital Market*

As a cultural and capital-intensive industry, funds are highly necessary for a film to be created, produced, distributed and finally, exhibited. Furthermore, a close integration of funds and creative talents serves as the prerequisite for a film to make a success, culturally and financially. In this regard, it involves film industry's access to the capital market, the architecture of a film company, and the impact of the capital market on the film industry. Liang Fengyi's Qin Jia Yuan Media Services Company Limited (hereinafter referred to as "Qin Jia Yuan") listing on the Hong Kong Stock Exchange, Beijing Poly Media Culture Limited and its subsidiaries (hereinafter referred to as "Poly") backdoor listing on the Hong Kong Stock Exchange, Huayi Brothers Media Co., Ltd. (hereinafter referred to as "Huayi Brothers") listing on the growth enterprises market in China, Bona Film Group Co., Ltd. (hereinafter referred to as "Bona") listing on the NASDAQ in the United States, China Film Co., Ltd. (hereinafter referred to as "China Film") and Shanghai Film Co., Ltd. listing on the Shanghai Stock Exchange, Bona's privatization and subsequent successful listing on the Shenzhen Stock Exchange in 2022, to name a few, are the typical cases that the capital market has been becoming increasingly closely intertwined with the Chinese film industry. That way, China's film industry has been significantly pushed forward in various aspects, constantly presenting new issues for China's film legal system to deal with.

### 2.2.1 Foreign Investment in Film Production

According to China's commitments made upon joining the WTO, both "broadcasting and television program production, publishing, distribution, and broadcasting companies" and "film production and distribution companies" have been listed in the "prohibited foreign investment industries" category in the "Foreign Investment Industry Guidance Catalog" implemented since 1 April 2002. However, the then SARFT and the MOFCOM released and implemented the "Interim Measures for the Administration of Sino-Foreign Joint Venture and Cooperative Production and Operation of Broadcasting and Television Programs" (referred to as "Order No. 44") on 28 October 2004, which lifted this ban and provided a legal channel for foreign investment in the television program production field. On 30 November of the same year, the National

Development and Reform Commission (referred to as "NDRC") and MOFCOM issued the "Catalogue for the Guidance of Foreign Investment Industries (Revised in 2004)", which included "broadcasting and television program production, distribution, and film production (Chinese majority ownership)" in the "restricted foreign investment industry catalog", allowing foreign investment in the film production field as well, albeit under a strict regulatory mechanism.

That way, major international audiovisual giants had been actively entering the Chinese film and television market. For example, in November 2004, Beijing Huasuo Film Digital Execution Co., Ltd. (referred to as "Huaso") was jointly established by Beijing Sony Pictures International Television Corporation, China Film Group Corporation and Huaxia Digital Production Co., Ltd. Huaso was established mainly to develop and produce Chinese language film and television entertainment programs, including television programs, sitcoms, TV series, and TV movies, and distribute them domestically and internationally. In Huaso, China Film Group holds 51% of the equity capital, while Sony holds 49%. The board of directors consists of six members, three from each side, with the Chairman of China Film Group serving as the Chairman of Huaso.

China Film Warner Hengdian Studio (referred to as "China Film Warner Hengdian") is the first Sino-foreign joint venture film and entertainment company in China's history. It is jointly invested by China Film Group Corporation, the largest State-owned film enterprise group in China, Warner Bros. Entertainment, a giant in the entertainment film industry, and Hengdian Group, the largest private enterprise in China's film and television industry. It was registered and established in Beijing in December 2004 with an office operating in the historic Beijing Film Studio as early as 2005. The senior management of the company is appointed by the three major shareholders, with the General Manager of China Film Group serving as the Chairman and Executive Vice President of Warner Bros. serving as the Vice Chairman. The company's business includes investment, production, distribution, and promotion of Chinese-language films, Sino-foreign co-production films, TV movies, and animation products.

With the promotion of Order No. 44, Viacom and Shanghai Media Group jointly formed Shanghai Oriental Nickelodeon Television Production Co., Ltd., with a registered capital of 6 million US dollars, with Chinese partner's holding of 51% and Viacom's holding of 49%. This company mainly produced localized children's television programs and introduced into China the market model, production concepts, and other aspects of well-known Nickelodeon children's channels such as "Blue's Clues" and "Kids' Choice Awards".

Against this background, on 13 May 2005, Yu Li Holdings Limited (hereinafter referred to as "Yu Li Holdings"), listed on the Hong Kong Stock Exchange, announced that it would acquire Anglo Alliance from its shareholders. Anglo Alliance is an investment holding company that owns 98% of the equity of Hao Ge Film and Television Media Culture Limited (hereinafter referred to as "Hao Ge"). Anglo Alliance group companies engage in various media-related businesses in China, including TV drama production, film investment, advertising agency, and advertisement production. After the equity acquisition accomplished, Yu Li Holdings will control 98% of Hao Ge's equity through Anglo Alliance, while Hao Ge holds 50% of Poly Huayi's equity. Poly Huayi is mainly engaged in TV drama production, film investment, advertising agency services, and production. Poly Huayi owns stakes in five companies with different shareholding ratios: Hainan Haishi Tourism Satellite Media Co., Ltd. (hereinafter referred to as "Hainan Satellite TV"), Beijing Ying Shi Film and Television Art Co., Ltd. (hereinafter referred to as "Ying Shi Film and Television"), Beijing Xin Bao Yuan Film and Television Investment Co., Ltd. (hereinafter referred to as "Xin Bao Yuan"), Beijing Huayi Shanhe Shui Advertising Co., Ltd. (hereinafter referred to as "Shanhe Shui"), and Beijing Qiansi Advertising Co., Ltd. (hereinafter referred to as "Qiansi Advertising"). Poly Huayi owns 49% of Hainan Satellite TV's equity. Hainan Satellite TV has the exclusive rights to manage and operate Hainan Satellite TV programs and advertising business and enjoy related income rights for 30 years. Poly Huayi owns 60% of Ying Shi Film and Television's equity. Ying Shi Film and Television is mainly engaged in the production of situational comedies. Poly Huayi owns 50% of Xin Bao Yuan's equity. Xin Bao Yuan is mainly engaged in the production of TV dramas directed by Zhao Baogang. Poly Huayi owns 51% of Shanhe Shui's equity. Shanhe Shui is mainly engaged in advertising agency services and production, primarily producing company videos and advertisements. Poly Huayi owns 55% of Qiansi Advertising's equity. Qiansi Advertising mainly provides advertising package services. The company uses various advertising media to provide advertising/promotion plans for clients. The overall revenue of Poly Huayi and its five subsidiary companies mainly comes from the sale of programs and film products, the licensing or sub-licensing of film copyrights and TV programs, and the provision of advertising services. According to Yu Li Holdings' shareholder circular, Poly Huayi's revenue in 2004 reached 77 million yuan. With the completion of the transaction, 50% of Poly Huayi's equity is incorporated into Yu Li Holdings, and the ultimate holder of 50% of Poly Huayi's equity, Dong Ping, receives 2.7 billion common shares issued by Yu Li Holdings, accounting for 27% of the issued shares at that time, making Dong Ping the second-largest shareholder of Yu Li Holdings outside of the public shareholders. Dong Ping is also appointed as an executive director of Yu Li Holdings, achieving the listing of the portion of Poly Huayi's equity held by Dong Ping through a reverse merger.

However, on 31 October 2007, the NDRC and the MOFCOM jointly issued the "Catalogue for the Gudance of Foreign Investment Industries (Revised in 2007)", which abolished the Catalogue for the Guidance of Foreign Investment Industries (Revised in 2004) by incorporating "broadcasting and television program production and operation companies" as well as "film production companies, distribution companies, and theater circuits" back into the "Prohibited Catalogue for Foreign Investment in Industries". As a result, after a brief period of allowing foreign investment in the form of physical investment to enter the Chinese film and television production market, the window was quickly closed. This made Poly Huayi's model an irreproducible history.

### 2.2.2 VIE Investment Structure

Currently, film and television production is still a prohibited area for foreign investment. Given that film production is the most substantial part for the film business, despite laws prohibiting foreign direct investment in film and television production, overseas investors have managed to enter this field through complex structural arrangments. Among them, VIE has become a commonly used structure for overseas investors to participate in the film production projects in China.

Early Case of Qin Jia Yuan

Qin Jia Yuan was listed on the Hong Kong Stock Exchange on June 30, 2004. Its main business was to provide media services in China. Qin Jia Yuan, production companies, and television program investors (mostly advertising agents) normally would sign investment agreements to ensure investment for a production project. According to this agreement, the production company, with the help of Qin Jia Yuan's television program services, was responsible for the production and distribution of television programmes in China, while investors (mostly advertising agents) were responsible for funding the production of television programmes. Qin Jia Yuan, as a bridge between production companies and investors, actually enjoyed a core position. Qin Jia Yuan earned commissions by providing services to production companies and advertising agents, earned income by providing television programme production services to production companies, and earned service income by providing market promotion services to advertising agents. In this way, through the implementation of the Variable Interest Entities (VIE) structure in the dual process of TV drama or television program production and advertising agents providing production funds, Qin Jia Yuan, as an overseas company, thus participated in the production of TV dramas and television programmes in Chinese mainland and obtained funding through advertising for the production of its TV dramas and television programs. This is an early investment case for an overseas investor tried best to obtain the access to the Chinese film and television production market through the VIE structure.

VIE Structure Adopted by Bona

Bona Film, a company incorporated in the Cayman Islands, operates its film business through three subsidiaries in the PRC. These subsidiaries, namely Bona Advertising, Bona Culture, and Baichuan Distribution, are established under the laws of the PRC. The equity interests in these companies are held by Yu Dong, the ultimate controller of Bona Film, his brother Yu Hai, or other subsidiaries. Bona Advertising stands as an exception, with 3% of its equity interest held by a third party natural person. Bona New World, a wholly-owned subsidiary of Bona Film, has entered into agreements with the three subsidiaries and their respective shareholders, defining the relationship between Bona Film and the subsidiaries. These agreements effectively give Bona

Film control over the subsidiaries and allow Bona Film to receive most of the revenues generated by them. Consequently, the three companies are considered VIEs under US GAAP, with their historical financial data being included in Bona Film's records. Two types of agreements were entered between Bona New World and the VIEs:

The first type of agreement was an "exclusive technical support and consulting services agreement" through which Bona New World provides technical support and consulting services to Bona Advertising, Bona Culture, and Baichuan Distribution. In return, Bona Advertising and Bona Culture pay Bona New World 100% of their net profit before tax as fees, while Baichuan Distribution pays 90% of its net profit before tax due to the 10% equity interest held by a company of the Poly Group. The payment of these service fees is governed by the agreements between Bona New World and the subsidiaries, subject to approval by the respective subsidiaries' board of directors. The term of each agreement commenced on the specified effective date and ended upon the dissolution of Bona Novia or the relevant subsidiary.

The second type of agreement was regarded as necessary to secure Bona Film's control over the relevant subsidiary. It consists of two contracts, namely the Voting Proxy and Equity Acquisition Option Contract and the Equity Pledge Contract. The Voting Proxy and Equity Acquisition Option Contracts granted Bona New World or a person designated thereby the right to exercise all voting rights of the shareholders in the subsidiaries. Additionally, Bona Film enjoyed the exclusive right, in accordance with PRC laws, to acquire all equity interests in the subsidiaries or designate other parties to do so. The price for such acquisition was determined based on the net assets of the subsidiaries or the lowest price permitted under PRC law, whichever was higher. The subsidiaries were obligated not to distribute profits without the prior consent of Bona Film. The contractual period for these contracts began on the specified effective date and ended when the related exclusive technical support and consulting services agreement was terminated.

The Equity Pledge Contracts were entered into between Bona New World and the shareholders of each subsidiary. These contracts secured the payment obligations under the exclusive technical support and consulting services agreements. Shareholders, except for the third-party shareholder holding a 10% equity interest in Bacera, pledged their equity interests in the subsidiaries to Bona New World. They were also restricted from transferring, selling, pledging, or creating any encumbrance on their shareholdings, except for transfers made in accordance with the Proxy Voting and Share Purchase Agreements or transfers between shareholders that did not affect the validity of the share pledge contracts. The term of each Equity Pledge Contract began on the agreed effective date and ended when the relevant subsidiary was no longer liable for its obligations under the related Exclusive Technical Support and Consultancy Services Agreement.

#### Uncertain Legal Status of VIE Structure

It is widely believed that the VIE structure, including its arrangement and structure, is in compliance with the regulations and laws of the PRC and does not violate any relevant provisions. However, there is some uncertainty regarding the application of the PRC regulations and laws. Therefore, it is possible that the regulatory authorities in the PRC may make a decision that contradicts the general consensus. If a PRC government authority determines that Bona Film's corporate structure and contractual arrangements, for example, violate the requirements of the relevant PRC regulations and laws, the VIE structure may be deemed invalid or unenforceable. This could result in Bona Film facing administrative penalties for violating PRC laws and being required to retroactively seek approvals from the relevant government authorities. The VIE structure was originally developed by foreign investors as a means to indirectly invest in the film, television, advertising, and performing arts industries in order to circumvent the restrictions imposed thereupon by PRC law. Although this structure can be deemed as not a foreign direct investment in these industries, there is still ambiguity in how it should be recognized in substance.

The VIE structure is a controversial issue in China's efforts to open up to the outside world. For once, China Unicom Corporation used so-called "Sino-foreign" financing structure to establish a GSM network. Under this structure, a joint venture was formed between a foreign company and a Chinese company, with the foreign company providing financing and technical support through a project cooperation contract. Once the network was built, China Unicom Group operated it, and the joint venture received a percentage of the cash flow generated by the project for a certain period of time. This cash flow was expected to cover the capital provided by the joint venture for the network construction, with the joint venture potentially earning a return as well. However, the "Sino-foreign" structure was seen as a way to bypass the restrictions on foreign investment in the telecommunications sector. In reality, foreign parties often participated in the network construction, and the financial system was controlled by the foreign party. The "Sino-foreign" structure allowed the joint ventures to share in the profits from the operation of the network through technical support and consulting fees, effectively constituting foreign investment and participation in the telecoms sector. The termination of the "Sino-foreign" cooperation contract resulted in significant losses for the Hong Kong-listed red chip company of the Unicom Group. The problem was eventually resolved, but at a cost to Unicom's financial resources.

In line with China's membership in the WTO and its commitment to opening up its telecommunications operations, a systematic approach has been adopted to allow foreign participation. This approach includes regulations on shareholding ratios, geographical areas, business scope, and timetable. To ensure the successful opening up of the telecommunication industry, the State Council issued Decree No. 333 on 11 December 2001, known as the Provisions on the Administration of Foreign-invested Telecommunications Enterprises. These provisions outline the forms, conditions, and approval procedures for foreign investment in China's telecommunication industry. They also specify the shareholding restrictions for foreign investors in basic and value-added telecommunication businesses. For basic telecommunication businesses, foreign investors' capital contribution should not exceed 49%, while for value-added telecommunication businesses, the limit is also 49%, except for wireless paging business, where the limit is 50%. However, to actively participate in the operation of the enterprise, foreign operators must have a controlling position in the joint venture, rather than being limited to receiving dividends. Despite these regulations, some foreign operators have chosen to invest in China's telecommunication market through VIEs, particularly in value-added telecom services. Additionally, multinational companies entering the China Internet market still rely on previous practices of "borrowing" ICP licenses from domestic companies, using domain name authorization and other means, to bypass the Regulations on the Administration of Foreign Invested Telecommunications Enterprises. In response to this, the former Ministry of Information Industry (MII) issued a notice in 2006 to regulate illegal cooperation between foreign investors and domestic value-added telecommunication companies. The notice requires that domain names and registered trademarks be owned by the operators in accordance with the law, that sites and facilities be established within the permitted business coverage, and that network information security measures be improved and implemented. As a result, companies like Google had to establish joint ventures with Chinese partners to obtain value-added telecommunications business licenses. However, even in these joint ventures, the foreign party effectively maintained control.

In the Internet industry, due to restrictions on foreign investors' capital contributions in joint ventures, many foreign investors have turned to the VIE structure to obtain licenses for value-added telecommunication businesses and secured control of enterprises. This situation has been kept going on under under the de facto consent from regulators and the concerned enterprises. However, on 12 May 2011, Yahoo, a US company listed on NASDAQ, issued a press release revealing that Alibaba Group had carried out two transactions without the knowledge and approval of its Board of Directors and Shareholders' Meeting. These transactions involved the transfer and divestment of shares of Alipay, a subsidiary of Alibaba Group. Yahoo had to enter into negotiations with Softbank and Alibaba Group regarding this matter. Alibaba Group transferred Alipay to a company controlled by Jack Ma, claiming that it was done to expedite the regulatory licensing process. Prior to June 2009, Alipay was a wholly foreign-owned company, but in June 2009, 70% of its shares were transferred to Zhejiang Alibaba Network Technology Co. The People's Bank of China issued an announcement in April 2009, stating that Alipay would not be a subsidiary of the bank. In June 2010, the Central Bank issued measures for the administration of non-financial institutions payment services, which specified the eligibility conditions and capital contribution requirements for foreign-invested payment institutions. The remaining 30% of Alipay's shares were transferred to Zhejiang Alibaba for 165 million yuan.[20] Despite the prohibition on foreign investment in non-financial institution payment services, Alibaba Group had been able to control Alipay and profit from it through the VIE structure. Meanwhile, Alipay had to make a written statement to the central bank confirming that it was not controlled by foreign investors. The

[20] Hou Jiyong, "Ma Yun defends the beginning and end of Alipay's decoupling: a correct but imperfect decision," http://www.21cbh.com/HTML/2011-6-20/xMMDAwMDI0NTQxMg.html.

transfer of Alipay to Zhejiang Alibaba at a price below market value caused dissatisfaction among Alibaba Group's shareholders, Yahoo and Softbank. After more than three months of negotiation, an agreement was reached. Under the agreement, Alipay would continue to provide preferential terms to Alibaba Group for its online payment services, and Alibaba Group would provide Alipay with intellectual property licensing and technical support services. Alibaba Group would be compensated for these services and receive a percentage of Alipay's pre-tax profit. In addition, Alibaba Group would receive a certain percentage of Alipay's equity upon its future IPO or other agreed events.[21] This solution represents a weakened version of the VIE structure, as Alibaba Group no longer has physical control over Alipay, but still benefits from its profits and equity transfer. This case highlights the legal challenges and significance of the VIE structure in overseas capital markets.

A VIE, or Variable Interest Entity, is an investment structure devised by foreign investors to bypass China's restrictions on foreign investment. Initially used primarily in the telecoms industry, the VIE structure has gradually expanded to other sectors where foreign investment is limited or prohibited, such as film, television, or the internet industry. By means of the VIE structure, foreign investors can exert significant control over companies operating in restricted or even forbidden industries and make a profit therefrom. This approach relies on the tacit approval of regulatory authorities and undermines the authority of China's legal regime governing foreign investment. However, an outright ban on VIEs could have repercussions on the investment model and cause disturbances in the international capital market.

Additionally, backhaul investment is a crucial method for China to access to foreign capital markets. Although China's tax law system has already clarified the legal position of backhaul investment, it has not been put into practice due to various considerations. Article 3 of the Enterprise Income Tax Law states that resident enterprises are required to pay enterprise income tax and defines a resident enterprise as an entity established in accordance with Chinese law or a foreign country's law with its actual management organ in China. Consequently, Chinese holding companies listed abroad, regardless of being "red chips" or "small red chips," may be recognized as resident enterprises under China's new tax regime. Circular No. 45 of 2011, issued by the State Administration of Taxation, further explains that overseas-registered Chinese-funded holding resident enterprises are those recognized as Chinese resident enterprises due to their actual management organizations being located in China.[22] These enterprises have the responsibility to fulfill tax obligations and withhold and pay enterprise income tax on behalf of non-resident enterprises when they receive income sourced from within China.[23]

In dealing with VIEs, a similar principle may be applied where the entire structure under the VIE is considered a resident enterprise as long as the controlling enterprise is a resident enterprise. This exempts it from the restrictions or prohibitions on foreign investment imposed by the PRC. However, if the controlling enterprise is

[21] See Yahoo! Inc.'s Form-K 8 filing with the SEC on 29 July 2011 for more information.

[22] Article III, Circular No. 45.

[23] Article IV, Circular No. 45.

not a resident enterprise, it may be subject to these restrictions or prohibitions. This approach allows for the listing of relevant Chinese industries abroad while upholding China's foreign investment regime. Treating the VIE structure in this manner also provides a clear path for the Chinese film and television industry to raise funds abroad, which certainly facilitates its development with inflow of the overseas professional equity capital.

On 25 August 2011, the MOFCOM issued the Announcement No. 53 of 2011, known as the Provisions of the Ministry of Commerce on the Implementation of the Security Review System for the Merger and Acquisition of Domestic Enterprises by Foreign Investors (the "M&A Security Review Provisions"). According to the M&A Security Review Provisions, the determination of whether a merger or acquisition is subject to the security review is based on the substance and actual impact of the transaction. Foreign investors are prohibited from circumventing the security review through means such as substitute holding, trust, multi-level reinvestment, leasing, lending, control by agreement, and offshore transactions.[24] As a result, mergers and acquisitions involving VIE structures, including those using control by agreement, are now incorporated into China's foreign investment legal system. This provision holds two significant implications. Firstly, it recognizes the concept of substantive mergers and acquisitions in China's foreign investment legal system, laying the foundation for the relevant legal framework. Secondly, it eliminates the ambiguities surrounding foreign investment and industry investment structures that existed previously. However, it remains to be seen whether the VIE structure, which relies on control by agreement, meets the requirements of China's legal regime for foreign-invested enterprises, as there is currently no established system for substantive acquisition in other aspects of M&A.

### 2.2.3 Growth Enterprise Market

On 27 September 2009, Huayi Brothers, the largest private film production company in China, received approval from the CSRC to go public and be listed on the Growth Enterprise Market (GEM) of the Shenzhen Stock Exchange. This approval, documented under No. [2009] 1039, allowed Huayi Brothers to issue 42 million RMB ordinary shares. The shares were offered through a combination of offline placement to inquirers and online pricing issuance to public investors. Out of the total shares, 8.4 million were placed offline and 33.6 million were priced online, with an issuance price of RMB 28.58 per share. The Shenzhen Stock Exchange listed the RMB ordinary shares of Huayi Brothers on the GEM Board, with the stock abbreviation "Huayi Brothers" and the stock code "300027". The 33.6 million shares issued through online pricing were made available for trading from 30 October 2009 onwards. This listing on the GEM demonstrates the capital market's provision of financing opportunities for the film industry in China. Besides its focus on film production, Huayi Brothers also enjoys a successful history in film distribution, exhibition, TV drama

[24] Article 9, M&A Security Review Provisions.

production, and artiste agency and related services. The successful listing of Huayi Brothers signifies a milestone in the formal integration between the capital market and the entertainment industry from a legal standpoint. Prior to this, China Film had also successfully issued corporate bonds to the public.

Given the volatile nature of the entertainment industry, companies involving in this sector, such as film and television companies, face higher than average business risks. In accordance with the Initial Public Offering Measures, which were implemented in the People's Republic of China on 18 May 2006, companies seeking to issue shares must adhere to the Company Law, Securities Law, and the additional requirements outlined in the Initial Public Offering Measures. Notably, these requirements include specific financial accounting criteria that must be met. The cumulative net profit for the past three fiscal years has to be positive, surpassing RMB 30 million. The net profit is calculated by considering the lower value before or after deducting non-recurring gains and losses. Additionally, the net cash flow from operating activities has to exceed RMB 50 million in total during the same period, or the operating income has to surpass RMB 300 million in aggregate. The total share capital must be at least RMB 30 million before the issuance. The ratio of intangible assets (excluding land use rights, water surface farming rights, and mining rights) to net assets at the end of the most recent period should not exceed 20%. Lastly, there should be no outstanding unrecovered losses at the end of the most recent period.

Based on the information disclosed in the prospectus by Huayi Brothers, the consolidated net profits for the years FY2006, FY2007, FY2008, and FY2009 from January to June were RMB23,564,114.94, RMB58,244,557.14, RMB68,064,536.13, and RMB31,634,415.25, respectively. These cumulative profits exceeded RMB 30 million, meeting the requirement of three years' net profit. However, the net cash flows from operating activities for the years 2006, 2007, 2008, and January to June 2009 were −34,389,203.59, −44,914,753.83, −61,122,829.31, and 13,127.188.61, which did not meet the standard of cumulative cash flows exceeding RMB 50 million in the last three accounting years. On the other hand, the cumulative operating revenues for FY2006, FY2007, and FY2008 exceeded RMB 300 million, meeting the standard of the three-year cumulative operating revenue. Additionally, the total share capital of Huayi Brothers before issuing new shares was RMB 126 million, complying with the requirements. However, as of December 31, 2008, Huayi Brothers had an inventory of RMB231,926,218.55 and a net asset of RMB248,012,409.59. According to the accounting treatment disclosed by Huayi Brothers, their inventory then included raw materials, products in process, goods in stock, and low-value consumables. The book value of their inventory as of June 30, 2009, was RMB285,390,500, accounting for 45.34% of current assets and 42.31% of total assets. Huayi Brothers explained that their capital was primarily used for making movies and TV dramas, hence the formation of inventory. The intangible assets in their assets exceeded 20% of the net assets. In these circumstances, Huayi Brothers would not be qualified to make an initial offering of shares in China and go public, as stated in Article 33 of the Measures for Initial Public Offerings.

To foster the growth of innovative enterprises and protect the rights of investors, the CSRC introduced the Interim Measures for the Administration of Initial Public

Offering and Listing on GEM in March 2009. These measures, also known as the GEM Administrative Measures, outline the requirements for companies seeking an initial public offering and listing on GEM. According to Article 10 of the GEM Administrative Measures, issuers must meet specific financial indicators. This includes having consecutive profits for the last two years with a net profit of at least RMB 10 million, or profits for the last year with a net profit of at least RMB 5 million, operating revenue of at least RMB 50 million for the last year, and a growth rate of operating revenue of at least 30% for each of the last two years. Additionally, issuers must have net assets of at least twenty million yuan, no uncompensated loss, and a total share capital of at least thirty million yuan. Unlike the Main Board, the GEM Administrative Measures do not limit the proportion of intangible assets to the net assets of the issuer. This accommodates R&D-based and copyright business-centered enterprises that seek capital market financing. The GEM Administrative Measures also reduce the profitability requirement from three years to two years, making it more accessible for high-growth and high-risk enterprises to go public. This creates opportunities for innovative enterprises and film and television companies to enter the capital market. For instance, Huayi Brothers, a film production company, meets the requirements of the GEM Administrative Measures and can issue shares publicly and be listed on GEM. The introduction of the GEM market has not only enriched landscape of China's capital market but has also provided a favorable capital platform for the film industry, which possesses lucrative opportunities but also carries significant risks. Huayi Brothers and Huace Film & Television are examples of companies that successfully listed on GEM, and Beijing Raycom Media Company Limited has also expressed its intention to pursue an initial public offering and listing on GEM. Overall, the establishment of the GEM market has greatly facilitated financing activities in the capital market for China's film and television industry.

### 2.2.4 Equity Investment from Financial Institutions

Various private equity funds are active in China's film industry. The involvement of private equity funds in the entertainment business also helps a film enterprise establish a complete set of production budget plans, auditing and financial management systems, and through the strong supervision of financial contributors on the use of funds, thus making the financing of a film project more standardised, which is of great significance in terms of private equity financing.

In China, private equity funds are normally sourced from financial institutions as well as from specialised investors in specific sector. Apart from the traditional credit service, banks in China have been exploring the other more convenient instruments to tap the gigantic capital pool maintained by themselves via deposit services provided. Given that traditional credit is not allowed to used for equity investment, private equity funds enable a bank to indirectly participate in the equity investment business under the general framework of asset management scheme, which can be dealt with by an separate subsidiary of this bank.

When the box office of China keeps hitting its historic record, film business has been a favourite choice for relevant equity funds. For instance, in the prospectus of China Film, various equity funds are found as the subscribers of the shares before the public offering, many of which are of bank background. Furthermore, China has promoted some so called leading equity funds to invest in the film sector, some of which are also substantially sourced from the capital pool maintained by banks. With the strict measures taken by China financial regulators since 2021 to oversee the equity investment activities of banks, the private equity funds have found it not easy to turn to the capital pool managed by banks. Accompanied with the strict regulation on leading actors or actress, who normally claim a substantial share of the budget of a film, the investment via private equite funds has been resceding from its tide.

However, equity funds specialised in film sector are still highly important for development of China's film industry. In 2007 and 2009, Sequoia Capital invested 10 million and 15 million respectively in Bona Film Group. The role of film funds in movie financing has gradually become prominent. Besides the financial resources necessary for a film production, these specialised funds have also provided invaluable support to streamlise China's film sector into a modern film industry, which is highly essential for development of China's film business. For once, given the rampant copyright violations, film producers expect little return in the whole life cycle of a produced film but only the theatre exhibition stage. This made the film producer desperately pursue the box office success of the film, come what may. This in turn raises the price of a film ticket, pushing away the potential theatrical visitors of the film, who may turn to other unauthoised means to enjoy a film. Thus, a negligent spiral has been formed and worsened. A specialised fund in film industry plays long term, otherwise it could easily be replaced by the quick money floating in the market. This may turn the tide to make the film prodocer to work more on the whole life cycle of a film.

Currently, domestic capital in China is relatively abundant, and the willingness of external capital to invest in the film industry is strong, creating a favorable development environment for the film industry, which heavily depends on capital investment. The expansion of investment and financing channels in the film industry not only benefits the development of film production but also provides important support for film companies to further extend their industrial chains. At the same time, the active participation of various domestic and international film industry funds, especially their rich experience in internal management, financial systems, and the use of financial instruments, has positively impacted the development of the entire Chinese film industry chain.

Specifically, the capital strength of enterprises in China's film industry has significantly increased. On one hand, film and television cultural companies such as China Film Co., Shanghai Film Group, Huayi Brothers, Huace Film & TV, and Enlight Media have successively gone public, enabling film companies to leverage capital market channels to gather abundant capital and high-quality resources from within the industry, resulting in positive resource synergy effects. On the other hand, due to adjustments and relaxations in national policies, an increasing amount of external capital has begun to enter various business segments of the film industry. Besides traditional general funds, numerous institutional investors, including various forms of funds such as trust investments, have started to enter the film market. Private equity investment funds have also become an emerging force within China's film industry. Currently, several funds, including IDG New Media Fund, China Film Fund, Sequoia Capital, SoftBank, A3 International Asia Film Fund, and the "Iron Pool" private film fund, are involved in the investment and creation of film and television products.

With the public offerings of some film and television enterprises and the influx of substantial external capital into the film industry, the next 3 to 5 years will be a crucial phase for Chinese film and television companies to integrate resources. Traditional small workshop-style film and television enterprises will face the prospect of mergers and acquisitions, or even being pushed out of the market.

## 3 China's Administration Licence System for Film Production

Although the economic reform influences heavily on the whole film area and has offered considerable autonomy to the film makers, the long lasting regulatory reliance and hesitance or straitjacketed mentality of the film regulators in China are still hindering the development of the film industry.

### *3.1 Regulators of China's Film Industry and the Regulatory Framework for Film Production*

China nationalized the previous private film companies between 1949 and 1953.[25] From the mid-1950s to the late 1980s, FBMC was the film industry regulator then.[26] In practice, FBMC was responsible for the planning, overseeing and distribution of the quotas and licence for film production in China.[27]

The integration of film and television industries, with complementary advantages and inherent request for unified management, had been a trend in the development of the film and television sector and a common practice in most countries. In 1985, the Central Committee of the Communist Party of China decided to transfer the Film Bureau under the Ministry of Culture in its entirety to the Ministry of Radio and Television, and renamed the latter as the Ministry of Radio, Film and Television ("MRFT").[28] Such institutional changes was approved by the National People's

[25] Shen Yun, "The Beginning and End of the Establishment of New China's Film Industry (1949–1957)", in "Contemporary Cinema", Issue 4, 2005, pp. 35–38.

[26] Ibid., pp. 32–33.

[27] Ibid.

[28] The preface of the "Notice on the Unified Assignment of Local Film Studios to the Radio, Film and Television Departments" jointly issued by the Publicity Department of the Central Committee

Congress.[29] The former MRFT was renamed the State Administration of Radio, Film and Television ("SARFT") during the institutional reform of the State Council in 1998. SARFT inherited the power of the FBMC to issue film production permits and perform other regulatory functions.

On 19 June 1996, the State Council promulgated the "Regulations on Film Administration" (hereinafter referred to as the "Film Regulations") for the first time. This set of regulations covered all three sectors of the film industry—film production, distribution, and exhibition—and had a strong administrative nature. On 30 December 2001, the State Council issued the revised Film Regulations, which were divided into the following parts: General Provisions, Film Production, Film Censorship System, Film Import and Export, Film Distribution and Exhibition, and Penalties. Although the resulting film regulatory system granted more autonomy to the film industry, its focus remained on the management of the film industry by regulators, which constituted the core of China's film legal system. Based on the Film Regulations, the SARFT also issues regulations and notices according to the actual development of the film market, which form an important part of the film regulatory system. Thus, the overall framework of China's film legal system is established relying on an administrative regulation. To further improve the film legal system in China, in the Spring of 2004, the SARFT proposed the formulation of the "Film Industry Promotion Law". It was reported that the first draft of the "Film Industry Promotion Law" would be completed in May 2004 and submitted to the public for comments in October 2004.[30] However, it was not until December 2011 that the draft of the "Film Industry Promotion Law" was published for public comments. After numerous rounds of discussions and redrafting, the Film Industry Promotion Law was finally passed at the 24th meeting of the Standing Committee of the National People's Congress on 7 November 2016.

## *3.2 Script Review System—Examination and Approval from Regulator Before Film Production Stage*

Before the founding of the People's Republic of China, the Central Publicity Department of the Communist Party of China issued the "Instructions on Film Work" to the Publicity Department of the Northeast Bureau in October 1948 based on Yuan Mu's two "Reports on the Film Industry". The instructions put forward specific

of the Communist Party of China, the Ministry of Radio, Film and Television, and the Ministry of Culture on 22 January 1996.

[29] The Fourteenth Meeting of the Standing Committee of the Sixth National People's Congress deliberated on the bill submitted by the State Council on changing the Ministry of Radio and Television into the Ministry of Radio, Film and Television. On 22 January 1986, it adopted a decision to change the Ministry of Radio and Television into the Ministry of Radio, Film and Television.

[30] Zhang Tianwei, "Draft Film Promotion Law to Take Shape in May, Legislation on Breaking Monopolies and Other Contents to Follow", in Beijing Youth Daily, 22 March 2004.

requirements for the review guidelines of film scripts and the scope of film script stories.[31] Among them, regarding the review of movie scripts, it was stipulated that politically, they should be anti-imperialist, anti-feudal, and anti-bureaucratic capitalist, and unreasonable criticisms should be rejected. Regarding the stories of movie scripts, "they should mainly be about the liberated areas, modern times, and China. However, at the same time, stories from the Kuomintang-ruled areas, foreign countries, and ancient times can also be adopted." It also proposed, "[R]egarding the review of movie scripts, a system must be established. Please have the Publicity Department of the Northeast Bureau organize a committee of three people to be responsible, with one designated as the director. This committee shall serve as the highest authority for reviewing movie scripts. Once a movie script is approved by it, it can be filmed, so as to avoid endless debates and disagreements, and at the same time, to clearly define responsibilities and facilitate the collection of public opinions for inspection and improvement of work."[32] This embodied the prototype of the censorship system established for the film industry after 1949.

According to the Decision of the Government Administration Council on Strengthening Film Production Work issued and implemented by the former Government Administration Council on 1 December 1954, the film censorship system was further strengthened: "A unified, centralized and hierarchical review system must be effectively established. The screenplays of feature films, the shooting synopses and completed films of large-scale documentaries shall be subject to a careful initial review by the Film Bureau of the Central Culture Department, and then be reviewed and approved by the Central Culture Department. After the approval of a feature film screenplay, the Film Bureau shall carefully review the shooting script to avoid major revisions after the film is completed. The screenplays or shooting synopses and completed films of other film genres shall, with the exception of special circumstances, generally be reviewed and approved by the Film Bureau. When reviewing the screenplays and completed films of large-scale feature films, large-scale documentaries and some short films of special significance, close cooperation with the main leaders of the relevant departments must be obtained, and basically consistent opinions shall be sought in the review comments. The annual film screenplay theme plan and screenplays or shooting synopses with major political content shall be submitted to the Publicity Department of the Central Committee of the Communist Party of China for review."[33] Here we can see that since 1954, the Chinese government has already established a dual censorship mechanism for screenplays and completed films.

The Interim Measures for the Examination of Film Screenplays and Films, issued and implemented by the Ministry of Culture on 15 December 1974, reiterated this

[31] Shen Yun, "The Beginning and End of the Establishment of New China's Film Industry (1949–1957)", in "Contemporary Cinema", Issue 4, 2005, p. 32.

[32] Cited from Meng Liye: "The Combination of Principle and Flexibility", published in Film Art, Issue 4, 2001, pp. 9–10.

[33] Decision of the Government Administration Council on Strengthening Film Production Work, Item 3.

dual mechanism of screenplay examination before film production and film examination after completion: First, each film studio should be responsible for reviewing and approving the movie screenplays prepared for production. After the review accomplished, they should be submitted to the FBMC for record before shooting starts, and simultaneously submitted to the relevant competent departments of the province, city, or autonomous region where the studio is located for record.[34] Secondly, after the production of various domestic films is completed, they should be initially reviewed by the film studios. After passing the initial review of the film studios, they would be submitted to the FBMC for final review.[35] Finally, for domestically produced films, foreign films translated and subtitled, and Hong Kong films reviewed and approved by the FBMC for national release or release in some provinces, cities, and autonomous regions, the FBMC would issue a screening permit.[36]

According to the relevant provisions of the Film Regulations, the State implements a film censorship system. Films that have not been approved by the film censorship institution shall not be distributed, screened, imported, or exported.[37] Film production studios shall, in accordance with the regulations on the prohibition of content in film works as stipulated in the Film Regulations, be responsible for the review of film scripts before production and of completed films before release. After reviewing the film scripts they intend to produce in accordance with the regulations, film production studios shall submit them to the film review institution for record. The film review institution can review the film scripts submitted for record and if any content prohibited by the Film Regulations is found, it shall promptly notify the film production unit not to proceed with the production.[38] In practice, regulatory agencies have the final say after reviewing film scripts to determine whether a film can enter the production phase. If a studio ignores the opinions of regulatory agencies, films made based on controversial scripts will ultimately not be allowed to be screened in theaters.

Under this script review mechanism, or the de facto film production permit system, review have been conducted on a film-by-film basis in practice without more specific criteria being stipulated in the relevant regulations. The regulatory agency thus enjoys an extensive discretionary power when making review decisions. In addition, since the regulatory agency should review the entire script, any handling and modifications to the script during the film production process also need to be filed with the regulatory agency. This has given the regulatory agency right to reject when the film production team files for record. This mechanism could delay the progress of film production and restrict the freedom of film creators, indirectly pose certain obstacles to the development of film industry in China.

---

[34] The first and second items of Article 1 of the "Interim Measures for the Examination of Film Screenplays and Films".

[35] The first and second items of Article 2 of the Interim Measures for the Examination of Film Screenplays and Films.

[36] The fifth items of Article 2 of the Interim Measures for the Examination of Film Screenplays and Films.

[37] Article 24, the Film Regulations.

[38] Article 24 Para. 2, the Film Regulations.

On 28 September 2003, after China's accession to the WTO, in order to meet the competition and challenges from Hollywood, the SARFT issued the Interim Provisions on the Project Approval of Film Scripts (Synopses) and the Review of Film Productions clearly stipulating the script review mechanism and laying out detailed provisions on the review procedures for completed films. Furthermore, according to the new rules, when the theme is not sensitive, the script review could be reduced to a mere review of the script synopsis.[39] In addition, the SARFT has since also delegated its review authority to local radio and television system institutions.[40] This way, the film production team has gained significant autonomy in the production of a film. Therefore, this shift has also made the censorship of released films implemented on a more friendly approach. As a result, throughout the entire film censorship system, although the censorship of film scripts and completed films is closely related, they are legally divided into two separate areas. This poses obstacles to the standardization of the film censorship system and actually makes film censorship retain more uncertainties.

On 22 May 2006, the SARFT issued the "Provisions on the Filing of Movie Scripts (Synopses) and the Administration of Film Productions" (hereinafter referred to as the "Provisions on Scripts and Film Productions"), which overhauled the film cencorship regime and replaced the Interim Provisions on the Approval of Film Scripts (Synopses) and the Censorship of Film Productions. The Provisions on Scripts and Film Productions defined the previous systems of script censorship and film censorship, and for the first time introduced the system of filing film scripts (synopses) and the system of film censorship: "The State implements a system of filing filing scripts (synopses) and a system of film censorship. Film scripts (synopses) not filed shall not be filmed. Films not passed the censorship shall not be distributed, screened, imported, or exported."[41] Secondly, the Provisions on Scripts and Film Productions have transformed the scripts review system as a script synopsis filing system. Although the channel for filing script synopses appeared in previous regulations, it was not clearly established as a system until the promulgation of the Provisions on Scripts and Film Productions. Admittedly, this facilitates the film creation activities of creators. On the other hand, the so-called filing is actually a kind of review system: after the film production company completes its review of the script, it then submits the filing to the CFA or the provincial radio and television departments implementing territorial review. The latter issues a "Receipt for Film Script (Synopsis) Filing" to the film production company within the period specified in the Administrative License Law. If the regulatory agency does not raise any concern within twenty working days after the filing, the film production company can proceed with the film making according to the filed film script (synopsis). If the film script needs to be reviewed by other relevant competent departments and experts, an additional twenty working days are allowed for the review while the film production company shall be informed

---

[39] Provisions on Scripts and Film Productions, Articles 2, 5 and 6.

[40] Provisions on Scripts and Film Productions, Article 10.

[41] Provisions on Scripts and Film Productions, Article 2.

of this in writing.[42] Provincial radio and television departments implementing territorial review shall report the filing of film scripts (synopses) to the CFA; the CFA will regularly publish the filings of film scripts (synopses) in relevant media.[43] Rejection or examination opinion of regulatory agencies constitute a review of the concerned film script synopses. At the same time, for films on key revolutionary and historical themes, major documentary films of literature, and Sino-foreign co-produced films, the whole scripts still need to be reviewed according to the so-called script project approval regime.[44] Although the Provisions on Scripts and Film Productions still retains the provisions for script review regime, it has basically established a filing system for film script synopses for the most film projects. Moreover, with the help of the territorial review system, the review of film scripts has been significantly relaxed, with the script project approval regime effective only as an exception.

However, the reformed regime then only applied to a film production company holding a Film Production License. For a domestic company, enterprise, or one of the other economic organizations (excluding foreign-invested enterprises) without a Film Production License, it had been required to establish a film and television culture company before producing its first film. The film and television culture company then applies to the relevant regulatory authority for a Film Production License (Single Film). Only a film and television culture company registered with the industrial and commercial administration departments at or above the prefecture-level city could be eligible to apply for a Film Production License (Single Film).[45] The company would provide a copy of the business license to the SARFT and submit an application for the Filming Permit for a Single Film. At that time, according to the "Interim Provisions on Access to Film Business Qualifications" (hereinafter referred to as the "Film Business Qualification Provisions") jointly issued by the SARFT and the MOFCOM on 10 October 2004, the SARFT should review the applied filming qualifications and the film literary script (story outline) within 20 working days. For those who pass the review, a Filming Production License (Single Film) would be issued. If not approved, the reasons would be offered in writing.[46] Although the production qualification of film and television culture companies had been reiterated therein, the focus of the whole regime was still the review of the film script synopsis. According to Article 5, Item (2) of the Film Business Qualification Provisions, the Film Production License (Single Film) should follow a one-film-one-filing system. At the same time, the holder of the Film Production License (Single Film) wound enjoy the one-time production right of the film, with which the producer could proceed its project independently or jointly with other qualified partners. This meant that if a film and television culture company would like to produce a second film, it would still need to apply for the Film Production License (Single Film) again. This also conforms to the stipulations relating to the Film Production License (Single

[42] Provisions on Scripts and Film Productions, Article 7.

[43] Provisions on Scripts and Film Productions, Article 8.

[44] Provisions on Scripts and Film Productions, Articles 9, 10, 11.

[45] Interim Regulations on Access Qualifications for Film Business Operations, Article 5, Item (2).

[46] Ibid.

Film) in the Film Regulations.[47] But in the Film Regulations, in addition to applying for the Film Production License (Single Film), a non-specialised company had to obtain the approval of the SARFT, which would be necessary for the company to complete the corresponding registration procedures at the industrial and commercial administration agency.[48] This stipulation was later weakened by the Film Business Qualification Provisions and the Provisions on Scripts and Film Productions. When a non-specialised company began to make a film for the first time, it was required to establish a film and television culture company registered with the administrative department for industry and commerce at or above the prefecture (city) level. Before the kick-off the production process, the regulatory authority would review the script submitted by the company, and issue a one-time Film Production License (Single Film) upon approval. Indeed the Film Regulations still required relevant registration procedures to be handled with the business registration agency after obtaining the Film Production License (Single Film). Upon the registration of the film production activities in the business license issued by the business registration agency, the necessity of these registration procedures herein would become questionable. In short, for a non-specialised company without a Film Production License, even if it had been reorganised as a film and television culture company, it would still need to obtain a Film Production License (Single Film) for each film it was to produce, let along a highly restrictive script (synopses) regime awaiting for it.

Under Article 13 of the Film Industry Promotion Law, the review of general film scripts has been be abolished, except for films involving major themes or national security, diplomacy, ethnicity, religion, military and other themes, which still need to submit the whole scripts to the film authorities of the State Council or the film authorities of provinces, autonomous regions and municipalities directly under the Central Government for review. Legal persons and other organizations that intend to produce films only need to apply for the filing of the film script synopsis. Those who meet the requirements of Article 16 of the Film Industry Promotion Law will be filed and publicly registered. Afterwards, a filing certificate or approval document will be issued, and the production of the filed film can move on afterwards.

## *3.3 Film Censorship*

If the filing of a film script synopsis is regarded as a prior review by the relevant regulatory authorities before the film production kicks off, then another crucial procedure for a film producer to face is the film censorship, also known as the review of the completed film. Regarding the censorship of films, the Decision of the Government Administration Council on Strengthening Film Production Work, issued and implemented by the former Government Administration Council on 1 December 1954, had

[47] Article 16, paragraph 2 of the Film Regulations.

[48] Ibid.

already established the system to review completed films.[49] The Interim Measures for the Examination of Film Screenplays and Films, issued and implemented by the Ministry of Culture on 15 December 1974, established a dual review system for film scripts and films. Regarding film review, after the completion of various domestically produced films, an initial review should be firstly conducted by the film studio itself. Once the initial review by the film studio completed, the film would then be submitted to the FBMC for final review.[50] Apart from that, the former MRFT issued the "Interim Provisions on Film Censorship" on 4 June 1993, which clearly laid down the procedures and standards for the review of completed films. However, it did not explicitly establish a film comprehensive censorship system, and such a regime only focused on the review of completed films.

The Film Regulations initially adopted in 1996 established officially the film censorship system: no film that has not been approved by the film censorship institution of the radio, film and television administrative department under the State Council should be distributed, screened, imported or exported.[51] According to this comprehensive film censorship system, in addition to the examination of the script by the film production company and the filing with the regulatory agency, the film production company should, after the completion of the film production, submit the completed film to the film censorship agency for examination. The film importer and operator should, after handling the temporary import procedures for the film, submit it to the film censorship agency for examination. The film censorship agency should, within 30 days from the date of receiving the submitted film for examination, notify the applicant of the examination decision in writing; for those that pass the examination, a Film Public Screening License for the film should be issued. The film production company and the film importer and operator should print the license number of the Film Public Screening License at the beginning of the first copy of the film.[52] The film censorship system installed in 1996 has thus established the basic principles of censorship as well as the specific censorship procedures, laying down the foundation for the subsequent development of the film censorship system.

On 16 January 1997, the former MRFT issued the Provisions on Film Censorship, which elaborated specifically on the film censorship system established in the Film Regulations in 1996. The provisions stipulate that film censorship should cover content review of films, including examination of the artistic and technical quality of films.[53] Moreover, the former MRFT established the Film Censorship Committee and the Film Re-examination Committee, which were responsible for the censorship

[49] Decision of the Government Administration Council on Strengthening Film Production Work, Item 3.

[50] Decision of the Government Administration Council on Strengthening Film Production Work, Items (1) and (2) of Article 2.

[51] Article 23 of the Film Regulation adopted in 1996.

[52] Articles 26 and 27 of the Film Regulations adopted in 1996.

[53] Provisions on Film Censorship, Article 3.

and re-examination of films.[54] Meanwhile, the Provisions on Film Censorship have further refined the censorship criteria and procedures.

On 12 December 2001, the State Council revised the Film Regulations with the revision coming into force on 1 February 2002. In terms of the film censorship system, the revised Film Regulations did not make substantial changes. On 28 September 2003, the Interim Provisions on the Project Approval of Film Scripts (Synopses) and the Review of Film Productions issued by the SARFT made detailed provisions on the censorship procedures for completed films. In addition to the provisions on the project approval of film scripts (synopses), the new rules also made some provisions on the censorship of films and the issuance of public screening permits, which overlapped with the still-effective Provisions on Film Censorship. The Interim Provisions on the Project Approval of Film Scripts (Synopses) and the Review of Film Productions re-issued by the SARFT on 6 July 2004 and implemented on 10 August of the same year established a territorial censorship system for the censorship of films: the provincial radio, film and television administrative departments with territorial censorship functions should establish film censorship institutions, set up corresponding film censorship systems, and censor some films produced by film production companies in their provinces (municipalities directly under the central government, autonomous regions) that hold Film Production Permits and are legally established.[55] Among the other things, in 2004, the Interim Provisions on the Project Approval of Film Scripts (Synopses) and the Review of Film Productions further stipulated the procedures for submitting completed films for review.

On 22 May 2006, the SARFT issued the Provisions on Scripts and Film Productions, which replaced the previous Provisions on Film Censorship and the Interim Provisions on the Project Approval of Film Scripts (Synopses) and the Review of Film Productions. Regarding the film censorship section, the Provisions on Scripts and Film Productions incorporated the film censorship criteria. Apart from this, there were no major changes compared to the Interim Provisions on the Project Approval of Film Scripts (Synopses) and the Review of Film Productions issued previously in 2004.

On 4 February 2010, the SARFT issued Document No. 19 of the "Notice of the SARFT on Improving and Perfecting the Filing of Film Scripts (Synopses) and the Examination of Film Works" (hereinafter referred to as the "Notice for Better Examination"). It reiterated the importance of the filing of film scripts (synopses) and the examination of films for the development of film industry in China. The system of "One Filing and Two Examinations" has been officially proposed therein for film examination. In this comprehensive film examination system, the production of a film requires the filing of the script (synopses) before shooting; once the film is completed, it has to undergo a preliminary examination and a final examination. The CFA is responsible for the nationwide film script (synopses) filings and general regulatory matters while its film examination institution is responsible for the

[54] Provisions on Film Censorship, Article 5.

[55] Interim Provisions on the Project Approval of Film Scripts (Synopses) and the Review of Film Productions, Article 14, Paragraph 1.

final examination of films. Meanwhile, the regulatory departments at the provincial level are responsible for film script (synopses) filings and the preliminary examination of films within their respective jurisdictions. For that the local government were required to establish corresponding regulatory institutions and film examination institutions, which are specifically responsible for approving, examining the film script (synopses) filings within their jurisdiction and submission those filings to the CFA, while dealing with preliminary examination and submission of completed films to the SARFT. The provincial film regulatory departments and film examination institutions implementing territorial examination (in Jilin, Guangdong, Zhejiang, Shaanxi, Hubei provinces, and Beijing) are responsible for submission and approval of the film script (synopses) filings within their jurisdiction, and the preliminary examination and final examination of some films.[56] Regarding the territorial review system established in the Provisions on Scripts and Film Productions, the Notice for Better Examination has streamlined its operation. In addition to conducting a preliminary review of major revolutionary and historical theme films, major documentary films, and films produced on the basis of co-operation between Chinese and overseas investors, submitting them for the final review to film examination institution under the CFA, the local film examination regulatory institution shall enjoy the authority to conduct final examination of the other films (although opinions from other relevant provincial-level competent departments are required for the films of special theme). Once a successful final examination accomplished at the local level, the film shall be issued the Film Review Decision and the Technical Appraisal Certificate for the Submitted Standard Copy from the local film examination regulatory institution. Afterwards, the film production company shall submit these documents, together with all the other relevant materials, to the CFA for the Film Public Screening License. Should a film required to be modified or having failed the final examination at the local level, the reasons elaborated in a written notice shall be issued to the film production company. If a provincial-level film examination regulatory institution is unable to make a final examination of an individual film or the film production company disagrees with the final examination decision thereon, the film should be submitted to the film examination institution under the CFA for a review, but a written opinion and reasons shall be provided.[57]

This territorial review system actually simplifies the film examination process, indirectly strengthens the autonomy of film creators to a certain extent, and facilitates the development of film production in China. On 10 May 2010, the Film Bureau of the SARFT issued the "Announcement on the Comprehensive Implementation of the 'One Filing and Two Reviews System' for Films". Starting from 1 July of the same year, the "One Filing and Two Reviews System" was expected to be fully implemented. The announcement further clarified the territorial review: The provincial radio and television departments of Jilin, Guangdong, Zhejiang, Shaanxi, and Hubei provinces, which piloted the territorial review, are responsible for the preliminary review of major revolutionary and historical theme films, major theoretical and

[56] Notice for Better Examination, Article 2, Paragraph 2.

[57] Notice for Better Examination, Article 2, Item 4.

documentary films, and Sino-foreign cooperative films produced by the film production company under their jurisdiction, and the final review of other films. The Beijing Municipal Radio and Television Bureau, which also piloted the territorial review, is responsible for the preliminary review of major revolutionary and historical theme films, major theoretical and documentary films, Sino-foreign cooperative films, and celluloid films among other films produced by the film production units under its jurisdiction, and the final review of digital films among other films.[58]

Article 17 of the Film Industry Promotion Law has acknowledged the One Filing and Two Reviews System in Article 17, "Legal persons and other organizations shall submit their completed films to the competent film department of the State Council or the competent film department of the people's government of the province, autonomous region or municipality directly under the Central Government for examination. The competent film department of the State Council or the competent film department of the people's government of the province, autonomous region or municipality directly under the Central Government shall make an examination decision within 30 days from the date of acceptance of the application. For films that comply with the provisions of this Law, they shall be allowed to be screened, and a film screening license shall be issued and announced; for films that do not comply with the provisions of this Law, they shall not be allowed to be screened, and the applicant shall be notified in writing and the reasons shall be stated. The competent film department of the State Council shall formulate and improve the specific standards and procedures for film review in accordance with this Law and announce them to the public. The formulation and improvement of specific standards for film review shall be publicly solicited for opinions from the public, and experts shall be organized to conduct demonstrations."

In this way, from script review to completed film review, and from film review to the "one filing and two reviews" system, the film censorship system not only meets the need of controlling content for the informative function of movies but also gradually adapts to the financial needs of the film industry and filmmakers. Although the current film censorship system still restricts the development of the film industry to a certain extent, the risks brought by the film censorship system are not specific to the film industry. Instead, they are a common phenomenon in the supervision of cultural industries and even cultural undertakings in China's current development stage. In this sense, the purpose of this book's research on film censorship is not to discuss the rationality or legitimacy of the film censorship system from the perspective of freedom of speech. Instead, it hopes to focus on the impact of this film censorship system on China's film industry, attempting to provide a certain perspective for the reshaping of the film censorship system at the present stage, and thus offering an idea for the improvement and development of the supervision structure of China's entire cultural industry.

On 18 February 2012, China and the United States reached an agreement on the implementation of the WTO publication ruling. According to this agreement, the

---

[58] Announcement on the Comprehensive Implementation of the "One Filing and Two Reviews System" for Films, Part 4 of Item (3) of Article 1.

United States agreed that China could retain the state-owned monopoly arrangement for film imports and exports. However, as an exchange, China promised to increase the number of revenue-sharing films by 14 over the next five years. These 14 additional imported films must be special films, namely so-called 3D or IMAX films. At the same time, the revenue-sharing ratio for imported blockbuster films was also correspondingly increased. Given the dominant position of the American film industry in the field of special films, this increased quota of revenue-sharing films is actually beneficial to the penetration of American Hollywood movies into the Chinese market.

Meanwhile, since film imports are mainly driven by the needs of China's film distribution and exhibition industries, the film production industry does not welcome an increase in the number of imported films or their market share. Thus, there is a conflict of interest between the film production industry and the film distribution and exhibition industries: the local film production industry hopes to restrict film imports so that the films it produces can enjoy the largest market share. For film distributors and exhibitors, their interest lies in distributing and exhibiting films with the greatest market potential to earn the most profits in the market. At this time, distributors and exhibitors do not care about the interests of the film production industry. In this way, unregulated film imports may run the risk of a winner-take-all situation.

Currently, China's relevant laws, regulations, and departmental rules do not provide for the diversification of imported films or the distribution and exhibition of the film market. Therefore, it is necessary to establish the principle of diversification in the film market or the film import market. This is to strike a balance between the market and culture while respecting the laws of the film market and fully considering its cultural attributes.

Judging from the Chinese film import market in the past three years, the principle of cultural diversity is being taken into consideration by film importers to a greater or lesser extent. In 2022, China imported 59 foreign films, of which 26 were Hollywood films; in 2023, China imported 82 foreign films, of which 40 were Hollywood films; and in 2024, a total of 92 films were imported, of which 40 were Hollywood films.[59] Without considering box office factors, foreign films released and screened in China still reflect a certain principle of diversity. At this time, although the film market can, to some extent, reflect the diversity of the world film market as reflected in imported films and meet the requirements of the cultural diversity principle of imported films in terms of multi-country, multi-genre, and multi-style, this has not been fully acknowledge in the law. From the perspective of film market delvelopment, if the cultural diversity of films in the film market can be established in the law, it will be more conducive to building a healthy legal system for the film market and can meet the relevant requirements of the WTO.

[59] Data Source: Dengta Professional Edition Data and its report "Inventory and Analysis of Hollywood Films in the Chinese Mainland Market in 2024".

### *3.4 The Basic Provisions of China's Content Review System*

There is no unified legal system in China to regulate content review in the cultural field. Instead, relevant regulations are scattered among the laws and regulations adopted for various cultural fields. For example, in the fields of publishing, film, and audio-visual products management, on 12 December 2001, the State Council promulgated the Regulations on the Administration of Publishing in the People's Republic of China (hereinafter referred to as the "Publishing Regulations"), the Film Regulations, and the Regulations on the Administration of Audio-Visual Products in the People's Republic of China (hereinafter referred to as the "Audio-Visual Products Regulations") respectively. Among them, the Film Regulations stipulate that no film shall contain the following contents: (1) content that opposes the basic principles established by the Constitution; (2) content that endangers national unity, sovereignty, and territorial integrity; (3) content that discloses state secrets, endangers national security, or damages national honor and interests; (4) content that incites ethnic hatred or discrimination, undermines ethnic unity, or infringes upon ethnic customs and habits; (5) content that promotes heresy or superstition; (6) content that disrupts social order or undermines social stability; (7) content that promotes pornography, gambling, violence or instigates crime; (8) content that insults or slanders others, infringing upon others' legitimate rights and interests; (9) content that endangers social morality or fine traditional ethnic cultures; (10) other content prohibited by laws, administrative regulations, and state regulations.[60] Commonly known as the "Ten Prohibitions". The same ten prohibitions are also stipulated in the Publishing Regulations and the Audio-Visual Products Regulations promulgated on the same day.[61]

In terms of film censorship, in addition to the "Ten Prohibitions" regulation, according to the Provisions on Scripts and Film Productions, if a film involves any of the nine major items, the concerned part in the film also needs to be deleted and edited.[62] These nine censorship items are:

(1) Distorting Chinese civilization and history, seriously deviating from historical facts; misrepresenting the history of other countries, showing disrespect for their civilizations and customs; denigrating the images of revolutionary leaders, heroes, and important historical figures; tampering with Chinese and foreign classics and the images of important characters in them;
(2) Maliciously denigrating the images of the people's army, armed police, public security, and judicial organs;
(3) Containing pornographic, vulgar, and low-level content, depicting promiscuity, rape, prostitution, solicitation, sexual behavior, sexual perversion, and other private body parts; including dirty and vulgar lines, songs, background music, and sound effects;

[60] Film Regulations, Article 25.

[61] Article 25 of the "Publishing Regulations"; Article 3 of the Audio-Visual Products Regulations.

[62] Provisions on Scripts and Film Productions, Article 14.

(4) Mixing in murder, violence, and horror content, distorting the value orientation of truth, goodness, and beauty, and confusing the basic nature of justice and injustice; deliberately showing the arrogance of criminal acts, specifically displaying the details of criminal behavior, and exposing special investigation methods; having highly stimulating plots of murder, bloodshed, violence, drug use, gambling, etc.; having plots of torturing prisoners of war, extorting confessions from criminals or suspects; having overly terrifying images, lines, background music, and sound effects;
(5) Promoting a negative, decadent outlook on life, world view, and values, deliberately exaggerating and highlighting the ignorance and backwardness of ethnic groups or the dark side of society;
(6) Preaching religious extremism, provoking contradictions and conflicts among religions, sects, and between religious and non-religious people, and hurting the feelings of the masses;
(7) Advocating the destruction of the ecological environment, animal cruelty, hunting, and eating of protected animals;
(8) Excessively portraying alcoholism, smoking, and other bad habits;
(9) Contrary to the spirit of relevant laws and regulations.

The nine censorship items are quite broad in scope. Meanwhile, the relationship between the nine censorship items and the "Ten Prohibitions" is rather ambiguous. The Regulations on Screenplay and Film Administration are departmental rules of the film regulator, ranking one level lower than the Film Regulations. Therefore, to some extent, the nine censorship items serve as the criteria for specifically implementing the "Ten Prohibitions" in the field of film censorship. For example, Item (6) of the nine censorship items states: "Advocating religious extremism, provoking conflicts and contradictions among different religions, sects, and between religious and non-religious groups, and hurting the feelings of the masses." This is actually a further elaboration of Item (4) of the "Ten Prohibitions", which states "inciting ethnic hatred, ethnic discrimination, and undermining ethnic unity".

However, in this way, the nine censorship items seem to have a tendency to over-strictly interpret the "Ten Prohibitions". For example, Item (6) of the nine censorship items stipulates content that "promotes a negative, decadent outlook on life, world view, and values, and deliberately exaggerates or highlights the ignorance and backwardness of a nation or the dark side of society", which does not seem to fall under any of the "Ten Prohibitions". Moreover, the catch-all clause in the nine censorship items classifies content that "violates the spirit of relevant laws and regulations" as a censorship item. The so-called "spirit of laws and regulations" itself is a grand topic in jurisprudence.

By using this concept to endow the film regulator with censorship power, its discretion is indeed very large. China's film censorship system fully is integrated with the market access system. Moreover, the core of the film censorship system is the film regulator's review and regulation of screenplays and films. Only after the review accomplished will the film be issued a Film Public Screening License. Regarding the purpose of this film censorship system, the Notice on Reiterating Film

Censorship Standards was issued on 3 March 2008, in which Article 1 reads, "The State encourages the creation of excellent films that integrate ideological content, artistic quality, and appreciation value, are close to reality, life, and the people, and are conducive to the healthy growth of minors. It vigorously develops advanced culture, supports healthy and beneficial culture, strives to transform backward culture, and resolutely resists decadent culture."[63]

If we adhere to such a purpose and rely on national administrative agencies to conduct censorship in a legal manner, it may fall short. Therefore, there has been a tendency for the interpretation of the nine censorship items based on the "Ten Prohibition" to be effective harsh and broad in scope, lacking a certain degree of foresight, which is not conducive to development of the film industry. On 3 January 2008, the SARFT issued the "Notice on Handling the Illegal Issues of the Film 'Apple'" (hereinafter referred to as the "Apple Notice"). According to the Apple Notice, due to the unhealthy and improper marketing practices of "Apple" during its distribution and screening, and the fact that it uploaded and spread a version of the film containing pornographic content that had not been approved for censorship on the Internet, produced audio-visual products of this version, and submitted an unapproved version of the film to compete in the 57th Berlin International Film Festival, the SARFT revoked the film's Film Public Screening License, stopped its distribution and screening in cinemas, halted its online dissemination, and recommended that relevant administrative departments stop the distribution of its audio-visual products. However, the illegal acts of "Apple" during its distribution and screening listed in the "Apple Notice" had no connection with the version of the film released in cinemas. Thus, the similar punitive measures such as revoking the Film Screening License and stopping the distribution and screening of "Apple" in cinemas did not correspond to the illegal acts listed in the Apple Notice, apparently violating the principle of proportionality.

## *3.5 Basic Regulations on Market Access System for China's Cultural Industry*

Meanwhile, in the cultural industry sector, China has strict and complex regulatory measures regarding market access. For example, Article 5 of the Film Regulations States that the state implements a licensing system for film production, import, export, distribution, screening, and public exhibition. Without permission, no unit or individual may engage in film production, import, distribution, or screening activities, and may not import, export, distribute, or screen films that have not obtained a license. The Film Industry Promotion Law leave this regime intact. Similar provisions can be

[63] Notice on Reiterating Film Censorship Standards, Article 1.

found in the Audio-Visual Products Regulations and the Internet Management Regulations.[64] In the Publishing Regulations and the Radio and Television Regulations, although there are no provisions that generally establish the market access licensing system, they do stipulate for complex approval conditions and approval authorities.

In the cultural industries, China has implemented a legal monopoly system for the product import and circulation business. These are normally operated by State-owned enterprises stipulated by law or established by the government, and are not open to enterprises of other ownership forms.

According to Article 30 of the Film Regulations, the import of films is managed by the film import and distribution units designated by the film administrative department of the State Council. Without such designation, no entity or individual may engage in the import of films. The Film Business Qualification Provisions jointly issued by the MOFCOM and the SARFT on 10 October 2004, reiterated this restriction, stating that the import and distribution of films is exclusively managed by film import and distribution enterprises approved by the CFA. The national distribution of imported films is carried out by distribution companies approved by the CFA and granted the right to distribute imported films nationwide. China Film Group Corporation (hereinafter referred to as "China Film Group") was once the only company authorized by the State to manage the import of films.

According to Article 2 of the Measures for the Administration of Imported Films, which was issued by the Ministry of Culture and the General Administration of Customs in 1981 and abolished in 1991, the import and distribution of films was uniformly managed by China Film Distribution and Exhibition Corporation (the predecessor of the Film Distribution and Exhibition Branch and the Import and Export Branch of China Film Group). On 1 August 2003, Huaxia Film Distribution Co., Ltd. (hereinafter referred to as "Huaxia") was established, thus creating an oligopolistic situation in the market for the distribution of imported films.

An Internet information service falls under the category of value-added telecommunications services.[65] According to Article 6, Paragraph 2 of the Regulations on the Administration of Foreign-invested Telecommunications Enterprises, which was issued by the State Council on 11 December 2001, and amended on 10 September 2008, for foreign-invested telecommunications enterprises operating value-added telecommunications services (including the wireless paging service in basic telecommunications services), the proportion of foreign investors' contributions in the enterprises shall not exceed 50% ultimately. This regulation is consistent with the Protocol on the Accession of China to the WTO.

According to Item (7) of Article 10 in the Catalogue of Industries Prohibited for Foreign Investment in the Guidance Catalogue for Foreign Investment Industries (hereinafter referred to as the "Guidance Catalogue") jointly issued by the National

[64] Please refer to Article 5 of the Audio-Visual Products Regulations and Article 4 of the Internet Management Regulations.

[65] Please refer to the provisions in the "Catalogue of Telecommunication Services" in the annex to the "Regulations of the People's Republic of China on Telecommunications" issued and implemented by China on 25 September 2000. Also, please refer to the provisions of Article 7 of the Internet Service Management Regulations.

Development and Reform Commission (hereinafter referred to as the "NDRC") and the MOFCOM on 7 December 2007, "news websites, internet audio-visual program services, internet cafes, and internet cultural operations" are prohibited from foreign investment. In the rulings regarding publications and audio-visual products, they mainly involve "internet audio-visual program services" and "internet cultural operations". In a sense, this can be interpreted as: foreign investors are not allowed to use the internet to engage in the import and distribution of audio-visual programs.

Linking China's existing market access to content review systems is China's foothold in the rulings on publications and audio-visual products. This is the first time that China has combined the State-owned monopoly on imports with the content review system in public documents, arguing that the State-owned monopoly is established for the purpose of content review, which is to protect China's public morality, and the State-owned monopoly is the only mechanism to effectively implement content review. At the same time, from China's defensive claims, it can be seen that this is an expansive review system, with its basis on the concept of "protecting public morality" acknowledged in WTO treaties. This concept not only involves content review of publications and audio-visual products, but also includes specific market access restrictions and arrangements, becoming part of "protecting public morality".

## *3.6 The Reshaping of Film Censorship System—WTO Rulings*

In April and July 2007, the United States successively requested consultations with the Chinese government regarding measures (hereinafter collectively referred to as "Measures on Publications and Audiovisual Products") of China concerning the import, distribution, market access, and national treatment of reading materials (such as books, newspapers, periodicals, and electronic publications), imported films for theatrical release, home audiovisual entertainment products (such as videotapes, VCDs, DVDs), and audio recordings (such as videotapes) of China. In July of the same year, China held consultations with the United States on relevant issues, but the consultations ended without any results. Subsequently, in October 2007, the United States requested the establishment of a panel to the World Trade Organization (hereinafter referred to as the "WTO"). On 23 June 2009, the WTO panel issued its final report (WT/DS363/R) China—Measures Affecting Trading Rights and Distribution Services for Certain Publications and Audiovisual Entertainment Products to China and the United States. On 12 August 2009, this final report was made public to all WTO member states. On 22 September 2009, China appealed the panel report to the WTO Appellate Body. On 5 October 2009, the United States also appealed an intermediate finding to the WTO Appellate Body. On 21 December 2009, the WTO released its Appellate Body report (DSB Report).

Notably, for the first time, this panel report and Appellate Body report (hereinafter collectively referred to as the "Rulings on Publications and Audiovisual Products") drew conclusions on the impact of content review systems in audiovisual products and related cultural industries on international trade. These conclusions involve the issue of market access for foreign investors in the development of China's relevant cultural legal system and even more so the status and functions of the review system within China's cultural legal system. On 12 July 2010, the delegations of the United States and China to the WTO issued a notice stating that they were willing to implement the Rulings on Publications and Audiovisual Products in accordance with the relevant treaty documents before 19 March 2011.

According to the final report that has been made public, the expert group reviewed certain specific provisions of 17 Chinese regulations and departmental rules. It accepted many of the claims raised by the United States regarding China's measures on publications and audio-visual products. On the other hand, due to procedural defects and insufficient substantive claims, the expert group also rejected some of the United States' claims. The details are as follows:

First, the United States argued that since China restricted the import of publications, home audio-visual products, sound recording products, and movies to state-owned Chinese companies, the import rights of foreign enterprises, individuals, and other Chinese enterprises and individuals for such products were restricted. In this regard, the United States listed a series of regulations and government rules, and claimed that the relevant provisions in China's measures on publications and audio-visual products violated China's commitment to opening up the right to trade in goods when joining the WTO, and thus did not comply with the provisions of the General Agreement on Tariffs and Trade 1994 (GATT 1994). China, on the other hand, argued that: (1) China's commitment to joining the WTO did not affect the Chinese government's power to regulate trade. The reason why the import of such products is monopolized by state-owned companies is mainly to conduct effective and comprehensive content review, which is the only feasible way to protect China's public morality from harm. (2) Sound recording products imported for digital distribution within China and movies imported for theatrical release within China are ancillary items for providing services and should not be regarded as goods but rather as part of the service. Therefore, they are not subject to the provisions of the GATT 1994.

The expert group believed that most of the arguments raised by the United States met the requirements of the Understanding on Rules and Procedures Governing the Settlement of Disputes (DSU) and fulfilled the burden of proof. When analyzing China's two main defenses, the expert group held that: (1) public morality requires content review, which, however, can be carried out without unduly restricting trade. Therefore, China's practice restricted the right to trade in goods and constituted a violation of its commitment to trade rights. (2) According to the customs classification rules and the classification code recommended by the WTO, movies and sound recording products imported for digital distribution within the territory are goods. However, when making the final decision, the expert group held that regardless of whether movies are goods, China's measures related to movie imports would affect the import of movies in the form of goods. Based on this, the expert panel concluded that the relevant provisions in China's measures on publications and audio-visual products violated the GATT 1994 and China's commitment to opening up the right to trade in goods.

Second, regarding the distribution services of publications, home audiovisual products, and recorded products, the United States believes that: (1) China prohibited foreign-invested enterprises from engaging in the general distribution of publications and electronic publications, the wholesale of electronic publications, and the distribution of imported publications; (2) China imposed more onerous restrictions on foreign-invested enterprises engaged in the distribution of publications and home audiovisual products than on domestic enterprises (such as requirements regarding the joint venture period); (3) China imposed a maximum shareholding ratio limit on Sino-foreign cooperative enterprises engaged in the distribution of home audiovisual products; (4) China prohibited foreign-invested enterprises from engaging in the digital distribution of recorded products through the Internet and mobile communication networks. China argued that it has not made commitments regarding the general distribution of publications in the commitment section of the General Agreement on Trade in Services, nor has it made commitments regarding the digital distribution of audiovisual products. The maximum shareholding ratio limit on Sino-foreign cooperative enterprises was based on agreements between the cooperative parties rather than on equity. While the panel agreed with most of the United States' arguments, it did not accept China's defense. However, because China had effectively prohibited foreign-invested enterprises from engaging in the digital distribution of recorded products through mobile communication networks, the United States' last argument in this part could not be fully supported.

Third, the United States believed that China did not provide national treatment to imported publications, imported recorded products intended for digital distribution, and imported movies. Specifically, this refers to: (1) China classifies imported publications and accordingly restricts the distribution channels of imported publications, allowing them to be distributed only through state-owned companies or wholly Chinese-funded companies, and not through foreign-invested enterprises, while there were no such restrictions on domestically published publications; (2) China implemented a more stringent and cumbersome content review process for imported recorded products intended for digital distribution than for domestic recorded products; (3) Imported movies could only be distributed through two State-owned companies, while there was no such restriction on domestic movies. China argued that classifying imported publications and restricting their distribution channels did not violate national treatment, but was instead necessary for effective content review and import supervision of imported publications. At the same time, China pointed out that it did not implement a more stringent and cumbersome content review process for imported recorded products intended for digital distribution than for domestic recorded products, but instead would review recorded products distributed in digital form. Finally, China believed that the situation where imported movies were distributed by two state-owned companies wss not a requirement of China's relevant measures, but a result of the current market development, which was not within the scope of the panel's review. Based on its view of import review in the first point, the panel first supported the United States' view that classifying imported publications and restricting their distribution channels violates the obligation to provide national treatment to imported goods. Regarding the United States' two subsequent requirements, the panel supported China's defense and concluded that the United States' arguments were unfounded.

Except for one intermediate conclusion of the United States' appeal, the Appellate Body overturned the panel's conclusion and determines that China's licensing requirements for foreign-invested enterprises regarding comprehensive balance violate relevant WTO regulations. Apart from this, the panel's conclusions were fully supported by the Appellate Body. This is the first time that the WTO has issued a panel and Appellate Body report on trade rights, and its significance is self-evident.

Regarding China's important defense regarding trade rights—content review, although the panel acknowledged that the public morality maintained by content review had the highest status, it rejected China's content review methods. On the one hand, the panel claimed that content review was crucial to a country's cultural life, national identity, and political life and therefor, of the highest status. On the other hand, the panel still insisted that there were theoretically alternatives that had a less impact on trade, thus rejecting this content review. This view actually examined the content review system at the trade level and concluded that this content review did not comply with relevant WTO treaties and China's commitments. This would have profound impacts on China's industries and even the relevant systems adjacent to the market.

The expert group believed that censorship for the protection of public morality did not violate the provisions of the General Agreement on Tariffs and Trade of 1994. In the Catalogue of Industries Prohibited for Foreign Investment under the Industrial Guidance Catalogue, Item 2 of Article 10 lists "the publication, general distribution and import business of books, newspapers and periodicals". At the same time, according to Article 41, paragraph 2 of the Publishing Regulations, "without approval, no unit or individual shall be engaged in the import business of publications; without designation, no unit or individual shall be engaged in the import business of newspapers and periodicals." Article 42 of the "Regulations on Publication" further stipulates that units engaged in the import business of publications must "be state-owned sole proprietorship enterprises and have the sponsoring units and their competent authorities recognized by the publishing administrative department of the State Council." These provisions excluded foreign enterprises, foreign-invested enterprises and even private enterprises from engaging in the import and operation of publications, which violated China's commitments on trade rights in the "Agreement on China's Accession to the WTO" and the "Working Party Report".[66] In this regard, China argued that such measures were "necessary to protect public morality." The expert panel did not raise objections to this, but first assumed the existence of this defense and examined whether it constituted "necessity." This had also become the way for the expert panel to review China's defense for other measures. Although this

[66] See Report of Appellate Body, WT/DS363/AB/R (09-6642), p. 66.

line of thinking saved the need examine whether China's defense was in compliance with Article XX(a) of the GATT, it did not violate Article XX(a) of the GATT when it was considered that China's relevant measures were "necessary" for the protection of public morality.[67] This retroactive approach shows that although the expert group may, for certain considerations, be reluctant to make a clear determination on this, the censorship system for the protection of public morality indeed has its legitimacy. To achieve the protection of public morality, censorship has to meet certain conditions. Assuming that China could rely on Article XX(a) of the GATT to defend the censorship system for the protection of public morality, the expert panel then examined the relevance of the relevant measures to the goal of protecting public morality and investigated the restrictive impact of these measures on trade. Taking Article 42 of the Publishing Regulations as an example, the expert group believed that China had failed to prove that excluding foreign enterprises and foreign-invested enterprises from the enterprises engaged in the import business of publications was conducive to protecting public morality; at the same time, China had also failed to prove that the alternative measures proposed by the United States could protect China's public morality, and these alternative measures could have less restrictive impact on trade than the measures under taken then by China.[68]

Here, the expert panel examined the content review system under the principle of proportionality. On the one hand, the application of the principle of proportionality made the rulings more targeted and conducive to the development of the WTO's legal system. On the other hand, the principle of proportionality would grant the expert group relatively expansive discretion, posing higher requirements for the independence and adjudication level of the expert panel. In the rulings on publications and audio-visual products, the principle of proportionality was actually a review of the review system and an examination of the impact of the review system on trade. This approach may expand the powers of the WTO as an international economic organization. This issue is not simply limited to the content review system involved in this case. On 2 November 2009, Pascal Lamy gave a speech titled "Environment First, Trade Second, the GATTzilla is Long Gone" at Carleton University in Ottawa, Canada. The speech positively responded to the concerns of developed countries about "carbon leakage" and argued that environmental issues are particularly important for a fair trade competition environment among countries.[69] This indicates that with the development of globalization, trade issues are intertwined with other issues, and the WTO tends to incorporate relevant issues comprehensively. After multilateral negotiations, this approach could prevail. However, without multilateral negotiations, the application of the proportionality principle may force the countries involved in the rulings to accept things they have been reluctant to agree with, and these things often fall outside the trade realm. The situation is not beneficial to developing countries.

---

[67] Ibid., p. 67.

[68] Ibid.

[69] https://www.ids.trade/files/news/2009/Lamy%20Remarks%20-%20Climate%20First,%20Trade%20Second%20-%20Nov09.pdf.

As previously mentioned, the determination on the content review system in the publications and audio-visual products ruling not only involves the review itself but also encompasses the market access system constructed to achieve content review. In this case, China attempted to prove that both the content review and the market access system are part of the review system and are necessary for protecting "public morality." Although the panel did not object to the defense raised by China based on Article XX(a) of the GATT 1994, it examined China's review system with the proportionality principle and concluded that China's statutory monopoly system of cultural product imports violated China's commitments for WTO accessment. The panel required China to modify the relevant legal systems to open up these fields to foreign investment. At this point, the content review system is no longer just a review issue but more of an industrial implication.

Given that the import and distribution of China's publications and audio-visual products are operated in the form of State-owned monopolies to facilitate content review, to implement the publications and audio-visual products ruling necessarily requires China to restructure its content review system, which needs to address two issues. First, is the content review system still relevant? Second, what are the ways and means for the estructur?

Judging from China's claims in this case, the United States' demands, and the panel's ruling, content review has been acknowledged as a way to protect "public morality," which is reflected in both the review and market access aspects of the regime. In other words, content review has both cultural and industrial significance. Content review helps maintain the cultural identity of a nation or a country while it also industrially protects the relevant cultural industries. The publications and audio-visual products ruling first acknowledges that protecting public morality is a policy goal of extremely high priority. The WTO has no intention of interfering with China's power of content review. However, for the purpose of the protection of public morality, content review needs to meet certain conditions. One of the conditions is that it should not impose undue restrictions on trade. After analyzing each of the measures at issue, the WTO overturned the statutory monopoly system in the import and circulation of cultural products (except for the film industry). At least, even under the framework of free trade, content review still enjoys certain legitimacy.

To this end, while abiding by the publications and audio-visual products ruling, it is necessary to transform the content review system to fulfil the purpose of content review, open up relevant markets to domestic private capital, and promote the marketization and industrialization of culture.

Regarding the publications and audio-visual products ruling, although the United States claimed a great victory in public opinion, it did not gain substantial benefits. When presenting its defense, the United States proposed an alternative method of content review by an independent institution, which still allows China's content review system to operate in a monopolistic form.[70]

Although the panel report and the Appellate Body report issued by the WTO were not without controversies regarding the ruling of the content review system, their

[70] See *Panel Report* WT/DS363/R (09-3798), pp. 64–66, 79, 81.

concerns about the market distortions caused by the review system are not unfounded. In fact, in terms of the import and export of goods and even services, the review system and the content classification system related will have a significant impact on trade. Currently, China's content review system is integrated with the import operations. Given that cross-border online business cannot be restricted thereby, it may lose its relevance in protecting domestic industries. At the same time, the lack of a classification system means that China's current content review system lacks depth. For some audio-visual products that are not covered by the current review system, there is a lack of effective and necessary supervision. Since the WTO requires China to separate the content review system from imports, while raising no objections to the content review system itself, China can take this opportunity to construct an independent content review mechanism and at the same time implement a content classification review system. This can ensure the content review on a right track and may also play a certain buffering role in mitigating the impact of imported books, audio-visual products, and movies on domestic industries. The rulings on publishing and audio-visual products would reshape China's content review system, which could be both a challenge and an opportunity for the development of China's relevant industries. The content review mechanism is not only about the content review itself but also about the market access regime that goes with it. This would prompt China to examine its content review mechanism for publishing and audio-visual products while fulfilling the relevant obligations under the WTO, in order to establish a competitive and vibrant cultural and media market.

On the 28th, September, 2003, facing the menacing competition from Hollywood after China's access to WTO, SARFT issued the Interim Provisions on the Project Approval of Film Scripts (Synopses) and the Review of Film Productions, which explicitly established the script review mechanism and also offers the detail procedures for a completed film to be examined. However, the new rules reduced the script reviewed to the abstract if the topic is not sensitive. Furthermore, SARFT also released his authority of review to some local branches. The film production team has since then obtained much autonomy in making a film. As a result, this change has also led up a loose-up of the regulatory examination of a film produced for the public exhibition and pushed forward for a gradual deregulation regarding film cencorship regime, which has now been happily acknowledged by the Film Industry Promotion Law.

## 3.7 A Loosed-Up Film Production Monopoly

Apart from the film censorship mechanism, a company was also required to obtain a qualification license issued by regulatory agencies before it could proceed with a film production project. At the beginning of the founding of New China, both the Central Committee of the Communist Party of China and the professionals in the film industry advocated the establishment of State-owned film studios. Under such circumstances, by the end of 1949, three major State-owned film production studios, namely the Northeast Film Studio, the Peking Film Studio, and the Shanghai Film Studio, had been successively established.[71] Meanwhile, there were still 8 private film companies. However, in February 1953, with the merger of the Shanghai United Film Studio, which was established by the combination of various private film companies, into the Shanghai Film Studio, the history of the Chinese film industry owned and operated in private hands, which had lasted for nearly half a century, came to an end.[72] In the 1950s, there were only three film studios in China.[73] By 1995, 16 film studios had already been granted permission to produce feature films.[74]

In 1993, Decree No. 3 clearly stipulated that film production should be market-oriented: "Film production, distribution, exhibition and other enterprises must adapt to the socialist market economic system established by the 14th National Congress of the Communist Party of China; as a spiritual product, the market for films lies in the audience (including cinema goers, rural projection enthusiasts, and audiences watching films and videos at home); the development of the film market should be judged by both social and economic benefits."[75] In addition, Decree No. 3 abolished China Film Group's monopoly on the distribution of domestic feature films, stipulating that "production units can conduct economic settlements with local distribution companies through methods such as selling regional distribution rights, individual film contracting, box office revenue sharing, and agency distribution."[76] The principle was thus established that producers could independently distribute feature films. On 5 January 1995, the former MRBT issued the Rules on Reforming Feature Film Production Work, which ruled that from 1 January 1995 onwards, except for film studios that had been approved by the State Council to have feature film production rights, other State-owned film studios in provinces, autonomous regions, and municipalities directly under the central government could also produce feature films. Before a film production kicked off, the script needed to be reviewed and approved by the publicity department of the Party Committee in each province, autonomous region, or municipality directly under the central government, and then submitted to the Film Bureau of the former MRBT for the production quotas. Only afterthese procedures accomplished, the film could be produced.[77] As a result, another 13 provincial film studios have received permits to produce films.[78] In addition, other social legal person organizations without film production permits might invest in feature film production with

[71] See Shen Yun, "The Beginning and End of the Establishment of New China's Film Industry (1949–1957)", in "Contemporary Cinema", Issue 4, 2005, pp. 33–35.

[72] Ibid., p. 38.

[73] See Lv Xiaoming, "Important Issues in Film Reform: Random Thoughts on Transforming Government Functions", in Zhang Zhenqin and Yang Yuanying (eds.), WTO and Chinese Cinema, Beijing: China Film Press, October 2002.

[74] See "A Major Reform in the Film Mechanism: Provincial Studios Gain Film Production Rights," in Film Literature, No. 3, 1995, p. 57.

[75] Decree No. 3, Article 1.

[76] Ibid., Article 3.

[77] Rules on Reforming Feature Film Production Work, Article 1.

[78] See "A Major Reform in the Film Mechanism: Provincial Studios Gain Film Production Rights," in Film Literature, No. 3, 1995, p. 57.

film studios that were of production rights. If their investment reaches more than 70% and they can comply with relevant regulations on film art creation and production management, upon approval from the former Radio, Film and Television Bureau, they could sign contracts with the film studio for that particular film and jointly use the term "co-production". The film would then be actually produced by the film studio with production rights.[79] After that, not only the enthusiasm of provincial film studios was mobilized, but also a large amount of social capital flowed into the film production industry. As a result, China's film production industry, which had been in trouble due to funding shortages in 1993 and 1994, caught a glimpse of hope in 1995. All film studios maintained a good production momentum and achieved relatively ideal market returns in that year. Taking Beijing Film Studio as an example, the studio set a record by producing more than 30 films in 1995, absorbing nearly 200 million yuan of social capital. In addition, since 1995, the implementation of the film and television integration policy (opening movie channels on TV stations, with part of the revenue returned to the film production industry) began to effectively promote the development of the film production industry.[80] These measures, together with the flexible system of profit distribution, led to the prosperity of the film market in 1995. The year 1995 saw the film industry in good shape. Many outstanding films were produced both at home and abroad. 75% of the production funds in the film market came from non governmental sources.[81]

Under these circumstances, State-owned film studios were not adapting well to marketization, while non-industry-specific capital was chasing film market profits. To address this, in March 1996, the National Film Work Conference was held in Changsha. The conference emphasized the spiritual value of film and implemented a strategy of producing high-quality works. The "9550 Project" was to be implemented, which aimed to produce 50 high-quality films during the "Ninth Five-Year Plan" period, or 10 films per year. Meanwhile, the strategy of producing high-quality works also included: "(1) Running key film studios well. First, build up Changchun Film Studio, Beijing Film Studio, Shanghai Film Studio, and August First Film Studio, making them the main force in producing high-quality films. Other studios should also fully utilize their advantages and make due contributions to the strategy. (2) Focusing on scriptwriting. The script is the foundation of a film, and it needs to be carefully crafted. We should organize creative teams well, establish scriptwriting centers, and organize creative exchanges. Increase the proportion of scriptwriting costs in film production costs. (3) Optimizing the combination of production elements. Every aspect of film production, including writing, directing, acting, cinematography, recording, art design, costumes, makeup, props, editing, post-production, and printing, can affect film quality if any is weak. We should

---

[79] Document No. 3, Article 3.

[80] Tang Rong. A Study on the Reform of China's Film System in the 30 Years Since Reform and Opening Up [J]. Modern Communication—Journal of Communication University of China, 2009, (02): 5–9.

[81] Li Duo, "Film Reform—A Life and Death Decision," published in China Newsweek, 2003, issue 46.

fully mobilize outstanding talents to participate in creating high-quality works and continuously promote stars. High-quality works produce stars, and stars produce high-quality works, making them mutually reinforcing. (4) Providing financial guarantees and policy support. National film funds should mainly support high-quality production. Give handsome awards and honors to studios and main creative personnel who produce high-quality works to encourage such production. (5) Strengthening publicity of high-quality works. Once high-quality films are released, media should vigorously report and review them to create widespread social impact."[82] While promoting the strategy of producing high-quality films, the Changsha Conference also continued to advocate for reforms. The conference identified several key areas for reform: First, measures were to be taken to promote the integration of film and television. Following this, after the establishment of the former Ministry of Radio, Film, and Television in 1986, the second focus was to establish film production bases. Third, measures were to be taken to expand funding channels for the film industry. Fourth, measures were to be taken to further deepen the reform of distribution and exhibition mechanisms. Fifth, measures were to be taken to actively promote international exchange and cooperation in the film industry. This policy shift to the govermental intervention in the following years led, however, to a decline in domestic film production and interrupted the reform process in the film industry.

In 2001, Document No. 17 was issued by the General Office of the CPC Central Committee and the General Office of the State Council, forwarding the "Several Opinions of the Central Publicity Department, State Administration of Radio, Film and Television, and General Administration of Press and Publication on Deepening the Reform of the Press, Publishing, Radio, Film and Television Industries" (hereinafter referred to as "Document No. 17"). This document summarized the experiences and lessons learned from cultural system reforms over the years, reflecting the understanding and thinking at the time. Document No. 17 proposed that cultural system reforms should focus on development, take structural adjustment as the main principle, and regard group construction as the key point and approach to breakthrough. It emphasized active exploration and innovation in five aspects: macro-management system, micro-operation mechanism, policy and legal system, market environment, and opening-up pattern, in order to further strengthen capabilities, enhance vitality, and improve competitiveness of the industry. Document No. 17 further clarified the goal of actively promoting media group reforms and establishing cross-regional, multimedia large-scale media groups. It also provided positive and specific responses to sensitive issues such as media industry financing, media investment with foreign capital, and cross-media development. This shows that the cultural authorities' emphasis on cultural elements in the film industry has not deviated from the cultivation and construction of the film market, and they are trying to achieve a balance between the two.

On 20 December 2001, the former SARFT issued the Implementing Rules for the Qualification Certification System of Obtaining the "Film Production License

[82] Ding Guangen, "Producing More Excellent Works to Prosper the Film Industry," in China Film Yearbook 1996, Beijing: China Film Press, 1997 edition, p. 8.

(Single Film)" (Trial) (hereinafter referred to as the "Single Film Rules"). The Single Film Rules further clarified that domestic film units at or above the prefecture (city) level, television stations, TV drama production units, and various cultural film and television legal person units registered with industrial and commercial departments at or above the prefecture (city) level (excluding wholly foreign-owned enterprises) can apply for and obtain the "Film Production License (Single Film)" to engage in film production business, with one application per film.[83] On 20 March 2002, Xu Jinglei's self-written, self-directed, and self-acted film 'I and My Father' (produced by Yi Nian Culture Development Co., Ltd.) obtained the 'Film Production License (Single Film)', becoming the first film produced by a private company to obtain this license since the release of the 'Single Film Rules'. In 2002, a total of 5 private companies or other non-production units applied for 'Film Production License (Single Film)' for 58 films. That year, China produced a total of 100 films, of which 32 were produced by private companies.[84]

On 29 October 2003, in order to fulfil china's commitments under the WTO Agreement, the SARFT issued Decree No. 20, the "Provisional Regulations on Access to Qualifications for Film Production, Distribution and Exhibition Operations" (hereinafter referred to as "Decree No. 20"), establishing legal channels for domestic private capital and foreign capital to enter the film market (excluding film distribution Sector). This would make the market more open, which means that the monopoly of State-owned capital in film production and distribution would come to an end. Firstly, Decree No. 20 encouraged domestic State-owned and non-State-owned entities (excluding foreign capital) to establish joint venture film production companies or independent production companies with existing State-owned film production units; it allows foreign capital to participate in joint ventures with existing State-owned film production units to establish film production companies.[85] Secondly, Decree No. 20 encouraged State-owned and non-State-owned units (excluding foreign investment) to hold controlling shares in or establish film technology companies on their own to transform film production, projection infrastructure and technical equipment; it allowed foreign-funded companies to participate in the operation of such businesses, and foreign-funded companies might also hold controlling shares in the operation of such businesses in approved provinces and cities.[86] Thirdly, Decree No. 20 encouraged both state-owned and non-state-owned film and cultural entities to establish companies exclusively engaged in the distribution of domestic films. These domestic film distribution companies enjoyed the same rights and obligations as provincial-level film distribution companies at the time.[87]

On 8 January 2004, the SARFT issued the "Opinions on Promoting the Development of Radio, Film and Television Industry", which stipulates: "Encourage eligible non-State-owned and non-State-owned capital (excluding foreign capital) outside

[83] Single Film Rules, Items 1 and 8.

[84] Yin Hong. 2002–2003 Chinese Film Industry Memo (Part I) [J]. Film Art, 2004, (02): 4–8.

[85] Decree No. 20, Article 3.

[86] Decree No. 20, Article 5.

[87] Decree No. 20, Articles 7, 8.

the film system to jointly or solely invest in film production, distribution and sales of domestic films, join or solely establish cinema lines, and renovate cinemas. Foreign film production institutions are allowed to establish film production companies with Chinese majority shareholding upon approval with domestic State-owned film production units; ……"[88] On 10 October 2004, the Film Business Qualification Provisions replaced Decree No. 20 and the "Single Film Rules" and adopted further liberalised provisions on the access to the film market. The Film Business Qualification Provisions were revised on the basis of Decree No. 20. To push forward the original liberalization of the business qualifications of the operators of the film production, distribution and screening, it further lowered the market access threshold, expanded the channels for investment and financing in the industry, and consolidated the practices for of the film industry reform in the form of department rules. The Film Business Qualification Provisions further relaxed market access for the film industry in four main aspects: allowing domestic companies, enterprises and other economic organizations to jointly or solely invest in filming films, establishing film production companies, distributing and selling domestic films, joining theater chains or solely investing in theater chains, and renovating theaters; allowing foreign production agencies to establish Chinese-controlled film production companies with domestic State-owned film production units upon approval; allowing foreign companies to establish theater construction companies or renovate theaters in the form of joint ventures upon approval; allowing domestic companies, enterprises and other economic organizations to establish film technology companies, or jointly or cooperatively establish film technology companies with foreign companies, enterprises and other economic organizations, and renovate film production, projection infrastructure and technical equipment. On 30 November 2004, the NDRC and the Ministry of Commerce jointly issued the Guiding Catalogue of Industries for Foreign Investment (Revised in 2004), which listed "film production" as a restricted foreign investment industry catalogue and stipulated that the Chinese investor should have a controlling position in "film production" enterprises.[89] This thus provided a legal channel for foreign investment in China's film production industry.

The Film Business Qualifictaion Provisions would allow domestic economic organizations to establish film production companies through the following means[90]:

- Jointly establish a film production company with domestic companies and enterprises that have obtained the "Film Production License". The registered capital of the joint venture shall be no less than 1,000,000 yuan.

[88] Opinions on Promoting the Development of Radio, Film and Television Industry, item (23) of paragraph 6.

[89] Catalogue of Industries for Guiding Foreign Investment (2004 Revised Edition), "Catalogue of Industries Restricted from Foreign Investment", Article 11(3).

[90] Article 5 of the Film Business Qualification on Provisions.

- Establish a 100% owned qualified film production company.[91] The registered capital of the film production company wholly owned here should not be less than 1,000,000 yuan either. However, before obtaining the film production license, the production company must have shot at least two films on the basis of obtaining the "Film Production License (Single Film)".

In this way, the Film Business Qualification Provisions not only clearly stipulated that the State allows domestic companies, enterprises and other economic organizations (excluding foreign-invested enterprises) to establish film production companies, but also further clarified the application conditions and procedures for establishing film production companies, and simplified the approval procedures and shortend the approval time in accordance with the requirements of the "Administrative Approval Law".

The Film Business Qualification Provisions only allowed overseas investors to establish production companies with existing production units that had certain qualifications by setting up joint ventures or cooperative enterprises.[92] Furthermore, the equity share held by overseas investors in such production companies shall not exceed 49%, and the total registered capital of all such production companies should not be less than 5,000,000 yuan.[93] This was a breakthrough in the film regulatory policy of China. In the past, China had only allowed foreign investors to co-produce films with domestic film production units. According to the Fim Business Qualification Provisions, foreign parties could form joint ventures or cooperate not only with units that had obtained the Film Production License, but also with units that had already obtained two Film Production Licenses (Single Film).[94]

If the Film Production License had been obtained, for newly established production companies, regardless of whether overseas capital was involved or not, they enjoy equal rights with State-owned production units.[95] After the release of the would Film Business Qualification Provisions, China Film Group Corporation, Time Warner and Hengdian jointly established China Film Warner Hengdian Film and Television Co., Ltd. as the first joint venture film production company set up in accordance with the "Interim Provisions on Market Access".

The entry of foreign capital into the field of film production would certainly prompt changes in the capital structure of the entire Chinese film industry, indicating that the reform of the Chinese film industry had begun to enter the level of capital structural reform. However, the entry of foreign capital also poses challenges to the content regulation of the broadcasting and film and television industries, in

[91] Here, a wholly-owned film production company refers to one whose registered capital does not come from the participation of a company or enterprise that has obtained a "Film Production License".

[92] It refers to those where the Chinese side has obtained the "Film Production License" or has obtained two "Film Production Licenses (Single Film)". Please refer to Article 6, Paragraph (1) of the Film Business Qualification Provisions.

[93] Article 6, Paragraph (3) of the Film Business Qualification Provisions.

[94] Article 6, Paragraph (1) of the Film Business Qualification Provisions.

[95] Article 7 of the Film Business Qualification Provisions.

particular the film industry. Furthermore, at that time, give that China had yet established a competition law system, the concentration of film capital without necessary antitrust check might also have an adverse impact on the development of China's film industry. Meanwhile, the Chinese film market was not open to private capital for a long time at that time. Under the circumstances where private capital was still relatively immature, adopting aggressive opening-up measures to foreign capital might not be conducive to the development of the Chinese film industry. Based on this, the Ministry of Culture, the SARFT, the General Administration of Press and Publication, the NDRC and the MOFCOM jointly issued and implemented the "Several Opinions on Introducing Foreign Investment in the Cultural Field" on 6 July 2005. According to these opinions, foreign investment in the establishment and operation of radio and television program production and broadcasting companies, film production companies, film import and distribution companies and video projection companies is prohibited.[96] In this way, within less than a year after the foreign investment access to the film production market opened, the legal channels for foreign investment in the film production industry were closed. Correspondingly, on 31 October 2007, the NDRC and the MOFCOM jointly issued the Catalogue for the Guidance of Foreign Investment Industries (Revised in 2007), abolishing the Catalogue for the Guidance of Foreign Investment Industries (Revised in 2004). All "radio and television program production and operation companies" and "film production companies, distribution companies and cinema chain companies" have thus been included again in the "Catalogue of Industries Prohibited from Foreign Investment".[97]

Since the implementation of the Film Industry Promotion Law on 1 March 2017, the approval of both film production qualification and Film Production License (Single Film) have been officially abolished. There is no longer a need to apply for the qualification for a company to produce a film. The market access system has been since significantly streamlined. Such a liberalisation of the market access regime has enabled more enterprises or even individuals to participate in film making business. The new regime is an breakthrough of the market oriented reform and is conducive to a more open environment for more creative input in the film industry. Lowering down the film production threshold instead of incessantly setting limits will release the professional power into the film production business. At the same time, simpler and more convenient approval regime with a decentralization of regulatory authority significantly facilitate the efficient operation of the film market, which will in turn lower down various costs for film production entities, while enabling them to focus more on creative production of the film itself. It also provides more favourable conditions for other entities to participate in the film industry and promotes market competition. After the regulations on film production licenses were abolished, the previous joint production business model of borrowing or relying on production licence held by the market incumbent have come to an end. More project companies

[96] Several Opinions on the Introduction of Foreign Capital in the Cultural Field, Article 4.

[97] Article 10, Items 5 and 6 of the Catalogue for the Guidance of Foreign Investment Industries and the Catalogue of Industries Prohibited from Foreign Investment.

with the aim of making and completing individual films may emerge. Under the legal framework of the project company business model, the rights and obligations of all parties involved in the film making are easier to define, and the operational management and revenue accounting are more standardized, which will be conducive to safeguarding the interests of all the stakeholders involved the film industry in China.

## 3.8 CEPA and Its Implications

HK had ever been regarded as a commercial film centre in the 1980s.[98] In Asia, Hong Kong is the most important film production base after India and Japan. The films it produces have performed well in the markets of East Asia, Southeast Asia, South Asia, as well as Europe and America. From the perspectives of economic value and cultural export, Hong Kong films have always been an important component of Hong Kong's service industry and cultural industry, and they are also a common cultural and entertainment product for multiple ethnic groups in Asia.[99] However, the late 1990s saw the decline of HK film production and box office.[100] In fact, according to the statistics of the Hong Kong Film Workers' Association, after entering the 1990s, the overall development of the Hong Kong film industry had shown signs of slowing down. Although the average annual box office of films in Hong Kong could reach 1.35 billion Hong Kong dollars during the seven years from 1991 to 1997, this figure covered the box office of both Hong Kong-produced films and imported films. Therefore, it did not tell the true situation of the Hong Kong film industry. Even so, the annual box office in Hong Kong dropped from 1.15 billion Hong Kong dollars in 1997 to 900 million Hong Kong dollars in 2000. The output value of the Hong Kong film industry dropped from 6.23 billion Hong Kong dollars in 1994 to 4.28 billion Hong Kong dollars in 1999. The revenue of the local film industry in Hong Kong mainly includes copyright fees for video tapes, DVDS, television and cinemas. Such revenue sharply declined from 1.1 billion in 1992 to 350 million Hong Kong dollars in 1999.[101] Moreover, the overseas market for Hong Kong films has also shrunk. The revenue from overseas markets dropped from 1.16 billion Hong Kong dollars in 1992 to 250 million Hong Kong dollars in 1998, which reflected the rapid shrinking of the export market for Hong Kong films. The reduction in the output value of the film industry, as well as local and overseas earnings, has also deterred investment in the Hong Kong film industry. In 1993, the total output of local films in Hong Kong was 242. Since then, it had continued to decline, and in 1997 and 1998, it dropped to 94 and 92 films per year respectively. Although the output of Hong Kong films rebounded

[98] Tyler Cowen.

[99] Hong Kong Film Workers' Association: "Policy Report on Revitalizing the Hong Kong Film Industry" (October 2002), p. 10.

[100] David Hancock.

[101] Hong Kong Film Workers' Association: "Policy Report on Revitalizing the Hong Kong Film Industry" (October 2002), p. 10.

during the three years from 1999 to 2001, it only reached 126 in 2001, which was far from comparable to the output during the heyday of Hong Kong films.[102] Meanwhile, according to a survey conducted by the Hong Kong Film Workers' Association in August 2002, the situation of unemployment and underemployment in the Hong Kong film industry was extremely serious. In July 2002, only 36.3% of the personnel were employed, 21.9% were underemployed, as many as 23.7% were unemployed, and the number of those who had changed careers had already reached 18.1%.[103] On 29 June 2003, in order to promote the common prosperity and development of the economies of Hong Kong and the Chinese mainland and strengthen economic and trade ties between the two sides and other countries and regions, the Financial Secretary of the Hong Kong Special Administrative Region and the MOFCOM signed the "Mainland and Hong Kong Closer Economic Partnership Arrangement" (hereinafter referred to as the "Closer Economic Partnership Arrangement" or "CEPA"). Thus, close trade and investment relations have been established between the Chinese mainland and Hong Kong. In the package of agreements signed for this purpose, amongst the others the Chinese mainland has been providing preferential treatment for the Hong Kong film industry.

First, since 1 January 2004, Chinese-language films produced in Hong Kong, after being reviewed and approved by the competent authorities in the mainland, are not subject to import quota restrictions for distribution in the mainland. The so-called Chinese-language films produced in Hong Kong refer to those produced by production units established or set up in accordance with the regulations of the Hong Kong Special Administrative Region and which hold more than 75% of the film's copyright. The main staff group of this film should have Hong Kong residents accounting for more than 50% of the total number of employees in the group. The so-called main staff group includes the director, screenwriter, male lead, female lead, male supporting role, female supporting role, producer, cinematographer, editor, art director, costume designer, action/martial arts director and original music composer.[104] This stipulation has secured a tremendous film market for this free trade port. Although there is still some room to manoeuvre about the definition of film produced in HK, the unlimited market access from HK to China is still attractive to the film makers from some western countries.[105]

Secondly, films co-produced between Hong Kong and the Chinese mainland should be regarded as domestic films being distributed in the Chinese mainland, provided that at least one-third of the members of the production team are from the Chinese mainland and the story characters and main plots are related to the mainland.[106] This regulation also enables co-productions between the Chinese mainland

[102] Ibid., p. 11.

[103] Ibid., p. 12.

[104] Please refer to Annex IV and Appendix I of the CEPA.

[105] Peisi Cheng, CEPA may help Hong Kong produce 100 films. Hong Kong Commercial Daily, 27 September, 2003.

[106] Ibid.

and Hong Kong to enjoy the treatment of domestic films, thus giving these co-productions the opportunity to utilize the distribution and screening channels of domestic films instead of only being distributed through designated companies like imported films.

CEPA opened up the increasingly prosperous mainland Chinese film market for the shrinking Hong Kong film industry. Before the implementation of the CEPA, due to strict reviews and restrictions on quotas, a large number of Hong Kong films were unable to enter the mainland. Before joining the WTO, the Chinese mainland imported 10 revenue-sharing films each year, among which there was generally only one film produced in Hong Kong. However, the increase in the quota for revenue-sharing films after joining the WTO failed to improve the difficult situation of Hong Kong film imports. In addition to importing revenue-sharing blockbusters, Hong Kong films can also enter the mainland in the form of "batch" films. The so-called "batch" films refer to the non-imported revenue-sharing blockbusters introduced to the Chinese mainland every year. Usually, they are bought out at a very low price (several tens of thousands of US dollars) by Chinese mainland film import companies in one go and then distributed and screened in the mainland. Because the licensing fees for Hong Kong films imported in this way are extremely low, the films introduced in this manner are generally old Hong Kong films with no big-name stars participating in the performances. Moreover, their production investment is relatively small, and most of them are independently produced by small companies. Therefore, the market influence cannot be compared with that of imported revenue-sharing films. Furthermore, before the signing of the CEPA, Hong Kong films also entered the mainland market through co-production, but the requirements for co-production were significantly stricter. Generally speaking, in China, a co-production film refers to a "jointly produced movie", which is a type of "co-produced film". The directors, photographers and other main creative personnel involved in the joint production of films must be approved by the film regulator and should generally be citizens within the territory of China.[107] According to the "Provisions on the Main Creative Personnel of Domestic Feature Films and Co-produced Films" issued by the former MRFT on 4 November 1996, for co-produced films, except for the director, screenwriter and cinematographer who should mainly be Chinese residents, the proportion of Chinese residents playing the main roles should generally not be less than 50%. If the proportion needs to be exceeded due to special requirements of the subject matter or characters, the production unit must report to the Film Bureau for approval. Without approval, the Film Review Committee would not accept the film.[108]

Before the signing of the CEPA, the Chinese film administrative department did not distinguish the types of co-produced films. Whether it was "joint production", "collaborative production" or "commissioned production", a production permit was

[107] Article 10 of the "Regulations on the Administration of Sino-Foreign Cooperative Film Production" promulgated by the former Ministry of Radio, Film and Television on July 5, 1994.

[108] Article 2 of the "Regulations on the Main Creative Personnel of Domestic Feature Films and Co-produced Films".

required before kick-off of the fim production, and the "License for Sino-Foreign Co-produced Films" was to be obtained. After the completion of the production, the finished film should be submitted by the China Film Co-production Company to the film administrative department for review in accordance with the relevant provisions of film censorship. After review and approval and issuance of the Public Screening License, it can be publicly screened within China or exported abroad. The film that has been reviewed and approved by the Chinese film administrative department should maintain its version as approved. The film may be cut as appropriate in accordance with the censorship regulations of the country and region where it is to be screened.[109] However, for double-version films that have not been reviewed and approved by the Chinese film administrative department or films whose original approved content has been altered without authorization during post-production, neither Chinese nor foreign parties or third parties are allowed to privately print, copy or reproduce them into other audio-visual products for public screening within or beyond China.[110] This kind of cooperative film production system that does not distinguish the participation of the Chinese side obviously fails to satisfy the industry and does not conform to the prevailing rules of the international film market. It is inevitable to be criticized. Therefore, on 8 October 2003, the SARFT issued the "provisions on the Administration of Sino-Foreign Cooperative Film Production" (hereinafter referred to as "Order No. 19"), stipulating that although the administrative licensing system is still to be implemented for cooperative film production, domestic and foreign organizations or individuals who have not obtained the "License for Sino-Foreign Cooperative Film Production" or approval documents are not allowed to cooperate or independently produce films within the territory of China.[111] Moreover, films completed through Sino-foreign cooperative production must be submitted to the film review institution of the SARFT for review after the provincial radio, film and television administrative department and the China Film Cooperative Production Company put forward the initial review opinions.[112] However, only jointly produced films, after passing the review and obtaining the "Film Public Screening License" issued by the SARFT, can be distributed and screened within or outside China. For collaborative production or commissioned production of films, those that pass the review can go through the exports procedures with the approval documents issued by the SARFT.[113] In response to Order No. 19, the SARFT issued the "Notice on the insurane of the Detailed Rules for the Implementation of the 'Provisions on the Administration of Films from Sino-Foreign Cooperative Production Sites' (Interim)" on 27, November 2003, making the following specific regulations on jointly produced films in Sino-foreign cooperative production: For jointly produced films, the place where the story takes place is not

[109] Article 15 of the "Regulations on the Administration of Sino-Foreign Cooperative Film Production".

[110] Article 16 of the "Regulations on the Administration of Sino-Foreign Cooperative Film Production".

[111] Order No. 19, Article 7.

[112] Order No. 19, Article 13.

[113] Order No. 19, Article 14.

restricted by regions, but the plot or main characters must be related to the Chinese mainland. For jointly produced films that employ foreign main creative personnel, approval from the Film Bureau is required. Among them, the main Chinese (mainland) actors shall not be less than one third of the total number of main actors in the film, and other main creative personnel shall, in principle, each account for one half. For films jointly produced by Hong Kong film producers (companies) and the mainland, apart from the main actors, other key creative personnel are not subject to proportion restrictions.[114] In addition, for collaborative production and commissioned production, it is stipulated that for films co-produced by Hong Kong film producers and those from the mainland, upon approval by the Film Council, the printing and post-production of the film's base samples can be completed in Hong Kong.[115] Later, On 6 July 2004, the SARFT issued Order No. 31 on Provisions on "Sino-Foreign Cooperative Film Production" (hereinafter referred to as "Order No. 31"), stipulating that production units within China holding the Film Production License and the Film Production License (Single Film) (including Sino-foreign joint venture production units established in accordance with the new policy) can all participate in the Sino-foreign cooperative film production Collaborate with foreign partners to produce films.[116] The principle that the proportion of foreign main actors should not exceed two-thirds of the total number of main actors is also established therein.[117] These measures have promoted the development of collaborative films, especially co-productions, and also driven the growth of collaborative films between the Chinese mainland and Hong Kong.

Overall, CEPA has enhanced the competitive level of the Chinese film market and provided Hong Kong with a huge and highly dynamic mainland Chinese market. Overall, CEPA has strengthened the Hong Kong film industry's grip on the mainland film market and, at the same time, greatly encouraged Hong Kong investors to collaborate with mainland production companies on films. This has further promoted the development of the mainland film market and played a positive role in pushing up the mainland film box office receipt exceeding 10 billion yuan since 2010.

However, it cannot be ignored that when Hong Kong films enter the Chinese mainland market through co-production and other means, they must be subject to the Chinese film censorship system. In the face of the film censorship system in China, Hong Kong filmmakers have shown a certain degree of maladjustment.

According to the Provisions on Scripts and Film Productions, films must avoid the "Ten Prohibitions" and nine major editing matters. On 3 March 2008, the SARFT issued the Notice on Reiterating Film Censorship Standards, reiterating The Ten

[114] Notice on the Issuance of the Interim Detailed Rules for the Implementation of the Provisions on the Administration of Sino-Foreign Cooperative Film Production, Article 3, Items (1) and (2).

[115] Notice on the Issuance of the Interim Detailed Rules for the Implementation of the Provisions on the Administration of Sino-Foreign Cooperative Film Production, Article 3, Items (3).

[116] Order No. 31, Article 8.

[117] Order No. 31, Article 13.

prohibitions and nine major cutting items.[118] For the Hong Kong film industry where film classification is implemented, the Ten Prohibitions and nine cuts have imposed certain constraints on its creative freedom. For example: "Misinterpreting Chinese civilization and Chinese history, seriously contrary to historical facts; Misinterpreting the history of other countries and disrespecting their civilizations, customs and habits; Belittle the images of revolutionary leaders, heroic figures and important historical figures; Tampering with the images of famous works at home and abroad and important characters in these works is one of the nine major items of editing. However, Hong Kong comedies—especially historical comedies like nonsensical ones, which sell themselves by spoof historical figures, are very likely to be caught by the cencorship system. If so, the tradition of nonsensical comedy in Hong Kong would not be able to find its place in the mainland in the form of co-productions. Police and gangster films are also two major types of Hong Kong films. However, "maliciously defaming the image of the people's army, armed police, public security and the judiciary" is a matter to be cut out. Furthermore, a the film should not contain "interwoven content of murder, violence and terror, reversing the value orientation of truth and falseness, good and evil, beauty and ugliness, and confusing the basic nature of justice and injustice; deliberately showing the arrogance of illegal and criminal activities, specifically presenting the details of criminal acts, and exposing special investigation methods; strongly stimulating plots such as murder, bloodshed, violence, drug abuse, gambling, etc. There are circumstances such as mistreating prisoners, extracting confessions from criminals or criminal suspects by torture; Matters involving overly terrifying scenes, dialogues, background music and sound effects." As a result, Hong Kong gangster films or criminal films that showcase gangster loyalty or reflect police corruption will find it very difficult to stand the censorship of Chinese mainland.

In order to specifically comply with China's film censorship system, many co-productions of related themes have to produce two versions. One is specifically provided for the Chinese mainland market, with relevant plots deleted or changed in accordance with the Provisionals on the Scripts and fim Productions, in order to pass the film censorship and obtain the "Film Public Screening License". The other version is the non-Chinese mainland version, in order to maintain its original Hong Kong film characteristics. However, in this way, Hong Kong films would lose their original market advantages. Moreover, this does not comply with the requirements of Order No. 31: Jointly produced films, after passing the review and obtaining the Film Public Screening License issued by the SARFT, can be distributed and publicly screened both within and outside China.[119] After the film has obtained the Film Public Screening License, if either the Chinese or foreign parties need to make any changes to it, they must report to the SARFT for approval.[120] This means that if a film that has passed the censorship is to be produced as an uncut or adapted version

[118] Article 3 of the "Notice of the State Administration of Radio, Film and Television on Reaffirming the Standards for Film Censorship".

[119] Order No. 31, Article 16.

[120] Order No. 31, Article 17.

for the Hong Kong and international markets in addition to the mainland version that has passed the censorship, it must be approved by the SARFT; otherwise, it would be considered a violation. However, its Cantonese version still retains its identity as being from Hunan. The Film Bureau of the SARFT regarded it as "in violation of regulations" in response to journalists' questions.[121] Because passing the review of the SARFT is itself a difficult task that Hong Kong filmmakers need to complete, obtaining the approval of the SARFT for the issues of the two versions has become something that ordinary filmmakers are reluctant to do.

A film can also be put on the Chinese mainland film market as an imported film. In 2004, at the beginning of the implementation of the CEPA, among the jointly produced films submitted to the SARFT for review, "Jianghu", invested by Eric Tsang, was the only film that failed the film review. Before this, "Jianghu" had already passed the script filing review.[122] In December 2008, it was reported that the film "Shinjuku Incident", starring Jackie Chan and directed by Er Dongsheng, had given up the Chinese mainland market as it had no hope of passing the film censorship. When the project kicked off, in order to comply with the regulations of co-production films, the investor added Polybona from the Chinese mainland and specially invited two Chinese mainland actresses: Xu Jinglei and Fan Bingbing. To meet the requirement that the production location be in the Chinese mainland, the production team also specially went to Changchun to shoot several scenes. However, the sensitivity of the subject matter and the bloody visuals still made the film unacceptable to the Chinese film censorship authorities.[123] The Shinjuku Incident was eventually scheduled for release in the Hong Kong market from April 2nd to May 6th in 2004, achieving a box office revenue of HK $13.91 million.[124] It is reported that "Shinjuku Incident" was made with an investment of nearly 100 million.[125] The previous co-production "Apple" had its Film Public Screening License revoked after its release, which also caused quite a stir in the market.

The development and predicament of co-productions between Hong Kong and the Chinese mainland after "CEPA" reflect the impact of the current film censorship system in China on the film industry. As a region with a relatively developed film industry and abundant talents, CEPA integrates Hong Kong into the dynamic market

[121] Xie Xiao, Chen Yiyi: the Chinese movie implementation of CEPA, film bureau answer eight questions, in the southern metropolis daily, January 20, 2005, http://ent.people.com.cn/GB/8222/42057/43636/3135543.html.

[122] Chen Yiyi: "Jackie chan" shinjuku>violence do not delete, the mainland must not release, in the southern metropolis daily, December 4, 2008, http://enjoy.eastday.com/e/20081204/u1a4023711.html.

[123] Chen Yiyi: "Jackie chan" shinjuku>violence do not delete, the mainland must not release, in the southern metropolis daily, 4 December 2008, http://enjoy.eastday.com/e/20081204/u1a4023711.html.

[124] Hong Kong Film Industry Association: "The Overall Situation of the Hong Kong Film Market in 2009", 2 January 2010.

[125] Chen Yiyi: "Jackie chan" shinjuku>violence do not delete, the mainland must not release, in the southern metropolis daily, 4, December 2008, http://enjoy.eastday.com/e/20081204/u1a4023711.html.

of the Chinese mainland. This is an opportunity for the Hong Kong film industry. Therefore, for a Hong Kong film makes, which already enjoys a mature classification system and developed market, if it wants to enter the Chinese mainland market through joint production, the films it makes must not only meet the hearts of mainland audiences but also comply with the film censorship system of the Chinese mainland. This is bound to cause serious discomfort to the film industry professionals in Hong Kong. Therefore, a distinction has emerged between the filmmakers who stay in Hong Kong to make pure Hong Kong films and those who go north to make films for co-productions. Current film criticists all hold that the former is more important for the future development of the Hong Kong film industry.

According to this, after the implementation of the CEPA, in the face of the entry of co-productions from Hong Kong and the Chinese mainland, the competition in the Chinese mainland's film market is undoubtedly fierce. However, the strict film censorship system makes it impossible for Hong Kong's diverse and rich genre films to smoothly enter the Chinese mainland's film market. Instead, more co-productions are produced that have no substantial difference from those produced in the Chinese mainland. Meanwhile, Hong Kong films have not gained nothing from it: The prevalence of co-productions has actually enabled the Hong Kong film industry to emerge from the shrinking situation in 2002 and given Hong Kong films that are popular in the local market a chance to survive.

## 3.9 Future Development of China's Regulatory System

The regulatory system for film production in China mainly consists of two parts: the market access system and the film censorship system developed with its focus on the issuance of the "Film Public Screening License". The market access system aims for the protection of existing market participants, while the film censorship system linked to administrative licensing reveals China's concerns about film content. On 27 August 2003, the Fourth Meeting of the Standing Committee of the National People's Congress passed the Administrative License Law of the People's Republic of China (hereinafter referred to as the "Administrative License Law"). In order to ensure the legal status of the film censorship system, the film censorship system is more closely linked to the Film Public Screening License, thus making film censorship one of the conditions for issuing the Film Public Screening License.

According to the provisions of the Administrative Licensing Law, the establishment of administrative licensing shall follow the logics of economic and social development, be conducive to releasing the full power to the enthusiasm and initiative of citizens, legal persons or other organizations, safeguard public interests and social order, and promote the coordinated development of the economy, society and ecological environment.[126] As an administrative license, it is hard to say that the Film Public Screening License meets this requirement. First of all, the film censorship system,

[126] Article 13 of the Administrative License Law.

as a system where a government department acts as the gatekeeper of film content, actually narrates the types of films that film creators or producers can create and produce. Therefore, the film screening license system, which is based on the film censorship system as a requirement, is not conducive to the initiative and creativity of the industry. Secondly, there are many matters that promote the coordinated development of the economy, society and the ecological environment. If any behaviour or matter that society pays attention to is listed as a matter that promotes the coordinated development of society and administrative licensing is set up accordingly, then the limits imposed on setting of administrative licensing would lose its significance. Here, when reviewing the relevant film content with the Film public Screening License as the licensing matter, it is necessary to consider whether this licensing system follows the logics of economic and social development and whether it safeguards public interests and social order. The issuance of the Film Public Screening License regards films as very special products and requires two separate regulatory reviews before production and circulation. On the one hand, from an economic perspective, these two regulatory reviews have reduced the supply of products, and their review criteria are ambiguous and uncertain. Therefore, it is difficult to say that the issuance of the "Film Public Screening License" follows the logics of economic and social development. On the other hand, if public interest and social order are taken as the theoretical basis for issuing the "Film Public Screening License", it is necessary to prove that the implementation of the film screening license is in line with the principle of proportionality. To achieve this is not that easy.

In fact, the Administrative License Law has imposed strict preconditions on the matters concerning the establishment of administrative licenses.[127] On the other hand, administrative licensing matters are regarded as a supplementary means. If the matters that is to be subject to administrative licensing can be regulated by means other than administrative licensing, then there is no need to set up such administrative licensing for them. The relevant methods other than administrative licensing are to be independently determined by citizens, legal persons and other organizations, are to be effectively regulated by the market competition mechanism, are to be self-regulated by industry organizations or intermediary agencies, or are to be resolved by administrative organs through other administrative management methods such as post-event supervision. This approach tries to strike a balance between the law and other social regulatory means: acknowledging the limitations of the law in regulating social relations, providing sufficient space for other market or social operations such as market competition and industry self-discipline, and voluntarily withdrawing when there are doubts about the operational efficiency of the law, leaving enough space for the entry of other means to work. Only in this way can the purpose that administrative licensing be realized: to follow the Logics of economic and social development and be conducive to releasing the full power to the enthusiasm and initiative of citizens, legal persons or other organizations.

As for the film review system attached to the "Film Public Screening License", by referring to the relevant provisions of the "Administrative License Law", it should

[127] See Article 12 of the Administrative License Law.

be possible to find a balance point that not only conforms to the development Logics of the film market but also protects the relevant public interests and the health of minors, thereby reshaping the supervision system in the film production process and promoting further development of China's film production industry.

Although China has made every effort to preserve its protection of the domestic film market, with the development of the globalization of service trade and under the pressure from Hollywood audio-visual giants to further open up the audio-visual field, it is unrealistic to expect the current regulatory system to remain unscathed in the future. If China further opens up its film market, the current film production license system in the Chinese film industry will face great challenges. The current legal system for film production in China is established with the "Regulations measures" at its core and cannot meet the demands of the current development of the film industry.

In 2004, the "Film Promotion Law" was included in the "Proposal on Formulating the Ten-Year Plan for Cultural Legislation in China (2004–2013)" issued by the Publicity Department of the Communist Party of China Central Committee. In 2006, it was listed as a legislative project in the "Outline of the National Cultural Development Plan for the Eleventh Five-Year Plan Period". Since 2007, it has been listed as an important project in the legislative work plan of The State Council for three consecutive years. In October 2009, the "Film Promotion Law" was renamed the "Film Industry Promotion Law". The draft for public comment prepared by the SARFT consisted of eight chapters and eighty-four articles. The main systems and measures to be stipulated are: the film market access system, the film administrative licensing system and regulatory responsibilities, the film support and guarantee system, and the safeguarding system for art films. All these four items are related to the film production process. Among them, the film market access system, the film administrative licensing system and the supervision of film shooting are closely related in particular.

Regarding the market access regime of the film industry, the "Film Industry Promotion Law (Draft for Comment)" specially prepared the so called "Industry Policy" clause, which held that the film industry should be a service industry. Film services fell under service trade category. The state formulated relevant policies to guide the formation of a unified, open, competitive and orderly film market, and to foster a pattern where public ownership is the mainstay and diverse forms of ownership develop together.[128]

After Film Industry Promotion Law was finally adopted, Article 5 therein stipulates, "The State Council shall incorporate the development of the film industry into the national economic and social development plan. Local people's governments at or above the county level shall, in light of actual local conditions, incorporate the development of the film industry into their respective national economic and social development plans. The state formulates policies for the film industry and related industries, guides the formation of a unified, open, fair and competitive film market, and promotes the prosperous development of the film market." This way, the service

[128] Article 6 of the Film Industry Promotion Law (Draft for Comment)".

industry status have been implicitly acknowledged by the Film Industry Promotion Law, which paved the way for further reform and liberalisation of the film industry.

On the other hand, the adopted Film Industry Promotion Law finally gave up the conclusion that the "Film Industry Promotion Law (Draft for Comment)" had treated film services involving trade as service trade. After China's accession to the World Trade Organization, this could actually be understood as an external declaration. However, traditionally, China has been a country where international treaties take precedence over domestic laws. In trade involving films, whether films are goods or services is covered in both the General Agreement on Tariffs and Trade and the General Agreement on Trade in Services without a clear cut definition. Moreover, in the rulings on publications and audio-visual products, the appellate body of the World Trade Organization has neither clearly defined nor been willing to clearly define the legal nature of the film trade. If such a declaration is inconsistent with the determination of the World Trade Organization in the future, it could lose its relevance in the field of international trade. In this sense, the determination of the overall nature of film services in the "Film Industry Promotion Law (Draft for Discussion)" might be too aggressive, and therefore, given up in the final law.

The Film Industry Promotion Law has a special chapter delineating the film censorship system. Perplexing is that the film censorship in its proposed film censorship system is interpreted as content censorship and technical censorship, while no further provisions are adopted for the elabaration of for technical censorship. The film censorship system stipulated in the chapter "Censorship Management" is a legislative summary of the currently effective "Provisions on Scripts and Film Poductions", relevant notices from the SARFT, and other normative documents. Among the prohibited contents in films, in addition to the "Ten Prohibitions" stipulated in the Film Regulations, the "Film Industry Promotion Law (Draft for Comment)" also stipulated three other prohibited contents: First, those that infringe upon the legitimate rights and interests of minors or are harmful to their physical and mental health; Second, the performance style is terrifying and cruel, and it damages the physical and mental health of the actors; Third, attracting audiences by taking advantage of human defects or by demonstrating human variations, etc. Neither the "Film Regulations" nor the "Provisions on Scripts and Film Poductions" stipulates these three contents. These three items are also hard to be classified into the "nine major cut items". The draft discussion did not further clarify whether these three items were intended to replace the "nine major cut Items" or as supplements outside the "nine major cut items".

These three prohibited contents would have three legal consequences in this regard. First of all, before this, protecting minors was merely one of the goals of the film censorship system. However, the "Film Industry Promotion Law (Draft for Comment)" listed it as prohibited content in films. This actually denied the legality of films that were unsuitable for minors and legally denied the possibility of the film classification system. Secondly, it is rather difficult to determine whether the performance style is "terrifying and cruel" and whether the physical and mental health of the actors has been "damaged", and this regulation seems to have the connotation of labor law. If the so-called "performance mode" is understood as "presentation mode", it can be understood that such a prohibitive regulation is made against the content contained in the film. However, highly emotional terms such as "terror", "cruelty" and "devastation", if implemented without a large number of cases and theoretical support, would be like putting the film censorship agency, a cat, in a pile of fish composed of films submitted for censorship, allowing it to relate and interpret the film content and these three regulations at will. Finally, the display of "human defects" or "human mutations" is a commonly used technique in films. For instance, in David Lynch's famous film "The Elephant Man" and the once very popular imported series "The Lion" in China, "human defects" or "human mutations" are involved, and they are used as artistic expression techniques to enhance their expressiveness. If the main creative personnel of a film make such artistic choices, the law cannot and has no right to interfere; otherwise, the boundaries between the law and artistic principles would be blurred. Considering that there were reports that the "Film Industry Promotion Law" included classification clauses during its drafting process, these three items might be the remnants of the original film classification provisions. This might be the reason why these three prohibitive regulations are so obsessed with details but also have great ambiguity.

The Film Industry Promotion Law has also made certain amendments to the "Ten Prohibitions". Some modifications even seem extremely strict. For instance, in the previous "Ten Prohibitions", violating the basic principles of the Constitution was counted as one item. However, in the draft for comments, "inciting resistance to or undermining the implementation of the Constitution, laws, regulations and rules" is listed as a prohibited item. The result of such regulations has enabled laws, regulations and rules to achieve the same status as the Constitution, and has excluded constitutional provisions, laws, regulations and rules from the scope of criticism. Such strict regulations are no less than a ban on realistic-themed films. There are several similar places in the draft for comments. Such review standards still need to be considered when determining the first law in the film legal system.

From this perspective, as a domestic industrial protection measure against market opening pressure, unless there is progress being made in the negotiations of the World Trade Organization, the existing market access system for film production in China will not change much. However, in the face of the current situation of the development of the film market, the film censorship system attached to the "Film Public Screening License" seems to have to make some changes. The disputes between the United States and China over audio-visual, publishing and entertainment products within the framework of the World Trade Organization in 2009 also indicate that the content censorship system implemented for Chinese audio-visual, publishing and entertainment products—including the film censorship system—needs to be reshaped. The Film Industry Promotion Law has made some attempts in this regard, but a crucial step has yet to be taken. Surely, before reforming the existing film censorship system, rigorous argumentation and long-term experience build-up are necessary. However, if the reform cannot even be initiated, the film censorship system has no chance to be improved, which will become a shortcoming of China's film industry and restrict the development of the entire film market.

# 4 State Aid for Film Production

Film production entails a large amount of investment. Sometimes, considering the cultural factors involved, the government provides financial support for the production of films so that they can be completed and put on the market. If the film production is regarded as partof film industry, then film production should also be subject to the market mechanisms and follow the rules of competition. Therefore, in addition to establishing a market access system like that in China, film production is also regulated by other legal systems, among which competition law is included. And government funding precisely gives specific producers in the market certain competitive advantages. In this case, should the film industry be funded by the government? Which films should be funded by the government? How can we ensure that government funding does not distort competition in the film market to meet the requirements of competition law? These are the problems that need to be solved.

## *4.1 Theoretic Modes of State Aid*

Should films be funded by the government? For this issue, it is necessary to examine it from the relationship between films and culture. In this regard, theoretically speaking, there are the following models for government funding of the film industry.

### 4.1.1 State Aid to the Films Only of Culture Value

If it is believed that films include pure entertainment films with no cultural value and art films with pure literary and artistic value, and a distinction can be made between them, financial support should be provided for art films. Even though entertainment films contain certain elements of popular culture, and such cultural elements are more likely to attract teenagers to buy tickets and enjoy them with a rush, entertainment films can survive easily in the film market without any other help. And so-called block buster productions with a large number of stars are even more lucrative in the film market. Compared with the aesthetic appeal and exciting scenes presented in blockbusters, art films usually have a relatively low production budget. Due to the limitation of funds, art films are generally low-key in marketing. When presenting the true yet embarrassing truth to the audience, they seem so awkward and so incompatible with the audience's longing for dreams and relaxation. After a tense day of work, art films are quite mentally demanding. This is the reason why art films are not as favored by funds in the market as entertainment films. In this case, if one wants to support art films with strong cultural elements, the most ideal choice is to fund art films. Like Sir Humphrey[129] said,

[129] This is one of the main characters in the BBC comedy series "Yes, Minister". Sir Humphrey was a calculating civil official who was good at leaving ministers who intended to do all kinds of

> Subsidy should only go to the art. It is not for what people want. It is for what people do not want but need to have.

Big-budget films dig a lot of money into the pockets of their producers so that they can invest the money in the next round of the cycle of making screen heroes. The audience's pursuit of blockbusters is the result of market choices. The government has no right to decide for the audience which film they should watch; otherwise, it would deprive the audience of their right to choose. The basic principle of competition law is to guarantee the audience's right to choose products or services. Furthermore, at both the constitutional and administrative law levels, there is no reason to prohibit people from enjoying films that embody popular culture. Otherwise, it would be a imfringement of the audience's right to choose and democratic principles.

For audiences who love blockbusters, the government cannot deprive them of the right to enjoy blockbusters. The only option the government can choose to intervene is to open another window, allowing the atmosphere of different types of films to reach moviegoers. This measure actually establishes two film markets: one is the physical film market established based on the audience's taste choices, where the market for art films may be very small; Another one is a virtual film culture market formed due to the cultural elements of physical films. The things circulating here are not only the cultural elements provided by blockbusters, but also should come from the cultural elements provided by other types of films. The intensity of competition in these two markets is not necessarily the same. For instance, the competition in the physical film market might be highly intense. All producers are scrambling to invest in big-budget productions, and one producer cannot dominate the entire film production market. However, in the virtual film culture market derived from this, there may exist a kind of cultural monopoly. Among the 20 highest-grossing films in Europe in 2010, 12 were produced solely by American producers, while the other 8 were co-productions between the United States and other countries. At the top of the list is the US-UK co-production "Avatar" directed by James Cameron. The film had 2200 million viewers in the European Union in 2009, while the number of viewers in 2010 exceeded 43 million. The last spot of the 20 highest-grossing films in Europe in 2010 was occupied by the US-China co-production "The Karate Kid", with 8.14 million viewers. Among the top 20 highest-grossing European films in the European Union in 2010, the US-UK co-production "Harry Porter and the Deathly Harrows" (Part 1) and "Robinhood" secured viewers of 31 million and 13 million respectively, ranking first and second on the list. There are three European films on the list with viewership ranging from 5 to 6 million, three with viewership ranging from less than 5 million to more than 4 million, and seven with viewership ranging from less than 4 million to more than 3 million. The remaining five films on the

---

things immobile. In one episode of the series, he strongly opposed the minister's motion to sell a second-rate museum to save a team on the verge of bankruptcy. In his view, business should not be subsidized—people will buy it when they need it, while art is a different story. Incidentally, in his eyes, films belong to business, and the minister did not raise any objection to this. He eventually arranged for the cabinet to appoint the minister of the Arts on the basis of the minister's existing powers, thus successfully preventing the minister from embarking on the implementation of what Sir Humphrey called a "barbaric" motion.

list all have viewership between 3 and 2 million. Meanwhile, the box office of the European Union reached a new record of 6.45 billion euros due to the popularity of 3D films, and the share of European films in the EU film market dropped to 25.3%.[130] Hollywood not only dominates the list of the top 20 highest-grossing films in the European Union, but also takes advantage of the European co-production system to dominate the European film market. This situation fully demonstrates the asynchrony between the virtual film culture market and the physical film market.

In this sense, if the government provides funding for certain films, it is also based on the consideration of safeguarding the competition in the virtual film culture market. However, since the virtual film culture market will actually be supported by the physical film market, the impact of these funding measures will ultimately have to be implemented in the physical film market. At this point, the possible action that can be taken might be: to select art films from the bustling, just as physical film market and protect them, just as the European nobility did to musicians in the past, in order to maintain competitiveness in the virtual market. Therefore, we need to establish systems to maintain a government's funding or subsidy system for art films. This actually offers protection to some films that cannot survive in the physical market, ensuring sufficient competition among various elements in the virtual market and preventing the monopoly of a single cultural element. However, before offering generous protection to it, the prerequisite that needs to be addressed is: selecting art films of great artistic value.

At this point, the topic becomes: What exactly are art films? Legally speaking, the right holder of an art film is its copyright owner. However, copyright law, which is most closely related to art, deliberately avoids addressing such a problem. The granting of rights under copyright law does not take whether the work has artistic value as a prerequisite. It is a very dangerous task to determine whether a work should be protected by copyright law based on its artistic or other values. This point has been fully acknowledged in the revision of Article 4 of China's Copyright Law in 2010.

In fact, art itself is also a term with variable meanings. How to determine the value of art is not a legal issue. What the Copyright law is concerned about is merely whether a work has originality, rather than making a judgment on the artistic value of the work. When dealing with the film market, the role of copyright law is merely to determine the tradable objects, the right to decide whether to trade or not, and the right to set a price during the transaction, rather than being constantly regulated by copyright law. Although the rules of the market are unpredictable, the transaction itself actually has nothing to do with artistic value. Throughout history, there seems to be a convention: truly epoch-making avant-garde art usually shines brightly in the public eye only after the death of its author. In this way, how can genuine art films be subsidized instead of ignoring those works that seem plain-looking? The copyright legal system cannot provide an answer.

---

[130] Please refer to European Audiovisual Observatory, 3D Drives EU Gross Box Office to Record High in 2010 as Market Share for European Films Drops, http://www.obs.coe.int/about/oea/pr/mif2011_cinema.html.

As for the successful films with market dominance of the Hollywood audio-visual giants, they are basically big-budget so-called blockbusters, and their success largely depends on stars and dizzying marketing battles. In a sense, it is actually the charming murmur of capital that fascinates teenage audiences. Large investments willing to take market risks naturally enabled producers to seize control of the film production process from directors.[131] Big stars, lively sales strategies—all of these have been integrated into mainstream and charming (that is, highly profitable) stories, making Hollywood known as the "King of the World". However, this king was not very daring to try something unconventional. Even if the Hollywood audio-visual giants hope to produce a different film, the generous remuneration demanded by the film stars may eventually significantly increase the film budget, making the film extremely vulnerable at the box office. For instance, "Fight Club" was originally planned to be a low-budget film. Laura Ziskin, the initial driving force behind the film, was a former senior executive of Fox Productions and was moved by the novel "Fight Club". However, Brad Pitt refused to lower his acting remuneration, and other actors followed suit accordingly. This made Fight Club one of the major productions whose box office revenue could not be guaranteed. Bill Mechanic, the head of Fox Productions, thus resigned under heavy pressure from Fox bigwig Rupert Murdoch.[132] Therefore, in terms of market considerations and their production models, Hollywood audio-visual giants are generally reluctant to invest in the production of films with limited market potential. Art films usually mean a smaller audience, so the box office performance of art films is usually not satisfactory. This situation conforms to the principle of competition among various producers in the physical film market and the need to make profits. However, once this situation is reflected in the virtual film culture market, it is the cultural factors attached to blockbusters that dominate it.

Therefore, legally speaking, based on the judgment of the competitive situation in the virtual culture market of films, encouraging creativity in the film industry might be the wisest approach and choice. Otherwise, who can guarantee that picking out art films for support in the physical film market will not be a rather arbitrary and blind choice?

The focus of film support is not on the physical film market, but on the virtual film culture market. In the physical film market, producers represented by Hollywood Audio-Visual companies are completely controlled by the power of capital when making films. Although this may lead to a monopoly in the virtual film culture market, in essence, it actually conforms to the market rules. If the creativity in films is to be encouraged, based on the virtual cultural market, the government should offer art film creators what Hollywood audio-visual companies cannot provide. According

[131] It is a very important strategy for Hollywood production companies to conduct preview screenings of films before their release to detect the reactions of potential audiences. The film "My Best Friend's Wedding" did not receive favorable reviews after its preview screening. The production company ordered the reshooting of Juliet Roberts' scenes, which eventually led to the film's great success. Please see BBC MMII.

[132] Ibid.

to this logic, the government can choose the simplest and clearest way to fund low-budget films without evaluating the cultural value of the films,[133] so as to liberate the main creative personnel of the film from the shackles of capital. In this way, the influence of capital on the film itself will be greatly weakened, and the film will return to the art world or the kingdom of creativity. If a low-budget film happens to be a commercial film, this form of government funding will also help the film industry cultivate its own talents, enabling these talents to maintain a certain degree of independence in the physical film market dominated by big-budget films. Such a situation will help the film industry maintain its vitality and lower the entry threshold of this industry.[134] If this policy also leads to the neglect of big-budget art films, there is no need to worry. If an investor is willing to invest a huge amount of money in an art film, the director of the art film or other artists involved in its production already have a market to realize their artistic dreams. At this point, is it still necessary for the government to bother to help them?

Generally speaking, there are two ways to implement government funding. Automatic government funding and selective government funding.[135] The government funds low-budget films precisely to prevent it from making arbitrary choices when selecting funding recipients. Therefore, in this sense, automatic government funding should be a relatively ideal choice.

However, sometimes, low costs in the film industry also mean low quality. Hollywood once helped the British film industry in a special way. Due to the ad-valorem tax imposed on Hollywood films,[136] in August 1947, Hollywood imposed a film embargo on the UK: Before the British government abolished this tax, Hollywood would not provide any films to the UK. The British did not give in: A large number of British films flooded in, filling the gap left by the withdrawal of Hollywood films from the screening market—but many of these British films were incompetent both culturally and at the box office. We should not rush to conclude that low-budget films are junk—such a conclusion is highly biased and extremely unfair. In fact, compared with Hollywood films, many avant-garde art films were produced with insignificant funds. However, if an indiscriminate policy prompts filmmakers to have the motivation to produce low-budget films, others will rush to do so, thereby diluting the art films that the government originally intended to fund. In this case, in fact, those film practitioners who make low-budget films should not be condemned. Instead, the government should be held accountable—it is the government's policies that give people the opportunity to discover ways to make money from government subsidies. In 2006, The State Council of China led its ten ministries and commissions

[133] As to the difficulty to ascertain the relevant market for art films, please see Christoph B. Graber, Handel und Kultur im Audiovisionsrecht der WTO, 156, 238; also Weber/Unternäher/Zulauf, 104–106.

[134] Thomas Elsaesser has made an insightful elaboration of this market barrier via the model of pinball machine.

[135] Weber/Unternäher/Zulauf, 108–113.

[136] This ad-valorem tax entitled the British Exchequer to 75% estimated earnings of the Hollywood films in the UK. This is part of the crisis austerity program announced by British government in August of 1947, aiming to reduce the trade deficit with US after WWII. See Geoffrey Macnab, 173.

to form the "Inter-ministerial Joint Conference on Supporting the Development of the Animation Industry" and issued the "Several Opinions on Promoting the Development of the Animation Industry" on 25 April 2006. The central government has accordingly provided financial support with a special development fund. By the end of 2009, 22 animation industrial bases had been established across the country. The number of domestic animated series had grown from 80,000 min in 2006 to 385 in 2010, totaling 220,530 min. This has enabled Chinese animation to take the pride of being the "world's number one" in terms of quantity. However, these animated films mainly survive for subsidies and do not pay attention to originality and quality, which makes the competitiveness of domestic animated films in the market rather unsatisfactory.[137]

This embarrassing result implies that some kind of technical selection and arrangement is indispensable for the government to fund low-budget films. Some people might advocate funding films that win awards at international film festivals, thereby achieving automatic government funding. However, the basis of this automatic subsidy arrangement is a role of film festivals in the government's funding system—they select the winners. In this way, the policy of government funding for low-budget films has to return to the original starting point of negation. As the patron of art films, the government must make some direct or indirect judgment on the cultural value of low-budget films. This compromise arrangement undermines the legitimacy of subsidizing low-budget films.

### 4.1.2 State Aid for Culture Diversity

The most damaging thing to the culture in a county is that the dominant one takes everything. In film industry, Hollywood is the dominant one and takes the best from the market.[138] Since the government can never be sure that what she funds is the true culture, she has to diversify risks. That is to say, the government has to ensure that the audience has enough choices. Moreover, before allowing moviegoers to make their final choices, the government has to ensure that they have the time and opportunity to make a choice after being fully informed of the information. This kind of government funding policy may not merely be direct funding. It enables the government to reserve a certain operational space for itself, just as stipulated in the "Law on Film Production and Film Culture" (Bundesgesetz uber Filmproduktion und Filmkultur, Filmgesetz) passed by Switzerland in December 2002.[139] In practices, it means more films but not just from Hollywood majors.

Before choosing any specific legal mechanism to keep a diversified film culture in the market, assuming Hollywood majors have created a unique culture with charming

[137] Jin Ju, "Development of china's An° ation industry", in Economic Research Guide 2016 (No.27): 35–36.

[138] Thomas Elsaesser; Wheeler Winston Dixon.

[139] Multiple film supply must be ensured in Switzerland; otherwise the state is entitled to take measures to install it. See Weber/Unternährer/Zulauf, 114. Roland Unternährer, 223–226.

stars and huge budget for promotion as well as for production, the films from Hollywood majors hold its own market. Both EU and US majors find the cinema goers are mainly the adolescence,[140] who seem to be locked in the market built up by the blockbusters and the shining stars.[141] If the culture diversity policy means just general market diversity instead of mainstream market diversity, culture diversity would be just a joke. The art film fans are the minority, even if there is no diversity in the film market; they can easily find the substitutes in other area, such as reading and etc. If the SSNIP method is adopted to determine the product market, assuming that the ticket prices of art films increase slightly but substantially, and if the majority of the audience who no longer watch art films turn to mainstream films, it proves that the audience of mainstream films and the audience of art films are in the same market, even if there is a monopoly of certain cultural factors in the virtual market. Nor should art films that compete with commercial films be funded to change the competitive relationship in the same market and distort the market. However, generally speaking, audiences of art films are usually not enthusiastic about watching mainstream commercial films. If the prices of art films rise, they may turn to other art consumption such as reading and fine arts, and thus leave the film market. In this sense, there are actually two sub-markets in the entire physical film market: the mainstream commercial film market and the art film market.

Actually, culture diversity problem exists in the locked up mainstream market, not in the general film market instead. Therefore, there seems to be a need for the state to keep the culture diversity of the top ten films' list. However, the danger is looming due to this conclusion. In 2009, Viviane Reding, the then European Commission's commissioner for media, said before the opening of the 2009 Cannes Film Festival: "We should not be content with screening European films at the French Film Week in Japan and at the film archive in Mexico City and Sydney. European films have won Oscars, which is indeed good, but it's not enough. We must ensure that our films are widely distributed through commercial channels."[142] This is actually encouraging European films to enter mainstream cinemas in third countries. This view actually reflects an attitude of the European Union towards promoting cultural diversity in the film market: European films must enter mainstream cinemas. This is essentially the result of marketization achieved through non-market means. Therefore, such a assertion also has implicit dangers.

The essential legal principle for state aid is not to distort the market and competition.[143] Otherwise, the market that relies on competition to achieve resource allocation will fail to function. When the government intervenes in the mainstream film

---

[140] FOCUS 2003, 6; Hot season for the film exhibition is normally in the summer holidays for students.

[141] In 2009, among the top 20 highest-grossing films worldwide, except for a French film that was extremely popular in France but had very little box office in North America, the other films were either produced by Hollywood or co-produced by Hollywood. Please refer to FOCUS 2009, 13.

[142] La commissaire européenne Viviane Reding se félicite du succès des films européens à Cannes et appelle au renforcement de la distribution du cinéma européen dans le monde, MEMO 09/228, http://europa.eu/rapid/pressReleasesAction.do?reference=MEMO/09/228.

[143] Richard Senti, 86–89; Americo Beviglia Zampetti, 11.

market and begins to implant the cultural diversity that the market originally lacked, the most convenient way is to achieve cultural diversity in the list of the top ten high-grossing films. If this is achieved, the proposition of cultural exception will already be shattered—culture has always existed in the market, and its decline or rise has relied on the power of the market. Although the view of the United States opposing cultural exceptionalism was not accepted by EU countries at that time, if cultural diversity is promoted in the physical film market, there is an implicit conclusion that in the globalized film market, culture has become integrated with goods and/or services. In this situation, cultural diversity cannot survive if there is no film market that supports cultural diversity. What an awkward situation this is for countries that advocate cultural exceptions!

How can a country maintain cultural diversity while neither violating the legal principle of government funding nor distorting the competition mechanism provided by the market guaranteed by competition law? Why can't we try another solution? If we do not regard film as an important cultural medium, then the government should not intervene in the film market for cultural diversity. Instead, it should stand idly by and do nothing about the competition among the participants, just as it does for other commodity or service markets. However, unfortunately, even market-oriented Americans have not made such radical assertions.[144] If culture diversity leads to a market being distorted, the fist is on the strong market players and the beneficiaries are the relatively weak film makers. In a globalised film market, this turns into the formula that reads like free trade against culture protection, global player against local player, or Hollywood majors against local film industry. The present world trade legal system may need to find another balance on the issue of film industry. It is quite understandable why Canada wants a new legal system covering this issue outside the WTO mechanism.[145] However, this choice may be not realistic—film is actually a two-folded concept, industry as well as the culture.[146]

Therefore, this problem cannot be completely solved in the existing world trade system—unless relatively weak film competitors grow into a strong market participant, that is, the competitive situation of the virtual film culture market and the physical film market can be synchronized. This requires the careful design of the entire legal system for film funding under the principles of competition law. Under the framework of the World Trade Organization, the audio-visual field is facing strong pressure for openness. For countries where the film market still needs improvement and the film industry is difficult to compete with Hollywood, to cultivate a strong film industry, that is, to make achievements in both maintaining cultural diversity and maintaining commercial vitality, this requires a mature mechanism achieved on a global scale. Under such a mechanism, the system of government funding for the film industry will eventually lead the future global film market to fully open to competition, rather than the other way around. When the General Agreement on Trade in

[144] Christoph B. Graber, Audiovisual Policy: The Stumbling Block of Trade Liberalisation? 3.

[145] Christopher Maule; Christoph B. Graber, Handel und Kultur im Audiovisionsrecht der WTO, 140–144.

[146] Recital C of the Parliament Film Resolution.

Services was signed in 1994, both the then European Community and France agreed to abide by the obligations and principles of "generality" stipulated in the General Agreement on Trade in Services of 1 January 1995.[147] This means that the market might be the ultimate choice for the film industry.

On the other hand, in the field of international law, the category of culture has gradually expanded. The 31st Session of the General Conference of UNESCO adopted on 2 November 2001 the Universal "Declaration on Cultural Diversity" submitted by its Executive Board in 2001, which holds that: culture should be regarded as the sum total of the different spiritual and material, intellectual and emotional characteristics unique to a society or every social group; In addition to art and literature, culture also encompasses lifestyles, ways of getting along, value systems, traditions and beliefs.[148] Coincidentally, at the same session of UNESCO, a general resolution was adopted, deciding that UNESCO would participate in 47 anniversary activities between 2002 and 2003, among in which the 28th item was to commemorate "the 100th anniversary of the birth of the film maker Max Ophuls (Germany)".[149] On 20 October 2005, the 33rd session of UNESCO adopted the Convention on the Protection and Promotion of Diversity in Cultural Expressions (hereinafter referred to as the "Convention on Cultural Diversity"). The previous statement of the Convention on Cultural Diversity states: "Reaffirm that freedom of thought, expression and information, as well as media diversity, enables all forms of cultural expression to thrive in society…" It is believed that cultural activities, products and services that convey cultural characteristics, values and meanings have both economic and cultural natures, and therefore should not be regarded as having only commercial value. It is noted that the globalization process driven by the rapid development of information and communication technologies has created unprecedented conditions for strengthening various cultural interactions, but at the same time poses challenges to cultural diversity, especially possibly causing various imbalances between rich and poor countries… Based on this, one of the goals of the Convention on Cultural Diversity is: "To reaffirm the sovereignty of all countries to maintain, adopt and implement on their territories the policies and measures they deem appropriate for the protection and promotion of the diversity of cultural expressions."[150] And the sovereignty of policies and measures taken for this purpose has been designated as the "sovereignty principle", which has become one of the guiding principles of the Convention on Cultural Diversity.[151] The Convention on Cultural Diversity fully emphasizes the position of culture in development, holding that culture is one of the main driving forces of development. Therefore, the development of culture is as

[147] When signing the Uruguay GATS Agreement in 1994, the EC and France have agreed to be subjected to the "general" obligations and disciplines as of the 1st, January, 1995 under GATS. See Emmanuel Cocq/Patrick Messerlin, 5.

[148] Please refer to UNESCO: Universal Declaration on Cultural Diversity, the Preamble.

[149] See UNESCO: Records of the Thirty-First Session of the General Conference—Volume I: Resolutions, Paris: 2002, p. 83.

[150] Article 1, Paragraph 8 of the Convention on Cultural Diversity.

[151] Article 2, Paragraph 2 of the Convention on Cultural Diversity.

important as that of the economy, and all individuals and nations have the right to participate in the development of both and benefit from it. And it was determined as the "Principle of complementarity between economy and culture".[152] While emphasizing the status of culture, the Convention on Cultural Diversity holds that culture is the foundation of sustainable economic development, and protecting cultural diversity will not hinder economic development. Thus, it puts forward the "Principle of Sustainable Development": "Cultural diversity is a kind of wealth for individuals and society." Protecting, promoting and maintaining cultural diversity is a fundamental requirement for the sustainable development of the present generation and future generations.[153] The reason why cultural diversity becomes a requirement is the "principle of equal enjoyment", which is the foundation of cultural diversity: "Equal enjoyment of the rich and diverse cultural expressions around the world, and all cultures enjoying various forms of expression and means of dissemination, are elements for enhancing cultural diversity and promoting mutual understanding."[154] Based on these principles, the Convention on Cultural Diversity confirms: "Cultural diversity is not only reflected in the various ways in which human cultural heritage is expressed, promoted and passed on through rich and diverse cultural manifestations, but also in the various ways of artistic creation, production, dissemination, sale and consumption through various means and technologies." This means that the Convention on Cultural Diversity also touches upon the protection of cultural diversity in the trade process, thereby forming a formal check and balance mechanism with the relevant principles and regulations of the World Trade Organization.

The United States voted against the Convention on Cultural Diversity and refused to join. In the minutes of the 33rd session of the UNESCO General Conference, the reason recorded by the United States was: "We are extremely concerned that the draft convention may be misinterpreted, and this may hinder the free dissemination of ideas in written and visual forms and affect other fields such as trade."[155] It can be seen that, on the one hand, within the framework of the World Trade Organization, the United States squeezes the application of other concepts such as cultural diversity through the concept of free trade. On the other hand, within the framework of the United Nations organization, the United States also warily guards its trade rights within the framework of the World Trade Organization, and this right is crucial to the position of American films in international trade.

[152] Article 2, Paragraph 5 of the Convention on Cultural Diversity.

[153] Article 2, Paragraph 6 of the Convention on Cultural Diversity.

[154] Article 2, Paragraph 7 of the Convention on Cultural Diversity.

[155] UNESCO: Records of the Thirty-third Session of the General Conference—Volume I: Resolutions, Paris: 2006, p. 291.

## 4.2 *From State Owned, Operated and Controlled Film Production to State Aided Chinese Film Production in China*

For now, perhaps the task of the Film regulator should be to prompt the country to withdraw from the film industry while maintaining the necessary public support mechanism for domestic films. Although the "Interim Provisions on Access" have created channels for domestic and overseas investors to invest in the film production industry, the Chinese government still seems content to use administrative regulations to avoid and defuse competitive threats from abroad in order to support the domestic film industry. Given that China has become a member of the World Trade Organization, this approach may bring about certain legal issues, which are very evident in the publication rulings aforesaid. Therefore, the current support system for the film industry, if not fragile, is not as powerful as that in Europe. Government funding is not sustainable without a dynamic film market. Only in areas where the market is not yet accessible can government funding play an effective role.

### 4.2.1 Private Capital Enters the Film Industry

Normally, the withdraw of the State owned capital from one industry goes on with the steps of restructuring the major State owned enterprises in the concerned industry into the company and then going public domestically or internationally, which have avoided the dramatic effects extending to the whole society while opening the door to the private capital on the securities market. In the meanwhile, Hollywood vertical and horizontal industrial model has been acknowledged as a viable template for the liberalisation of the China's film industry from the centralised state monopoly.[156] The establishment of China's Group Company of Radio, Film and Television on the 6th December 2001, which held film production, distribution, and Television companies together, indicated a new trend toward the vertical integration of the audiovisual industry of China.[157] The Film Business Qualification Provisions had also offered an alternative, which is supposed to dilute the state owned capital in the film industry, especially in the film production sector.

At the beginning, the PRC government did not treat the film industry as an ordinary industry, but regarded it as a cause with a strong promotional function. Therefore, the process of private individuals entering the film industry has not been a smooth sailing. However, with the development of the market economy and the deepening of reforms, the entry of private capital into the film industry and the connection between the film industry and the capital market have increasingly become an unavoidable choice. The Film Business Qualification Provisions not only clearly stipulated that the State

[156] Ying Zhu, 22.

[157] This is not an isolated case. Even before that, the provincial studios and TV channels had conducted six major integrations. See Ying Zhu, 146.

should allow domestic companies, enterprises and other economic organizations (excluding foreign-invested enterprises) to establish film production companies, but also further clarified the application conditions and procedures for establishing film production companies, and simplified the approval procedures and shortensed the approval time in accordance with the requirements of the Administrative Licensing Law. Furthermore, as Film Industry Promotion Law takes effect in 2017, China has abolished the requirement that an enterprise should obtain the licence before producing a film. This specific liberalisation measure further released the private capital for film business.

### 4.2.2 Public Support System

Special Fund for the Development of the National Film Industry

In 1979, in the report "Reforming the Management System of Film Distribution and Screening" forwarded by The State Council from the Ministry of Culture and the Ministry of Finance, it was stipulated that the ticket prices of films would be comprehensively balanced by the China Film Distribution and Screening Corporation. On 9 January 1991, the former MRFT, the Ministry of Finance, the former State Price Bureau, the State Taxation Administration and the Industrial and Commercial Bank of China jointly issued the "Notice on Clarifying the Management Authority of Film Ticket Prices and Establishing a Special Fund for the Development of the National Film Industry" (hereinafter referred to as the "Ticket Price Notice"), which stipulated that film ticket prices were still managed by each province, autonomous region and municipality directly under the Central Government. At the same time, a special fund for the development of the national film industry was established. Starting from 1 January 1991, after the authority to manage ticket prices was delegated, on the basis of appropriate adjustments to ticket prices, cinemas in counties and cities above the county level (including cinemas and theaters that sell tickets to the public, open clubs, etc.) should extract five cents from each ticket price sold (for poverty-stricken counties confirmed by The State Council, two cents should be temporarily extracted). As a special fund for the development of the national film industry, the basic ticket price could be appropriately raised if it is relatively low. The special funds for the development of the film industry paid by each cinema should be deducted before the income tax with the exemption from education surcharge, key construction fund for energy and transportation, and budget adjustment fund. With the development of the film industry, the "Administrative Measures for Special Funds for the Development of the National Film Industry", which was issued in 1996 and revised in 2006 by the Ministry of Finance and the SARFT through Document No. 115 of CAI Jiao [2006], revised the Ticket Price Notice. It is stipulated that cinemas at the county level and above in county-level cities must remit 5% of their box office revenue to establish a special fund for the development of the national film industry.[158]The special Fund for the development of the national film industry is managed by the film Special Fund Management committees established by the central and provincial governments (hereinafter referred to as "National Management Committees" and "Provincial Management Committees" respectively) in accordance with their respective duties.[159] The special funds for the development of the national film industry shall be organized and collected by the provincial management committees, and the funds shall be fully remitted to the central Treasury on the spot within the same day after receiving them. The National Management Committee will return 40% of the amount remitted by each province to the province on a quarterly basis, which will be arranged for use by the provincial management committee. The remaining part will be arranged for use by the National Management Committee.[160] The State Administration Committee should formulate the annual revenue and expenditure budget and final accounts of the special fund for the development of the national film industry. After being reviewed by the CFA, they should be submitted to the Ministry of Finance for approval.[161]

In terms of the use of the special funds for the development of the national film industry, the funds arranged for use by the State Administration Committee are mainly used to support the screening of domestic films in urban cinemas, the renovation and upgrading of urban cinemas, the computerized ticketing systems in cinemas, the translation and production of ethnical minority films, and other projects approved by the Ministry of Finance and the SARFT that have a significant impact on the development of the film industry. The funds arranged and used by the provincial management committee are mainly used to support the renovation and upgrading of urban cinemas.[162]

Therefore, it can be seen that the Special Fund for the development of the national film industry reflects a principle: subsidies should be provided to the film production field from the film screening stage—just as the EU countries have done, and instead subsidies should also be given to the screening of State supported films and other films and the establishment of related cinema chains. This reflects the current thinking in China: After the reform of the film production industry, the production of films is no longer a weak link in China's film industry. The subsequent distribution and screening have become crucial links for the growth of China's film industry. Facing the influx of imported films and the competitive pressure from foreign film industries, cultivating and developing the Chinese film distribution and screening market has become a major issue for China's film industry. Therefore, shifting the focus of government support to the distribution and screening stages, especially for domestic films, has become a policy orientation.

---

[158] Article 2 of the "Administrative Measures for Special Funds for the Development of the National Film Industry".

[159] Article 4, ibid.

[160] Articles 8, 9, ibid.

[161] Article 6, ibid.

[162] Article 10, ibid.

### Special Fund for High-Quality Films

On 18 December 2000, the State Council issued Guo Fa [2000] No. 41, "Notice on Several Economic Policies to Support the Development of Cultural Undertakings" (hereinafter referred to as "Document No. 41"), reiterating: "5% of the income from film screenings will be extracted to establish the 'National Film Industry Development Special Fund', which will be used for the macro-control of the film industry." And clearly summarized other measures to assist the film industry.[163] First of all, the income from the sale of film copies by film studios approved by the State Council is exempt from value-added tax. Secondly, the distribution income collected by film distribution units from screening units is exempt from business tax. Thirdly, 3% of the net income from TV advertisements will be extracted to establish a "Special Fund for High-Quality Films", which will be used to support the production of high-quality films. Fourth, a certain proportion of funds should be extracted from the revenue of imported films to support film production and translation.

Document No. 41 has expanded the means of public support for the film industry. In addition, the establishment of the "Special Fund for High-quality Films" also reflects another principle: Television operators should subsidize film producers. As a system, the "Special Fund for Film Masterpieces" was established by the former MRFT and the Ministry of Finance on 18 March 1996, through the issuance of the "Notice on the Relevant Provisions for Establishing Special Funds to Support the '9550' Project of Film Masterpieces" (hereinafter referred to as the "Notice on Special Fund for Film Masterpieces") (Guangfa Jili Zi [1996] No. 125).

Firstly, the Notice on Special Funds for Film Masterpieces stipulates that the special funds for film masterpieces shall be established by extracting a portion of the television advertising revenue: First, CCTV the china's national TV station, shall calculate and remit 3% of the net television advertising revenue to the national radio, film and television administrative department each year, and the remittance amount shall not be less than 30 million yuan. Second, provincial TV stations of each province, autonomous region and municipality directly under the Central Government shall calculate 3% of their net television advertising revenue and remit it to the provincial radio and television administrative department for special account storage to support the production of high-quality films. Thirdly, whether the TV stations of cities with independent planning status and provincial capitals undertake the obligation of remittance is determined independently by each province and autonomous region. Among them, the so-called net income from television advertising refers to the portion of television advertising income after the business tax has been paid in full.

Secondly, the Notice on the Special Fund for Film Masterpieces stipulates the scope of use of the special fund for film masterpieces: it is exclusively used to support the production of film masterpieces. In provinces, autonomous regions and municipalities directly under the Central Government without film studios, it is used

[163] Article 4, Document No. 4.

to support the film production in the "Five Ones Project", a title list to be supported by the state.

Finally, the Notice on Special Funds for Film Masterpieces stipulates the nature of the special funds for film masterpieces: The special funds for film masterpieces are national fiscal funds and should be managed as part of the national Special Funds for the development of the film industry. Funds must be stored in dedicated accounts and used for specific purposes only. The radio and television administrative departments of all provinces, autonomous regions and municipalities directly under the Central Government shall, before the end of February each year, report the collection and use of the special funds of the previous year to the financial departments at the same level, and at the same time copy the national radio and television administrative department and the Ministry of Finance. All levels of financial departments should strengthen supervision over the use of this fund. However, in the "Administrative Measures for the Special Fund for the Development of the National Film Industry", it is stipulated that the source of the special fund for the development of the national film industry is a 5% levy on the box office revenue of films in county-level and above urban cinemas. It does not mention the source of 3% of the net income from television advertising. The Notice on Special Funds for Film Masterpieces has been abolished by the SARFT in the Notice on Announcing the Abolition of Some Regulatory Documents on Radio, Film and Television issued on 17 December 2003. Apart from the Special Fund for Film Masterpieces mentioned in Document No. 41, no other laws, regulations or normative documents have made any provisions. According to the response to journalists' questions by the spokesperson of the SARFT in 2009, it was pointed out that the Chinese government was collecting special funds for the development of the national film industry and high-quality films. Each year, 3% of the net income from TV advertisements is extracted to establish a special fund for high-quality films, which is used to support the development of the film industry.[164] However, in the Film Industry Promotion Law, no specific provisions have been made on this.

The Chinese film support system mainly reflects the selective thinking, but no clear regulations are made on the criteria for making choices. Although a support fund system has been established, there is a lack of necessary transparency in the allocation and application of the funds. Although China has a full understanding of the marketization development of the future film industry, the lack of a meticulously established assistance system is not only detrimental to the growth and improvement of the Chinese film market, but also to the competition within it, posing a risk of distorting market competition. Recently, China has strengthened its cooperation with the European Union, but the film industry seems to be an overlooked area. Perhaps it is because the most-favored-nation treatment in the General Agreement on Trade in Services makes it impossible for China to join future MEDIA projects. However, cooperation through other means and channels, such as cooperative training programs, still has room for maneuver in the future.

[164] Chinese news: the State Administration of Radio, Film and Television special funds to support domestic film, http://www.chinanews.com/cul/news/2009/09-15/1868012.shtml.

## 4.3 Tax Matters

The Film Industry Promotion Law has stipulated that tax measures may be adopted to promote the development of the film industry of China. However, against the background of China's tax reform, the film industry of China still need to find the tax measures suitable for its real needs.

### 4.3.1 Valaue-Added Tax Reform

On 31 July 2013, the six major Hollywood studios jointly rejected box office revenue shares after the implementation of the business tax reform (VAT) because they were dissatisfied with the reduction of revenue from shared films. Meanwhile, the Motion Picture Association of America sent its former vice president to Beijing for negotiations and contacted the U.S. Trade Representative, claiming that China violated its WTO commitments and hoping the U.S. government would pressure the Chinese government.

The reason that the six major Hollywood studios refused to accept their box office revenue shares is not aimed at China Film Group but rather at China's legal measure of business tax reform.

When the business tax system was implemented in the film and television industry, Hollywood exported films to China in a revenue-sharing format without bearing business tax. According to China's business tax system, a business tax rate of 3% was levied on the total ticket revenue earned by film screening units. After that, no business tax was levied on the revenue charged by film distribution units to screening units, but the rental income from copies provided by the film distribution departments during the distribution process was still subject to a business tax at a rate of 5%. Consequently, Hollywood studios involved in revenue sharing did not bear business tax when receiving revenue shares since they did not have to deal with the rental of copies and theater screenings, allowing them to fully reclaim their revenue shares according to the box office revenue sharing ratio. In February of 2012, China and the United States reached an agreement regarding China's imported film system, one of which was to raise the revenue share ratio for foreign distributors from 13 to 25%. Hollywood held high hopes for this agreement.

Starting in 2012, China began pilot programs for the VAT reform in some regions. From 1 August 2013, the pilot program began to be implemented nationwide. This marked significant progress in the VAT tax reform. The reform is an important measure in China's tax system reform, with significant impact for the upgrade of China's economic structure and the improvement of the fiscal system. The pilot policy clearly states that the "broadcasting and film services industry" is also part of the pilot industries for the VAT reform. Each aspect of production, distribution, and exhibition in broadcasting and film business that involves value addition falls under the VAT collection, with a tax rate of 6%. According to the pilot policy, "before 31 December 2013, film production, distribution, and exhibition companies approved by the administrative departments of broadcasting film and television (including member enterprises), film studios, and other film enterprises that transfer film copyrights, distribute films, and screen films in rural areas" are exempt from VAT. This means that besides the cinemas paying VAT on box office income, domestic film enterprises distributing films and transferring film copyrights do not have to pay VAT before the end of this year. This was a transitional arrangement implemented under the VAT reform structure for the distribution and rural screening sectors in the broadcasting and film industry.

However, Hollywood studios are not China's national enterprise, so they cannot enjoy the tax exemption benefits of this transitional arrangement. After Hollywood producers receive 25% of the box office revenue according to the revenue-sharing arrangement, they still need to pay a 6% value-added tax (VAT) on the revenues obtained from box office distribution in China. Specifically, since they do not have a business entity based in China, Hollywood producers should pay VAT at a ratio of 25% * 6% / (1 + 6%), which is approximately 1.41% of their share of box office revenue. This portion must be withheld and paid by China Film Group. As a result, Hollywood producers did not receive the full percentage of profits they anticipated.

The value-added tax system is not unique to China. As a globally prevalent turnover tax, it is widely applied in developed countries. All EU member states implement VAT. The absence of a VAT in the United States might be one reason Hollywood producers were confused by China's reform and tax change. Nonetheless, this could not be a reason for Hollywood to deny the applicability of PRC reform and tax change policy to the broadcasting and film industry.

China's VAT reform framework does distinguish between domestic distributors and Hollywood producers regarding the collection of VAT on film revenue sharing. Specifically, before 31 December 2013, domestic film distributors were exempt from VAT on their distribution revenues, while foreign film producers and distributors were not. Hollywood could indeed protest this. However, this was merely a transitional arrangement and not a fixed policy. The revenue sharing of foreign films involves the profits derived from box office revenues allocated to distributors and producers, and it is also a profit distribution mechanism in film copyright trade. Therefore, it is necessary to adhere to the national treatment provisions of the General Agreement on Trade in Services (GATS) as well as the Agreement on Trade-Related Aspects of Intellectual Property Rights (TRIPS).

The national treatment principle established by TRIPS is stronger than the provisions in GATS: "In the context of protecting intellectual property rights, each member shall provide treatments to other members that are at least as favorable as those it provides to its own nationals." Although TRIPS specifies limited exceptions, it is difficult to apply these exceptions to the discriminatory treatment issues related to VAT collection. After 31 December 2013, the different treatment of domestic and foreign film companies in terms of revenue sharing from films under the VAT reform has no longer been an issue since a tax heaven has been created for the whole film industry so that this is no longer an trade issue.

### 4.3.2 Valaue-Added Tax Heavon Clause

Since the VAT reform has significantly increased the tax burden of the film companies, China has to create a tax heaven for the film industry and extended it twice. This tax heaven clause gives a pause for the film industry to fit in the new tax regime, while reflecting China's resolution to make good what the Film Industry Promotion Law has in vision.

According to the provisions of the "Transitional Policies for the Pilot Reform of Business Tax to Value-Added Tax in the Transportation Industry and Certain Modern Service Industries" in document Cai Shui [2013] No. 37, before 31 December 2013, the administrative departments of broadcasting, film, and television (including central, provincial, municipal, and county levels) are authorized to approve film groups (including member enterprises), film studios, and other film enterprises engaged in film production, distribution, and screening to transfer film copyrights, distribute films, and screen films in rural areas exempt from value-added tax.

According to the "Notice of the General Office of the State Council on Printing and Distributing the Two Provisions on the Transformation of Operating Cultural Institutions into Enterprises and Further Supporting the Development of Cultural Enterprises" (Guobanfa [2014] No. 15), the following are exempt from value-added tax: income from the sale of film copies (including digital copies) and the transfer of copyright obtained by film production companies, income obtained by film distribution companies from film distribution, and income from film screenings in rural areas by film screening companies. Urban film screening services provided by general taxpayers may choose to calculate and pay value-added tax using the simplified tax method according to current policy regulations. The implementation period of this document is from 1 January 2014, to 31 December 2018.

According to the notice "Further Supporting the Development of Cultural Enterprises" (Guo Ban Fa [2018] No. 124), the income from the sale of film copies (including digital copies) and the transfer of copyright by film production companies, the revenue from film distribution obtained by film distribution companies, and the income from film screenings in rural areas by film screening companies are exempt from value-added tax (VAT). Urban film screening services provided by general taxpayers can choose to pay VAT using the simplified tax calculation method according to the current policy regulations. The implementation period for the tax policies stipulated in this notice is from 1 January 2019, to 31 December 2023.

According to the provisions of the document "Notice on Continuing the Implementation of Value-Added Tax Policies to Support the Development of Cultural Enterprises" (Ministry of Finance and State Administration of Taxation Announcement No. 61 of 2023), the film authorities (including central, provincial, municipal, and county levels) are authorized to grant approval for film production, distribution, and screening by film group companies (including member enterprises), film studios, and other film enterprises. These entities shall be exempt from value-added tax on income from the sale of film copies (including digital copies), transfer of film copyrights (including transfer and licensing), film distribution income, as well as income from film screenings in rural areas. General taxpayers providing urban film screening services may choose to calculate and pay value-added tax using the simplified taxation method in accordance with current policy regulations. The implementation period for the tax policies specified in this announcement is until December 31, 2027.

The broadcasting and film industry is a crucial part of China's cultural industry, making it necessary to continue providing preferential treatment to it after the VAT reform. Representing China's cultural industry, the broadcasting and film sector serves as an important market vehicle for the inheritance and development of Chinese culture, as well as playing a leading role in cultivating influences of national soft power. This is also the reason for implementing a transitional arrangement for the exemption of VAT in the broadcasting and film sector. After the transitional arrangement expires, continuing to provide certain tax incentives to China's broadcasting and film industry will help achieve the goal of healthy development of the cultural industry, facilitate a smooth transition of the VAT reform, and support the continued development of China's film industry. Therefore, establishing a VAT collection system for the broadcasting and film industry that complies with international trade rules is a matter that China needs to consider during the transition period.

### 4.3.3 A Chinese Work Tax Preference Regime Needed

Using certain qualifying Chinese broadcasting and film works as the basis for tax exemption will help establish a VAT preferential system that adheres to international trade regulations, thereby promoting the development of China's film industry. This requires to abandon the taxpayer-centric concept and to re-establish tax incentives for the production, distribution, and screening of Chinese broadcasting and film works. For example, it could be stipulated that the distribution, screening, and copyright transfer of Chinese broadcasting and film works are exempt from VAT, thus promoting their distribution and screening. At this point, determining what constitutes Chinese film works becomes an important technical issue.

On 3 October 1989, the Council of the European Union adopted Directive 89/552/EEC ("the Television Directive"), which establishes broadcasting quotas for European works. This directive requires member states to ensure that their television stations dedicate the majority of their specific broadcasting times to European works.

European works must meet four criteria: First, they need to be predominantly created by authors or performers who reside in EU member states or countries that are signatories to the European Convention on Transfrontier Television; Second, the works must be produced by producers established in EU member states or in countries bound by the European Convention on Transfrontier Television; Third, if the works do not meet the production criteria, their production must be overseen or actually controlled by producers established in EU member states or countries that are parties to the European Convention on Transfrontier Television; Finally, if the works do not satisfy either the production or control criteria, the producer established in EU member states or the countries that have ratified the European Convention must hold a predominant position in the financing of the co-production project, and the project must not be controlled by other producers outside of these countries.

The European Union's approach to defining "European works" is noteworthy for to refer to. For instance, when imposing value-added tax (VAT) on film and television production, distribution, and broadcasting in the broadcasting and film market, we could consider granting VAT exemptions for the production, distribution, and broadcasting of "Chinese works." This could be determined based on the residence and nationality of the authors and performers, the location of the producer's registration, production control and financing control factors, among other relevant criteria, thereby promoting the development of our broadcasting and film industry's growth through tax reform.

With a transition of promotion from the film producer to national film, the tax regime may help Chinese culture to find a stronger hold in the film industry. Moreover, it may also make China more open to the global production or distribution operators, forseeing an more opening up film market to the world.

## *4.4 Maintaining a Balance Between Support and Free Competition under the Cultural Legal System as a Requirement of Cultural Security*

As a very important and prominent cultural industry, from every aspect, the formation and development of the support and market systems related to the film industry also fully demonstrate how to maintain a balance between cultural support and free competition when designing a legal system governing the cultural market. This is not only the requirement of the construction of the cultural legal system, but also the specific manifestation of cultural security to be ensured in the law.

### 4.4.1 Acknowledging the Market Attributes of the Cultural Industry—The Prerequisite for Balancing Cultural Support and Free Competition in the Law

To sum up, as a cultural industry, films not only possess industrial characteristics but also play a cultural role. In China, films have always been regarded as a form of art with educational functions. From the development of the aforementioned regulatory framework for Chinese film production and the evolution of the film censorship system in China, it can be seen that the film regulatory system in China is gradually weakening the educational function of films and striving to establish a film regulatory mechanism that conforms to the development logics of the film industry. However, the cultural role of films has not been suitably reflected in the legal system. In this way, not like ideological, industrial characteristics, the cultural function a film can have has not been fully reflected in the legal framework. Meanwhile, the market-oriented legal system development of the cultural industry is not entirely satisfactory. However, this problem is not specific to the film industry. It exists in many cultural sectors including publishing and audio-visual products. Although the decision of the Sixth Plenary Session of the 17th Central Committee of the Communist Party of China proposed to "promote the leapfrog development of the cultural industry, making it a new growth point, an important fulcrum for strategic adjustment of the economic structure, and an important focus for transforming the economic development mode", it still needs to be reflected in the corresponding cultural legal system construction and improvement.

In fact, other cultural industries also have both cultural functions and industrial characteristics. The developing cultural legal system in China has long recognised the public welfare and commercial nature inherent in culture, and thus views it as cultural undertakings and cultural industries in various contexts. The aim of China's cultural legal system is to promote the development of cultural undertakings and cultural industries. For cultural undertakings, due to their non-business purposes as public welfare, fundamentality, equality and convenience, it maybe necessary to adopt some regulation-oriented measures within the system. For the cultural industry, however, its profitability determines that market conditions are the prerequisite for its development. Therefore, legal guarantees must be provided for the market conditions of the cultural industry's development. The legal system developed for the cultural industry should not only build and improve the legal system of the cultural market, but also provide state support for related industries when necessary. Striking a balance between State support and free competition is an important aspect in the legal system developed for the cultural industry. Therefore, establishing the marketability and cultural functions of the cultural industry in the development of cultural legal system is the prerequisite for building a cultural market and taking supportive measures when necessary.

### 4.4.2 The Balance Between Competition and Support in the Form of Law is a Manifestation of Cultural Security in China

The Relationship Between Cultural Security and the Legal System of Cultural Support

The concept of cultural security was officially incorporated into the decision of the Sixth Plenary Session of the 17th Central Committee of the Communist Party of China. In terms of cultural legal system, it is reflected in the balance between competition and support in the cultural market. It is precisely because the cultural industry is highly characteristic of the industry and has cultural functions that the legal system of the cultural industry cannot merely consider the requirements of the pure cultural market, nor can it rely solely on competition law to maintain the competitive order of the cultural market and ensure the development of the cultural industry. In this regard, the Convention on Cultural Diversity and relevant treaties of the World Trade Organization work hand in hand to maintain the balances, emphasizing the power of governments of various countries regarding cultural diversity, with the aim to ensure the balance of competition and support in the cultural market in the global context. Within a country's legal system developed for its cultural sector this pair of balanced relationships must also be reflected. In the context of the development of the global cultural industry, it is necessary to not only develop the cultural market but also support products or services that reflect relevant cultural factors, so as to safeguard the country's cultural identity, diverse cultural resources and thus its cultural security.

#### The Interaction Between the Physical Cultural Market and the Virtual Cultural Market

Just like in the film industry, capital and cultural elements in the cultural industry are not necessarily unified. Therefore, a physical cultural market and a virtual cultural market have been formed. The former is dominated by capital, while the latter is formed by the competition among different and diverse cultural elements. However, the physical cultural market is the foundation of the virtual cultural market. The interaction between the physical cultural market and the virtual cultural market can be categorised into three situations.

First, both the physical cultural market and the virtual cultural market are in full competition. The market does not need extenal intervention. In this case, the development of the physical cultural market can already guarantee the competition in the virtual cultural market. At this point, apart from the necessary supervision of the cultural market, the competition law system has been sufficient to ensure the operation of the cultural market and the development of the cultural industry. In this regard, the government no longer intervenes.

Secondly, if there is full competition in the physical cultural market while the virtual cultural market is dominated by a single cultural force, it indicates that the competitive situation in the physical cultural market can no longer provide diverse cultural elements. Government intervention is thus needed to support cultural products that cannot survive in the competitive situation of the physical market so as to maintain competition in the virtual cultural market. When the competition in the virtual cultural market is unbalanced and monopolies emerge, it will cause the physical cultural market to lose its role in developing a country's own cultural identity and cultural diversity, thereby endangering a country's cultural security. At this point, the government's intervention to maintain competition in the virtual cultural market is both necessary and legitimative. However, the intervention reflected in the former through government support cannot distort the competition in the physical cultural market, while the latter is providing the essential support for the formation and operation of the virtual cultural market. Here, the relevant legal systems with regulation orientation and the competition law system must be connected to a certain extent. At present, the legal system regarding cultural support in China has not developed into a system and cannot be connected with the competition law system represented by the Anti-Monopoly Law. Therefore, establishing a systematic legal system for cultural support has become an important part of the legal system development for the cultural industry.

Thirdly, the physical cultural market has not been fully competitive, and neither has the virtual cultural market see the effictive. competition. At this point, it proves that there is a monopoly in the physical cultural market itself, or that the physical cultural market has not yet been opened up. Since the virtual cultural market exists and develops in full reliance on the physical cultural market, without a competitive physical cultural market, there will be no competitive virtual cultural market either. The development of China's cultural industries vary. Due to its business characteristics, the publishing industry is highly competitive. Leaving aside market access restrictions, it is hard to say that there is a substantive monopoly in the physical market. In terms of the physical film market, there is no obvious monopoly either. However, the film regulatory system indicates that the physical film market has not been fully opened up. Film regulation remains relatively strict, and the autonomy of enterprises is not prominent. In 2001, the General Office of the Central Committee of the Communist Party of China issued Document No. 17 of 2001, Document No. 17 summarize the experiences and lessons learned from the cultural system reform over the years and basically reflected the understanding and thoughts at that time. Document No. 17 propose that the reform of the cultural system should take development as the theme, structural adjustment as the main line, and group construction as the focus and breakthrough point. It should actively explore and innovate in five aspects: the macro management system, the micro operation mechanism, the policy and legal system, the market environment, and the open pattern, so as to further strengthen The industry, enhance its vitality and improve competitiveness. Document No. 17 further clarifie the goal of actively promoting the reform of media groups and establishing large-scale cross-regional and multimedia groups. It has made positive and specific responses to sensitive issues such as financing in the media industry, cooperation between media and foreign capital, and cross-media development. Document No. 17 indicate that China's cultural industry, especially the media industry, would further move towards marketization. At present, China Film Group has been restructured and gong public, while other cultural institutions have also been undergoing restructuring one after another. The completion of the reform of cultural enterprises would further promote the opening up of the cultural market and lay a solid foundation for the developments and improvement of the cultural legal system.

The Sixth Plenary Session of the 17th Central Committee of the Communist Party of China proposed to make the cultural industry a new growth pillar of the economy and a strategic fulcrum for economic structural adjustment. This is an inevitable requirement of China's economic development and also an inevitable result of the growing cultural demands of the public. In this sense, the balance between competition in the cultural market and the support provided by the government when necessary is an important goal and principle of the current cultural legal system. To this end, it is necessary to further promote the legal system development for China's cultural industry, ensure the openness and competition of the cultural market, and guarantee the national cultural identity and cultural diversity based on the market mechanism, so as to make the cultural market more dynamic and promote the further development of the cultural industry.

# 5 Creative Personnel

Creative personnel in the film industry is the driving force of the film industry. The regulatory measures specific to the creative personnel are, at moment simply too general to target what the whole mechanism needs to offer. Furthermore, the policy to limit the remuneration for stars in a film project also have some implications for the whole industry.

## *5.1 Regulatory Legal Framework and Its Limits Felt in Practices*

The regulatory authority for the business of artist management and related services resides in the Ministry of Culture of the People's Republic of China. According to Article 2 of the "Provisions on the Administration of Commercial Performances," issued by the State Council on 7 July 2005, and amended on 22 July 2008 (State Council Order No. 439), commercial performances refer to live artistic performances held for the public with the aim of making a profit. According to Article 2 of the "Implementation Regulations for the Administration of Commercial Performances," issued by the Ministry of Culture on 28 August 2009, and effective from 1 September 2009 (Ministry of Culture Order No. 47), commercial performances are defined as live artistic performance activities held for the public with profit making purposes through the following means: (1) selling tickets or accepting sponsorship; (2) paying fees to performing entity or individuals; (3) using performances as a medium for advertising or promoting products; and (4) organizing performances through other profit-making methods. Since the artist management and related service industry related to commercial performances is an emerging service sector, the industry supervision system is still in a process of gradual development and improvement. According to State Council Order No. 439 and Ministry of Culture Order No. 47, an application to establish performing artist management agency must have at least three full-time performance agents and sufficient funds that are appropriate for its business, and must be approved by the provincial-level cultural authority where it is located. Foreign investors can establish joint venture or cooperative performing artist management agencies in partnership with Chinese investors, with the Chinese side holding a controlling stake (not less than 51%). The establishment of joint ventures or cooperative agencies must be approved by the Ministry of Culture, after which a commercial performance license will be issued. In practice, aside from agencies that have obtained commercial performance licenses being able to engage in artist management services, many individuals with professional capabilities and resources are also engaged in artist management services, and there are currently no clear laws and regulations governing and supervising individual artist managers. However, according to Article 6 of the "Administrative Measures on Agents," issued by the then State Administration for Industry and Commerce on 28 August 2004: "Those who meet the 'Provisional Regulations on the Management of Urban and Rural Individual Industrial and Commercial Households' shall apply to the industrial and commercial administration for an individual business license to become individual agents." Therefore, strictly speaking, individual artist managers should apply for an individual business license.

In addition to handling the artist management and related service business related to commercial performances, private film production companies also provide agent services for artists participating in film productions. This type of agent service exceeds the scope of the State Council Order No. 439 and the Ministry of Culture Order No. 47. There are no specific laws, regulations, or administrative rules covering this artist management service industry, resulting in a relatively relaxed regulatory environment. Currently, the only applicable regulation concerning film-related agent services in China is the Administrative measures on Agents. Article 2 of the Administrative measures on Agents states: "An agent refers to a natural person, legal entity, or other economic organization that engages in intermediary, dispatch or agency business for the purpose of earning commissions and facilitating trades in economic activities." The Administrative measures on Agents clarifies that agents may conduct agency business in the forms of individual, sole proprietorship, partnership, limited liability company, and other economic organizations, while standardizing the names and business scope of agency enterprises. Additionally, Article 12 of the Administrative measures on Agents stipulates: "After agents obtain their business licenses and hire or dismiss agency practitioners, they should, within 20 days from the date of hiring or dismissal, submit the employment contract and the details of hired agency practitioners, including their name, photo, address, agency project, practice record, and dismissal contract to the local administrative department for industry and commerce for record." Furthermore, Article 13 of the "Administrative measures on Agents" states: "Agents shall prominently display the names, photos, agency projects, and contact numbers of the agency practitioners they employ at the business premises," to prevent agency practitioners from harming the interests of clients and other parties during their agency practice. While the "Administrative Regulations on Agents" establishes that agency practitioners have the right to collect commissions, it also outlines the scope of agents' activities, types and requirements for entering into agency contracts, rules that agents must abide by and prohibited actions, as well as the regulatory authorities for agents. The "Administrative measures on Agents" lays down the basic regulatory framework for agents in the form of departmental regulations.

Overall, private film production companies have entered the upstream artist management industry to acquire scarce actor resources, which provides them with the capability for vertical integration in the industry and a certain talent pool for their film and television productions. It can be seen that Huayi Brothers' artist management business mainly serves its film and television productions. In some aspects, this management business resembles an employment relationship. Regarding such a relationship, whether it is necessary to sign intermediary, agency, or entrust contracts to meet the requirements of the "Administration Measures on Agents" is by on means lear. Moreover, the "Administration Measures on Agents" is currently merely departmental rules, with a relatively low legislative status, making it difficult to provide a comprehensive legal framework. A careful examination of the position of the artist management industry within the entire industry chain of Huayi Brothers reveals that, in some respects, their artist management business is more akin to the star system previously adopted by Hollywood studios. The Chinese film industry currently operates with producers, well-known directors, and renowned actors as its core. For Huayi Brothers, the contribution of a few contracted producers and directors to the company's performance is relatively significant. For example, in the film business, Feng Xiaogang's studio produced films "Assembly" and "If You Are the One 2," which, as of June 30, 2009, had generated a total box office split income of 188.965 million yuan, accounting for approximately 40% of Huayi Brothers' film business revenue and 18% of total operating income from January 1, 2006, to June 30, 2009. This indicates a certain dependency of Huayi Brothers on Feng Xiaogang's team. To address this dependency, Huayi Brothers' solution is to grant equity. Feng Xiaogang, Zhang Jizhong, Li Bingbing, Huang Xiaoming, and other stars hold certain shares in Huayi Brothers. However, such a shareholding arrangement does not provide a solid legal guarantee for Huayi Brothers' star model.

On one hand, the interests of Huayi Brothers as an agency and production company need legal protection; on the other hand, stars are only a part of the production staff composition, and a competitive market for all personnel should be ensured to protect the creative and economic interests of personnel other than the stars. In this regard, the "Management Measures for Agents," which adjusts relationships between equal parties, cannot meet the requirements for balancing these interests. Given that the relationship between production staff and production companies resembles an employment relationship, introducing labor law into the artist management business of film production companies and establishing comprehensive legal rules might be a legal guarantee for further development of artist management in film production companies, thereby promoting business integration within the film industry.

## 5.2 *Remuneration Limits for "Stars"*

Even before the film production licence was abolished by the Film Industry Promotion Law, private capitals had crammed into the market via various channels. It stirred up the whole film market and made the box revenue of China's film souring up. However, since the capital then was not in the hands of the professional investors, many project yielded in some films with high box revenue but with a poor quality in the eyes of film critics. A lot of film stars were courted frenzily by the capital.

Some film star could have a price which would drain up the budget of a film. The inflation of the remuneration of film stars was an easy excuse for the failed producer to complain when the investment from the lay investor flop up.

On 31 October 2018, the National Radio and Television Administration ("NRTA") issued a notice on "Further Strengthening the Management of Radio, Television, and Online Audiovisual Arts Programs," proposing to "strictly control guest remuneration": "The total remuneration for all guests in each program should not exceed 40% of the total program cost, and the remuneration for main guests should not exceed 70% of the total remuneration for guests." "For each TV drama and web drama (including online movies), the total remuneration for all actors should not exceed 40% of the total production cost, with the main actors not exceeding 70% of the total remuneration." On 6 February 2020, the NRTA reiterated the limits on actors' remuneration in its notice on "Further Strengthening the Management of Creative Production in TV Dramas and Web Dramas." On 15 October 2020, the NRTA issued opinions on "Promoting the Strengthening and Improvement of Broadcasting Institutions in the New Era," emphasizing "strict control over actors' and guests' remuneration, and advocating for actors and guests to participate in public welfare programs without remuneration out of a sense of social responsibility and mission." These three normative documents from the NRTA, along with the self-regulatory norms of performance self-discipline organizations, have effectively constrained the excessively high salaries of stars, making it difficult for successful performers to obtain substantial economic benefits through previously high remuneration agreements. It is evident that the salary limitation system has made marketing and even advertising revenue outside of the performing arts increasingly important for successful performers. This has encouraged stars to actively participate in online live broadcast marketing activities, thereby indirectly enhancing the public acceptance of online live broadcast marketing models.

In fact, the stars participating in content production realize further monetization of their economic value through advertisements and other marketing activities, which is an important aspect for successful performers in the entertainment industry to gain profits: on one hand, stars earn compensation from their performances, while on the other hand, they gain economic income by leveraging the personal image established through their artistic work into the advertising market. This is almost a universal practice in the global entertainment market, but no country has seen as many stars participate in online live streaming marketing as China does: either directly promoting related products or services as live streamers or appearing as guests to interact with live streamers in order to increase the visibility of related live streaming marketing activities. For the former, due to the lack of mature professional team support for stars, there are few successful cases, which has led the latter to gradually become the way for stars to participate in online live streaming marketing besides the content production business.

This indeed illustrates the success of commercialization in China's internet live streaming sector. China has the largest number of internet live streaming users worldwide, accounting for about 50% of the global internet live streaming user base in 2019; the average daily active users of Chinese internet live streaming platforms reached 213.4 million during the same period, with each daily active user spending an average of 33.2 min per day on these platforms.[165]

However, this also indicates that performers in the entertainment business field have limited channels for receiving compensation in their as professionals. For content producers who have not achieved sufficient recognition in the industry, actively seeking advertisements or participating in marketing activities has become an important or even primary source of income; for stars, China's "salary caps" system might well explain why they are eager to engage in online live streaming marketing activities.

Remuneration of a creative personnel should have been a contractual issue to be solved by the agreement between the producers and the concerned personnel or more specifically, a film star. In a film market where tremendous amount of investment is not in the hands of professionals, a film investor may be willing to contract the personnel with the great fame. The less professional a film investor may be, the higher remuneration a film star could claim in a film production project. To solve this problem, the more appropriate solution may be to cultivate a more professional investment environment for the film financing. Simply to order a film star cannot claim a remuneration exceeding an amount determined by the regulatory agency may just miss the point. On the other hand, if a creative personnel in the film industry could not obtain the deserving reward from his or her contribution to a film project, this personnel may turn to other ways to make up his or her loss in the film industry. The advertising industry may help such a personnel to get some reward in this regard. It seems that no one is hurt even if this personnel could not obtain its full remuneration for his or her contribution to a film. However, if a personnel could not fully remunerated from her or his job, the remuneration mechanism in the film industry may be distorted. When the market could not deliver the signal that the job could pay a personnel back, the whole mechanism may fail to give the positive stimulus to those who eager to contribute to the film industry full-heartily. Be ware of what you wish for. The starting point of the salary cap for a creative personnel may be from a good intention, but it may lead to some result beyond expectation.

[165] Kuaishou Technology "Prospectus submitted Version," page 162.

# Chapter 3
# Film Distribution and Exhibition in China

The financing of films is a very complex process. Not only because of the unpredictable return on investment in a single project, but also because films involve multiple legal relationships, and the complex legal structure implies numerous stakeholders. Generally speaking, the financing of a film can be divided into the financing for film production and the recovery of film funds. The relationship between film production financing and the recovery of film funds is very close. For example, if a film distributor signs a contract and provides funds before the completion of film production, its payment under the contract is regarded as part of the film financing. If the film distributor signs a contract with the producer after the completion of the film production, the licensing fee paid by the film distributor constitutes the recovery of the film funds. The former is manifested as pre-sale of films, while the latter is manifested as "Negative Pick Up". In the former case, the distributor can exert influence on the production of the film, but not in the latter. However, the relationship of presale is even more complicated. Before the completion of the film, the funds paid by the distributor to the producer usually come from bank financing, and the distributor repays the bank after obtaining the finished film.

## 1 Film Distribution

In a globalised film market, a film produced in any place theoretical enjoys the global audience. The lubricating oil for the film showing worldwide is offered by the film distributors, who have maintained a decisive position since the birth of the film industry.[1] With the worldwide distribution channels, Hollywood majors have established a global distribution-oriented film industry, which prevails over the fragmented EU market as well as China's liberalising market.

---

[1] Weber/Unternäher/Zulauf, 34–35; Roland Unternährer, 3–5.

© Social Sciences Academic Press 2026

J. Wu, *Legal Mechanisms for Film Financing and Support in China*,
https://doi.org/10.1007/978-981-95-0922-5_3

## *1.1 Legal Relations Between Film Producers and Film Distributors*

It is really a daunting task for a company to produce a film, in both financial and regulatory terms. To obtain economic return, this film has to perform well regarding its distribution and exhibition. Without a popular film in hand, a film distributor, together with the exhibitors, will not stand firmly in the competitive market. Apparently, a strong film producing sector is essential to a sustainable development of a resilient film industry. This also entails that a film distributor or exhibitor would like to take any film, so long it is popular.

### 1.1.1 Competition Issue Rather Than Licence Issue

In an ideal market, each market participant's decision on price should only affect the price of its own products and cannot have an impact on the prices of others' products in the market. In the case where the market is monopolized, the price of a certain product in the market is determined by the monopolist. In reality, the film market is neither an ideal perfectly competitive market nor a monopolized one. It is almost a common rule in various countries, regions and stages, the film market is in a state between these two extreme situations. The HHI index used in economics can conduct a quantitative assessment of the structure of the market.[2]

"The content of any medium is another medium." The shooting of any film is based on the script. And the script might be based on the novel. This accurately describes the interrelated situation among the media. Besides, although in the entertainment industry including films, it is generally believed that content is king, content is of course very important for the film industry. However, with the expansion of the film market and the development of globalization, the importance of content is increasingly giving way to the channels for delivering content to consumers. The reason for this change lies in the fact that "content creation does not require a large amount of capital investment, that is, it is not economies of scale." Compared with content creation, distribution requires efforts such as establishing channels and market promotion, involving a large amount of capital investment. This kind of capital investment sets a relatively high threshold for market access, thus making the issuance market dominated by a limited number of companies.

Distribution means film producers license the copyright (or authors' right) to the others for film exhibition. The film making is a capital extensive activity and longing for reward, i.e. the film must be exhibited in the cinemas as many as possible. Otherwise the film artists find no one to support them to continue with another expensive creative event. The producers who are focusing on film production may have no further resources to pick up every cinema available to do the talk. Therefore, the producer needs a channel for the film rolling into the cinemas or other exhibition

[2] Obach, Barack Y. and Einav, Liran, Uniform Prices for Differentiated Goods, 27 Int'l Rev. L. & Econ. 129.

vehicles against the licence fee. Distributors serve as the vital connection which transports the film produced for the producers to the exhibit vehicles, only via which can films see their audience. In film industry, if a producer is more powerful than the director, who commands all the staff in the production team, a distributor is more powerful than the producer because a successful distribution determines how much profit (or honour) the producer could receive. This situation has tremendously turned the issue of copyright licence into an issue more related with competition law. Even if copyright licence also involves competition law issue when the licensor has imposed anti-competitive clauses in the licence agreement, film distribution agreement is made in the situation just the opposite, where the distributor is the one who can voice his will on the producer if the producer has no control on this distributor via any direct or indirect means like Hollywood majors do.

On the other hand, the film industry is a business full of risks. Although many films have made astonishing profits, for the majority of them, achieving box office success commensurate with their investment has become a luxury. In the United States, generally speaking, among ten films shown in cinemas, six or seven can be said to be unprofitable, and one is neither profitable nor loss-making.[3] In this situation, for the producer of one film, the distributor of multiple films has a strong ability to resist risks. This also explains from one aspect why Hollywood film giants operate distribution businesses while engaged in production. This production-distribution model has obvious positive significance for the survival of film enterprises. Therefore, when applying the relevant principles of competition law to the film distribution market, especially when determining whether it constitutes a vertical monopoly, careful consideration must be given to the economic basis and rationality of the production-distribution model.

This has created such a situation: Film producers hope to find distributors who can deliver their works to the audience to the greatest extent, while distributors hope to find films that can be loved by the audience to the greatest extent. The distribution network controlled by film distributors becomes a necessary element for a film to achieve commercial success. The degree of competition among film distributors is very important for film producers.

At this point, the core facility refers to the distribution network rather than the copyright in the films produced. When producers and distributors sign contracts, the so-called "Blind booking" and "block booking" were not originally problems. The proportion of film distribution in a film's budget is actually quite considerable. A successfully released film may require not only a distributor with a significant market position, but also a large amount of marketing promotion, which cannot be supported by films with medium or small budgets. Therefore, telecommunications operators can acquire a large number of users as long as they obtain the network access rights of fixed-line operators. However, it is not certain that films can obtain the vast audience that producers dream of just by being handed over to distributors controlled by Hollywood audio-visual giants. In fact, the budget of the film has

[3] Vogel, Harold L., *Entertainment Industry Economics, A Guide for Financial Analysis,* 8th Ed., New York: Cambridge University Press 2011, 71.

become another substantive entry threshold besides film distributors. In the European Union, for the distribution of the so-called 20 European blockbusters, distributors directly or indirectly controlled by the United States have captured 54% of the share.[4] If European producers are willing to invest in a film, Hollywood audio-visual giants are also willing to serve European films. Therefore, the obstacles to market access are caused by the budget size of the film rather than the distribution network.

The essential facility means the distribution network instead of the copyright contained in the film produced.[5] Blind booking and block booking are not at the issue when a contract is entered into between the producers and distributors.[6] Therefore, the distributors subordinated to Hollywood majors could meet rather tricky situation in EU, where 64% films are distributed by the subsidiaries or the joint ventures of the Hollywood majors. However, why not a single suit is raised successfully against these market dominants for refusing offer services for the films produced by the independent or any directive issued from Commission, like they did in telecommunications area, to require the Member States shall open the access to the film distribution network?

Distribution occupies a substantial portion of the whole budget for a film.[7] A successfully distributed film may need not only a well positioned distributor but also a considerable marketing campaign, which is normally not bearable by the middle or low budget films. Therefore, it is not the case that the film put on the track of the distributors controlled by the Hollywood majors will meet the mass audience the producers are dreaming of, like a telecom operator gets access to the fixed line operator to let his business flourish. Actually, it is the budget of the film which serves as another essential threshold apart from the distributors. In EU, as to so-called 20 leading European blockbusters distributed in EU, US related distributors held 54 contracts in 2004.[8] If the European producers invest heavily in a film, the Hollywood majors are willing to serve for their films. Therefore, the barrier for the market access is laid down by the size of the film budget, not by the distribution network.

[4] The Fragmented Universe of Film Distribution Companies in Europe, European Audiovisual Observatory, Contribution to the Workshop "Distribution of European Films", Venezia, 29–31 August, 2003, downloaded from http://www.obs.coe.int on 23rd, April, 2024.

[5] As to the access to the essential facilities, see D. G. Goyder, 346–350.

[6] If there is a blind booking exists between powerful distributor and the producers, this may constitute a joint production, like the TV channel does in a not real entrusted film production, see Harald Dörfler. It is possible that a stronger producer may force the weak producer to do the blind booking or block booking, when the Hollywood producers face a local distributor in Europe and China. Then the competition law applies. See Weber/Unternäher/Zulauf, 106, 107; Roland Unternährer, 90–94.

[7] In 2002, the total average investment per film made by Hollywood major is USD 89.4 million while the printing, advertising and promotion ate USD 30.6 million. See FOCUS 2003, 13.

[8] The Fragmented Universe of Film Distribution Companies in Europe, European Audiovisual Observatory, Contribution to the Workshop "Distribution of European Films", Venezia, 29–31 August, 2003, downloaded from http://www.obs.coe.int on 23rd, April, 2004.

### 1.1.2 Sectors of Distribution

With the advance of technology, in addition to the traditional distribution of films in cinemas, TV and video products are now available to producers as indispensable means for film distribution.

TV plays an increasingly important role in film exhibition thanks to the emergence alongside traditional broadcast channels financed by advertising and/or licence fees, of encoded channels for which a charge is made and whose arrival has been made possible by the development of cable and satellites. This category of channels may itself be divided in two, those charging by monthly subscription (premium channels) and pay per view channels.

However, the video sector is an expanding method of film exhibition. This sector principally covers the purchase and rental of pre-recorded film cassettes or DVD-RWs. The proceeds rolled back from video sector have exceeded those from cinema and TV channels.[9]

The traditional vehicle for distribution remains to be the cinema, though this sector has seen significant changes. There is a trend towards the grouping of cinemas within a small number of national or regional circuits with independent cinemas not part of a circuit now being the exception. This development is explained primarily by the very substantial investment entailed by the modernisation of existing cinemas and the boom of multiplex cinemas.[10] Cinemas in these networks, mainly located in urban areas, either in town centres or in the suburbs, are designed to meet the diversifying demands of the public in terms of comfort and services. Moreover, the multiplex cinema normally has comfortable auditorium with large screens, offer easy access and parking, and are well-served by shops, restaurants and other related services. However, the emerging of digital cinemas and the speedy development of digital TV set may transform this sector or even impair the market share of this distribution sector.

## *1.2 Liberation of the Film Distribution Sector in China*

The distribution and exhibition of Chinese films had long been operated under a planned economy system, with a low degree of marketization, primarily managed by state-owned film enterprises. Since 2001, with the introduction of relevant laws and regulations such as the Film Regulations, Decree No. 20, Film Business Qualification

[9] In 2003, MGM obtained revenue of USD 1651.9 million, in which cinema exhibition brought in USD 220.9 million while home video products (including DVD and other video products) brought in USD 1051.6 million. See the Form 10-K Annual Report filed by MGM for 2003, 40, 41.

[10] Although there is as yet no official terminology, from a practical point of view wide consensus has been gained in the profession for the definition adopted by MEDIA Salles, according to which the term multiplex cannot properly be used unless the complex has at least 8 screens. See MEDIA Salles, European Cinema Year Book, 2003 advance edition.

Provisions, Document No. 17, and Several Opinions on Introducing Foreign Investment in the Cultural Sector, the film industry has gradually opened up to private capital and foreign investment. Currently, restrictions on the operation of private capital participating in film distribution and exhibition have significantly decreased, and foreign investment is allowed to participate in cinema construction and investment without holding a controlling stake. However, relevant industrial policies still emphasize a primarily public ownership structure and the leading role of state-owned cultural enterprises (groups). In practice, State-owned film enterprises, with their long operational history, possess certain historical advantages in industry layout and talent pooling. Consequently, large State-owned film enterprises still maintain a degree of competitive market power in various aspects of film distribution, theater chains, and cinema operations. On the other hand, although private enterprises have been involved in the film industry for a relatively short period, they are gaining ground in the distribution sector, leveraging their flexible operational mechanisms.

The film distribution sector is divided into the national film distribution sector and the imported film distribution sector. From the perspective of market concentration and competitive landscape, in the import film distribution segment, due to the exclusive import film distribution qualifications of China Film Group and Huaxia Film, both companies enjoy monopolistic position. In the domestic film distribution segment, private film distribution companies have secured a significant portion of the market share.

### 1.2.1 Domestic Film Distribution Sector

Initially, FBMC was in charge of the film distribution. A national distribution network was established in 1950 in the form of regional film management companies while the SFDC was founded in Beijing in 1953 to take over the functions of film distribution from FBMC. Acting as a central film distribution agency overseeing the film distribution nation-wide, SFDC purchased the complete film prints from the studios at a rate based on the film's length. Thereafter, SFDC assigned the prints to the local film management companies formed by the local film bureaus, who exhibited the films according to the exhibition period fixed by SFDC.[11]

After 1979, SFDC was restructured as CFC. CFC purchased the original prints at a mandatory rate of RMB 900,000 per film and then distributed nation-wide through its local branches to the cinemas and obtained 80% of the box office proceeds since 1979. In the next three years, CFC and its local branches re-invest 50% of their proceeds in the cinemas' renovations and expansions. Although this profit share system appeared to be at the sacrifice of the studio's interest, CFC purchased the entire studios' productions with an indiscriminate rate. In 1980, this studio payment system was adjusted that CFC should pay RMB 90,000 per print for the first 110 copies sold to the cinemas. CFC should pay RMB 99,000 per print to the copies which

[11] The local film management companies might adjust the exhibition period according to the profit potential of each film even though it was against the central management system. Ying Zhu, 51.

was sold beyond the first 110 copies.[12] Thus, the first profit-sharing system according to the market situation was established. However, CFC was then the monopoly holder of the film distribution nation-wide, who distributed film, paid fees to the studios and footed the bills for promotion. In 1984, the local branches of CFC were required to shoulder the costs of extra prints exceeding the first distributed ones. China's government announced she would not allocate money to the studios since they were actually enterprises.[13] In 1987, the mandatory prices for purchase from the studios and the distribution price to the local branches were dismissed. This led to a qualified box office receipt sharing mechanism between studios, CFC, CFC's local branches and cinemas.[14]

In 1993, MRFT issued Decree no. 3, which pushed for a market oriention approach for the film industry reform,[15] dismissed the domestic film distribution monopoly of CFC and allowed the studios to negotiate with the local distributors (CFC local branches) nation-wide for distribution via selling of distribution rights, flat rate, box office receipt sharing and commissioning while loosing up the central control of the ticket price.[16] In May of 1993, a film trading market was established in Beijing. Although the dismissal of the monopoly was welcomed by some film distributors and acknowledged by some scholars,[17] the nation-wide distribution system was fragmented. This inflicted tremendous suffering to the little private studios, which had to find the distribution channels province by province.[18] The big studios were also upset for the uprising distribution cost. In the context of globalisation and in comparison with the objectives in distribution sector set by MEDIA Plus, this reform aimed for an aggressive liberalisation. A fragmented domestic distribution market swelled the distribution cost of the national film while the distribution channel for the famous and well promoted Hollywood blockbusters imported remained intact.[19] A dramatic sliding-down of the national film market was the bitter fruit the reformers' rash plans.[20] Further measures to reform or to modify the popular reform policy, embodied in Decree No. 3, was urgently needed.

In the meanwhile, the distribution market opened the door for the private capitals. In June of 2003, BRFT granted the distribution rights to seven private enterprises

[12] Ibid., 53. Guo Yujie: "It's Hard to Bid Farewell to Monopoly and Break the Rules of the Film Industry", published in Caijing on April 27, 2002.

[13] Guo Yujie: "It's Hard to Bid Farewell to Monopoly and Break the Rules of the Film Industry", published in Caijing on April 27, 2002.

[14] Ying Zhu, 72–75.

[15] Article 1, Notice Three.

[16] Ibid., Article 2 and Article 3.

[17] Ying Zhu, 76.

[18] Xiaoling Zhai; Yujie Guo.

[19] For which CFC still enjoyed the nationwide monopoly.

[20] In comparison with 1992, for national films, film exhibition in 1993 dropped 50%, cinema admissions dropped 60%, and distribution income as well as box office returns dropped 40%. Nine of ten films with the best box office performance for national films were co-productions with Hong Kong and Taiwan. These statistics please find in Ying Zhu, 77 and Yujie Guo.

after loosing up the non-State ownership control in the film distribution sector.[21] With the adoption of Film Business Qualification Provisions, China began to encourage the private capital to flow into the distribution sector. Those companies with the registered capital no less than RMB 500,000 and have ever acted as an agent for the distribution of two films or two TV plays should have right to apply for the film distribution business licence from the film regulator of China. At the moment, the distribution sector was closed from the overseas capital.

The adoption of the Film Industry Promotion Law abolished the license requirement for a company to go into the film production business, but has retained the film distribution business licence regime established by the Film Business Qualification Provisions. Articles 24, 25, 26 reiterate the stipulations of the Film Business Qualification Provisions regarding film distribution licence system. Accordingly, enterprises with capabilities appropriate for the film distribution activities may engage in film distribution activities with the approval of the State Council's film regulatory department or the film regulatory department of the local government at the provincial level. With the adoption of the Film Industry Promotion Law, the Film Business Qualification Provisions has since secured a solid legitimate basis to be still effective in both distribution and exhibition sectors of the film industry.

According to the Film Regulations, to establish a film distribution entity, an application must be submitted to the film administration department of the provincial, autonomous region, or municipal government where the entity is located; for establishing a film distribution entity that operates across provinces, autonomous regions, or municipalities, an application must be submitted to the State Council's film administration department. Upon approval, a Film Distribution Business License will be issued. The State implements an annual inspection system for the "Film Distribution Business License," with specific methods formulated by the State Council's broadcasting and film administration department. According to the Film Business Qualification Provisions, domestic companies to act as agents for the distribution of two or more films (excluding foreign-invested enterprises) may apply to establish a film distribution company specializing in the distribution of domestic films. Such companies can obtain a specialized Film Distribution Business License for domestic films only after approval by the CFA. CFA implements a biennial inspection system for the Film Distribution Business Licenses it issues, while local film administration departments conduct annual inspections of the Film Distribution Business Licenses and Film Exhibition Business Licenses they issue according to their management authorities.

### 1.2.2 Distribution of the Films Imported

After surrendering the distribution monopoly of national films, CFC still reserved the monopoly for the distribution of the films imported and the children's films with certain percentage. In 1994, just after the loss of the monopoly of national

[21] Hongyu Li.

film distribution, CFC obtained the monopoly of film import, which led to the first Hollywood film, *The Fugitive*, rushing into the market. Since 1995, China loosed up the content examination controls for the film imported and CFC began its import of foreign films, mainly the so-called "big films" from Hollywood. With the nation-wide distribution network and the overwhelming promotion efforts, Hollywood films quickly claimed their dominant power in China's film market. Until 2002, the films imported on the basis of box office receipt sharing should not exceed the annual import quotas of 10 films.

However, in some sense, this quotas system was actually a sham if it was for the protection of the national film industry. A loosed-up content examination system without the qualification from rating system and the streamlined distribution mechanism nation-wide via the biggest distribution company, CFC, made the film imported easily to defeat those national films, which have to found way through the fragmented market. The worse thing was that, since the quotas was only 10, after the 1995, CFC imported only the box office hits or those films with a monstrous production investment, which are impossible to be non-Hollywood films.[22] Furthermore, this quota covered only the films imported with the box office receipt sharing model, the flat rate model and the exhibition through TV or DVD selling is not covered. From 1995 to 2001, China imported 134 US films, in which 61 films shared box office receipt. With the development of digital technology and the increasing share of DVD products in the distribution market of Hollywood majors, Hollywood majors' profit potential was actually unchained in China. The combined film import and distribution monopoly has dramatically weakened the choice of China's film audience.

On 11 December 2001, China notified WTO that she had rectified the membership terms and became the 143rd Member thereof. As to the film distribution sector, China has committed to allow 20 films imported per year in the first three years after the access to WTO and then the films imported under the quotas will be increased to 50 films, of which 20 films shall share the box office receipt.[23] WTO brought great challenge to China's film industry.

CFC's distribution monopoly of film imported actually offered the unfair advantage of the films imported against the national films. On 8 August 2003, Huaying Film Distribution Company, Ltd. ("Huaying") was established in Beijing. Since then, Huaying and CFC share distribution market of the film imported and began

[22] In 1995, the ten films imported were *Natural Born Killers, Broken Arrow, Twister, Toy Story, True Lies, Water World, the Bridge of Madison County, Jumanji* and two other HK commercials, which totalled 70–80% of the national box office proceeds in China. See Ying Zhu, 86. In 1998, this situation turned to be a bit better, *Titanic, Home Alone III, Saving the Private Rayne, Crash* and etc., which accounted 2/3 of the total box office proceeds in China. See Hong Ying. In 2002, the box office receipt was about RMB 1 billion, the imported blockbusters took RMB 0.5 billion. See Zhui Li.

[23] Zhonglun Ren.

to compete with each other.[24] These two new distribution companies are in charge of the imported film supply to the 35 cinema chains formed under new reform policy.[25]

Currently, the management of imported films in china is based on the principle of one importer and two distributors. CFA authorizes the Film Import and Export Division of China Film Group Corporation to uniformly handle the import of foreign films and films from Hong Kong, Macao, and Taiwan. After the films are reviewed and approved by the Film Review Committee of the CFA and brought in, the Film Import and Export Division of China Film Group Corporation is responsible for distributing the films to the original China Film Distribution Corporation and Huaxia Film Distribution Co., Ltd.

In summary, according to relevant regulations, and departmental rules the film import business is operated by China Film Group, while both China Film Group and Huaxia Film hold the national distribution rights for imported films. Other film distribution companies, including the private distribution companies, can distribute domestic films and assist in promoting imported films. Given the fact the promotion constitutes the essential item of the distribution operation, private companies are also deeply involved in the imported film distribution of China. In this sense, competition in the market for distribution of imported film is highly intensified.

### 1.2.3 Cinemas Rushing into Chains

According to the Implementation Rules for the Reform of Film Distribution and Screening Mechanism (Trial) issued by former SARFT and the Ministry of Culture, and the Opinions on Further Promoting the Reform of Cinema Chain Companies, China implements a distribution and screening mechanism primarily based on cinema circuits, formed by a distribution entity and several cinemas subordinated. This mechanism enforces a unified brand, unified scheduling, unified operation, and unified management, with distribution companies and production units supplying films directly to the cinema chain companies.

This reform policy has been initiated from the crisis the domestic film faced in distribution market. The market for the national films had shrunken dramatically partly due to the fragmented distribution market for the national film in comparison with the streamlined distribution network for film imported. The fragmented national films distribution market was actually the monopoly fragmented into the provincial levels. The studio still had to negotiate with just one distributor in one province and the box office receipt were shared between the studios, the distributors and the

[24] However, Huaying and CFC each enjoy the exclusive distribution of different films imported according to the range of "CFC, Huaying, Huaying, CFC", See Hongyu Li. This system actually constitutes no competition but oligarchy. However, there is also the requirement that each of Huaying and CFC's films to be distributed shall be decided according to their achievement of the national film distributions as well as the distribution of the assigned imported films. This partly offsets the edge obtained by the films imported.

[25] Yujie Guo.

cinemas in equal proportion. Since studios could not supervise the box office receipt, box office fraud was also a problem.[26]

In 2000, some officials of SARFT claimed there should be a second nation-wide cinema chains. Before that, some provinces began to see the second distributors in 1998.[27] In December, 2001, SARFT issued the Rules 1519, which ruled that there must be a second distributor or cinema chains in the provincial level except some western province. Provinces refusing to do this would have no right to distribute the blockbusters imported.[28] On 1 June 2002, the first batch of 30 cinema chains in the country officially began operations, marking the start of a new operating mechanism for the film market in China. The comprehensive reform of the cinema chains system broke the previous model of film supply based on administrative regions, transforming the single, multi-level distribution into a primary distribution model centered around cinema chains. Distribution companies and production units now supply films directly to cinema chains, reducing distribution costs and optimizing the industry structure. By the end of 2021, there were a total of 51 cinema chains across the country's urban areas.[29] With the continuous relaxation of industry regulations, private enterprises represented by Wanda Film and Hong Kong-funded companies represented by UME are constantly growing and developing. This has significantly changed the competitive landscape of the Chinese cinema market and has also promoted the marketization of the cinema group.

However, since the imported Hollywood films dominate the film market, it is possible that the two distributors for the film imported could control the cinema chains newly established. Therefore, the appropriate legal form of cinema chains is of great importance to the healthy competition market dreamed by the film makers.

A cinema chain is a form of horizontal integration between cinemas, which are encouraged in China. According to the Film Business Qualification Provisions, the present cinema chains' mergers are allowed to establish cinema chains by the tightly or loosely networking, which is encouraged to go beyond provincial level. The merger between all the cinema chains within one province is forbidden. Furthermore, the merger of the cinema chains must be approved by the CFA.[30]

In the meanwhile, the film or TV operators are encouraged to establish the cinema chains by equity control or participation. There are two modes according to the approval authority they are subject to.[31]

- The establishment of cinema chains at trans-provincial level shall be approved by CFA.
- The establishment of cinema chains within a province shall be approved by the provincial branch of CFA.

---

[26] Hongyu Li. It was said the studios could only get 22% of the box office receipt, which means an 11% gap between what they were entitled to. See Hong Yin.

[27] Yujie Guo.

[28] Hongyu Li.

[29] For the data, please refer to the Prospectus of Bona Film Company signed on 8th August 2022.

[30] Article 12, Film Business Qualification Provisions.

[31] Ibid.

According to the Implementation Detailed Rules for Reforming the Film Distribution and Screening Mechanism (Trial) by the SRAFT and the Ministry of Culture issued on 18 December 2001, as well as "Opinions on Accelerating Cinema Construction to Promote the Prosperity and Development of the Film Market," issued by the CFA on 11 December 2018, the establishment of a cinema chain must meet the following conditions: the number of controlled cinemas must be no less than 50 or the number of screens must be no less than 300; the total box office revenue of the controlled cinemas in the previous year must not be less than 500 million yuan; the affiliated cinemas must normally pay into the special fund for the development of the film industry; the applicant entity must not have had any illegal or irregular business activities in the past three years and must not have received any administrative penalties or other sanctions; and no more than three affiliated cinemas must have been subject to administrative penalties or other sanctions in the past three years due to illegal or irregular business activities, with the penalties having been completed and the corrective measures fully implemented.

The establishment of cinema chain company must follow the relevant procedures set forth by CFA. The establishment of inter-provincial cinema chain companies must be approved by the CFA; the establishment of intra-provincial cinema chain companies must be approved by the provincial film authorities where they are located and reported to the CFA for filing.

The cinemas in China are thus running to chains. Concerned about the dominant distribution power of Hollywood, China does not allow the overseas capital participate in cinema chains at the moment.[32] The vertical integration encouraged between studios and exhibitors appears to suggest that the studios' control in exhibition sector will be strengthened. This serves as a preparation for the possible liberalisation of the global film market as well as the beginning of the overhaul of the whole film industry in China. Since China's consolidation of its film distribution market is an issue within a country, it may be easier for China to achieve an intensively integrated local market than EU accomplish a single internet market. However, the shortage of capital has forced China making some concessions to the overseas capital.[33] In the future, the balance between capital and protection for national industry has to be kept with efforts.

---

[32] Ibid.

[33] Although foreign investors are not allowed to invest in cinema chains directly, China permits foreign entities to invest in cinemas in collaboration or joint venture with domestic companies and enterprises. In seven major cities, including Beijing, the proportion of foreign capital in the registered capital cannot exceed 75%, while in other cities, it cannot exceed 49%. Please refer to Article 4, Section (3) of the "Interim Regulations on Foreign Investment in Cinemas." Additionally, see Zhu Yongde and Shen Shan's article "Dreamlike Industry Breaks Monopoly," published in the Economic Observer on 17 June 2002. However, as of 1 January 2005, investors from Hong Kong and Macao Special Administrative Regions are not subject to the aforementioned investment ratio restrictions. This is stipulated in the first item of the "Supplementary Rules on Film Business Qualification Provisions" jointly issued by the SARFT and MOFCOM on 7 March 2005.

# 2 Film Exhibition

The growth of cinemas and screens is one of the important foundations for the steady development of China's film industry. The number of cinemas nationwide increased from 2800 in 2011 to 12,387 in 2021, with an average annual compound growth rate of 16.03%. The number of screens grew from 9286 in 2011 to 82,248 in 2021, with an average annual compound growth rate of 24.37%. Although the Chinese film market has been impacted by the COVID-19 pandemic, the number of screens and cinemas continues to maintain a relatively stable growth rate. By 2021, the number of screens reached 82,248, with an increase of 6667 screens throughout the year, representing an 8.82% growth compared to 2020.[34]

## *2.1 General Legal Framework and National Film Exhibition Preference in China*

According to the provisions of the Film Industry Promotion Law, enterprises and individual businesses that have the necessary personnel, venues, technology, and equipment suitable for film screening activities may engage in film screening activities at fixed venues such as cinemas, subject to approval by the film authority of the county-level people's government where they are located. According to the Film in Regulations and Film Business Qualifications Provisions, the State encourages domestic companies, enterprises, other economic organizations, and individuals to invest in the construction and renovation of cinemas and to operate in film screening businesses. To establish a film screening operator, an application must be submitted to the film administrative department of the county or district-level municipal people's government. After approval, the operator can obtain a Film Screening Operation License for registration. The national government implements an annual inspection system for the Film Screening Operation License, and the specific methods are to be formulated by the CFA.

From the perspective of box office and landscape of individual cinemas, the concentration of the cinema market in China is relatively dispersed. Cinema investment management companies are management companies that invest in and hold multiple cinemas, managing their subordinate cinemas through capital management, operational management, personnel management, and other forms. According to data from Maoyan, a top Chinese film business datebase platform, the top 10 film investment companies by box office from 2019 to 2021 held over 30% of the market share.

China has been gradually open up its cinema exhibition sector to the foreign investment. The Film Regulations stipulate that the State allows the construction and renovation of cinemas through joint ventures or cooperative agreements between

[34] For the data, please refer to the Prospectus of Bona Film Company signed on 8th August 2022.

Chinese and foreign Investor. According to the Interim Regulations on Foreign Investment in Cinemas issued by the SAPPART on 28 August 2015, foreign investors are not allowed to establish wholly foreign-owned cinemas or to form cinema chain companies; the registered capital of foreign-invested cinemas must not be less than 6 million yuan; for Sino-foreign joint venture cinemas, the Chinese party's investment proportion in the registered capital must not be less than 51%; for pilot cities nationwide, in Sino-foreign joint venture cinemas, the foreign party's investment proportion in the registered capital must not exceed 75%; the duration of joint ventures and cooperations must not exceed 30 years.

In the cinema exhibition sector, China adopts a national film preference policy. According to Article IV of GATT, the Member States are permitted to carry out the screen quotas in favour of national film exhibitions. Just after the access to WTO, China adopted amended Film Regulations, which requires that the national film shall enjoy at least 2/3 exhibition time annually.[35] This system has been acknowledged in the Film Industry Promotion law in Article 39. In 1996, the central State TV Channel launched a speclised film channel and it is required that the film imported shall not be exhibited more than 25% of the volume of films exhibited generally and during 19:00 to 20:00, the foreign films cannot be exhibited for 15% of the volume of the films exhibited in the same period therein.[36] These measures are aimed to ensure a market proportion for national films and maintain the culture diversity in the meantime.

## 2.2 *Potential Interest Conflicts Between National Film Producers and National Film Distributors/Exhibitors*

Even Department of State of US admitted in 1950 that films are different than other products; it is more related to domestic cultural policies than to economics and trade because their value lies in the film itself and not in the income it generates.[37] Therefore, economic value must bend down a little to the culture values, i.e. the exhibition sector must make a little sacrifice for the national film producers. This implies that film producers and distributors/exhibitors have different interests in the chain of film industry.

For the convenience of argument, without considering the copyright issues, assuming that the film producers are the authors of the films, who care no film marketing but just the film making, then distributors and exhibitors of the films constitute the market for the film. If the authors make the films just for market potentials, which are the favourites of the distributors and exhibitors, they shall be no conflicts. Maybe the best practice for the film makers to do, if involving no competition law

[35] Article 44, Film Regulations.

[36] Article 1 (5), the Notice for Film Channel issued by the BRFT on 14 June 1996.

[37] Although US later On the 18th, December, 2000, in their Communication on audiovisual and related services to the WTO Council for Trade in Services omitted this and admitted only the economic significance in this regard. See Ivan Bernier.

issues, is the cross ownership between all these three sectors, like Hollywood majors did.[38] Then, there will be no conflicts between the authors and market. However, the works with no popular potentials would find no way in the market. In some cases, these kind of unpopular films are either of experimental nature or of high culture value. If films are like novels or pictures, which involves only individual efforts and not so much capital required in production stage, an unpopular film does not matter much to the authors. A hobby with no tremendous expense is enjoyable even without audience. However, at the moment, a film is never cheap. If no market is available for the art in film, no art film can survive. This conflict is of no competition nature. More likely, it is a relation between the control and the controlled. However, there is still a balance point between the producers and distributors/exhibitors, money. The former needs money for works creation while the later needs money for the reservation or expansion of cinema or distribution networks. Thus, the concern for market becomes an overwhelming element for the whole film industry.

In China, the box receipt split mechanism reveals the conflicts between film producers and its distributors/exhibitors.

Normally, the film release schedule is submitted by the distributor to the CFA, which then issues the film schedule to major cinema chains. The box office revenue of the film is primarily realized within this release window, and the sales costs are also concentrated during this period. In China's film market, the scale of subsequent sales revenue such as internet broadcasting rights after the film screening is relatively small; most of the film's sales revenue comes from box office earnings. According to current industry practices and market structure, the box office revenue is mainly distributed among the production, distribution, cinema chains, and theaters through a box office sharing model. The distribution procedure of box office revenue generally works as follows: The cinema deducts the value-added tax and additional charges, as well as the national film special fund, from the box office revenue to calculate the net amount (i.e., net box office revenue). This net amount is then distributed to the theater chain company according to an agreed-upon ratio. After the theater chain receives the box office split payment, it deducts its service fee before distributing the remainder to Huaxia Film or China Film Digital. Huaxia Film or China Film Digital collects the distribution service fee as per the agreement and then pays the

---

[38] By the 1930s the US major distributors, and through them the studios themselves, were vertically integrated into exhibition, or ownership and operation of movie theatres. In the late 1930s and 1940s the Antitrust Division brought a series of cases against eight distributors alleging various horizontal and vertical violations of the Sherman Act. Eventually, judicial decrees were entered in the cases, collectively called the "Paramount" decrees (Paramount, Inc. was one of the defendant distributors). The decrees are not identical, but they share many common elements. Those distributors that were vertically integrated into exhibition were required to divest their theatre assets, and some (but not all) were prohibited from re-entering the exhibition business. The decrees also contained certain injunctive provisions intended to prevent discrimination against small, independent exhibitors and to prevent vertical re-integration by contract. The distributors could not engage in "block booking," or conditioning the licensing of a desired film on the simultaneous licensing of other films, or in other specified types of contractual arrangements that effectively bound a theatre or chain of theatres to a distributor. See U.S. v. 20th Century Fox, 882 F.2d 656 (2d Cir. 1989), cert. den. 110 S. Ct. 722 (1990). See OCDE/GD (96) 60, 49–51.

box office split to each distributing company. After the distributing company receives the box office split payment (i.e., distribution revenue), it then divides the distribution revenue with the production company according to an agreed-upon ratio.

Box office revenue split targets the income generated from ticket sales after a film has been completed. The film producers reach a distribution and screening cooperation agreement with domestic cinema circuits in China, and the box office revenue from screenings is shared between producers and cinema circuits. Generally, film producers can receive about 40% of the box office revenue.

According to the Document No. 866 Guidance of Box Receipt Split Ratio of National Films issued by the SARFT on 19 December 2008, which adjusted the revenue sharing ratio for domestic films, the producers' share should not be less than 43%, while cinemas typically do not exceed 50%. In November 2011, when negotiations over the box office revenue sharing ratio for "The Flowers of War" were deadlocked, the Film Bureau of the SARFT issued Document No. 992 "Guiding Opinions on Promoting Coordinated Development of Film Distribution and Screening," to the China Film Distribution and Exhibition Association and the China Film Producers Association. Document No. 992 states that cinemas' share of the revenue for first-run screenings should not exceed 50%, reaffirming the cinema revenue sharing ratio outlined in Document No. 866. It further proposes gradually reclaiming advertising rights for cinemas and suggests that producers no longer operate promotional advertisements. Additionally, it addresses the issue of rental costs affecting cinema revenues, recommending that annual real estate rent should not exceed 15% of annual box office revenue. Document No. 992 attempts to regulate the sharing of box office revenue and the corresponding balance of interests across various stages of film production, distribution, and screening. In actual practices, the specific revenue-sharing ratio is determined through negotiations among the film participants, taking into account relevant guidelines, the specific case of the film, etc., and it often fluctuates based on the guidelines provided by the CFA.

## 2.3 *Multiple Channels Offered by the Technology*

Historically, the "Paramount" decrees[39] firstly denied the vertical integration between producers, distributors and exhibitors. However, with the development of technology, TV, audio and digital products has begun to share substantially the film distribution or exhibition market. Film exhibition becomes a chain of business, first-run film exhibited in cinemas, then video products and digital products, then the pay-for-view TV channels and at last the free TV channels. Although many first-run film are still exhibited in the cinema, whose box office receipts determine the profit the producer may obtain later, DVD selling increased its share in the whole distribution and exhibition market and enjoys the highest share of the profits a film brought in for Hollywood majors while TV channel becomes the biggest income source

[39] Ibid.

for film producers in EU.[40] Therefore, the film exhibition market is divided into three sectors, cinema exhibition, and video or digital products sales sector and TV exhibition. Theoretically, the time gap between these three sectors should be decided by the film producer or the film copyright holder. For example, a film produced by MGM normally is exhibited in the cinema sector. Six months later, they will distribute the DVD and other home video products. One year after the starting date of cinema exhibition, the pay TV will obtain the right from MGM to exhibit the film. Three or five years after the starting date of cinema exhibition, the film will be available via other means.[41] A film goes through the chain of distribution/exhibition in this order to ensure that the producer could obtain the utmost profit.

The basis of this distribution system is that the cinema sector, the video or digital products[42] and the TV sector for the exhibition of film are three different exhibition markets. Otherwise the time gap between the exhibitions of a film in these three sectors would not attract more audience than a film could get. A film exhibited in the cinema is regarded as a service, not only the big screen with incomparable pictures, but also the convenient restaurant and bar services and etc. in the modern cinemas and multiplexes.[43] A cinema success means also the success in TV and video or digital product sector lately. Therefore, although the cinema renovation and expansion cost heavily for the investors, still more investors are swarming in to build more expensive cinemas. Technology appears to offer more and more exhibition channels for a film without changing the substantial role the cinema plays.

However, if a film is screened simultaneously in cinemas, on TV channels and through the home audio-visual market (the sale of video tapes and DVDS), the profits obtained by the film's producers are less than the profits obtained by the film in sequence through the normal distribution and screening chain. In this sense, the classification of the film screening market mentioned above may not be accurate in a legal sense: When services are allowed to be provided simultaneously in three markets, if audiences shift from the cinema market to the movie channel and home audio-visual market, or from the home audio-visual market to the movie channel market, or vice versa, it indicates that there must be some overlap in the parts of these three markets. The number of screening channels that technology provides for a film determines the number of overlapping parts among these channels. In a sense, technological development has blurred the boundaries between each other in the film screening chain and has increased both the economic and legal costs of maintaining the film screening chain.

The group that can give up the cinema and switch to DVD discs or television (the "switching group") will make the decision to switch when the film is shown simultaneously in these three screening segments. But when the film goes through the distribution and screening stages in sequence, they have no choice. If they want to be the first to watch the film, they can only go to the cinema to watch it. Perhaps

40 COM (2003) 784 final, 3–5.

41 Form 10-K annual report issued by MGM on the 24th, February, 2004, 31.

42 Also home video sector, ibid.

43 Thomas Elsaesser.

there are still some people who would rather wait until the DVD is on sale or when it is broadcast on TV to enjoy the movie than go to the cinema to watch it in the first release period ("non-cinema audience"). True movie lovers ("movie fans") might choose to watch movies in the cinema even when they can buy DVDS or watch movies on TV, because they value more the effects provided by the big screen and other services that come with the cinema, which neither DVD discs nor TV can offer them. When a film passes through the screening process one after another in order to obtain the maximum profit, the right to turn to the group is deprived to some extent. Therefore, the screening chain is actually a way for group or family audio-visual product operators and television operators to provide subsidies to movie fans. This kind of subsidy is actually what competition law strives to avoid. However, the undeniable fact is that both the European Union and China recognize the legitimacy of the exhibition chain.

In 1980, ECJ decided that the exclusive assignee of the performing right in a film for the whole of a Member State may therefore rely upon his right against cable television diffusion companies which have transmitted that film on their diffusion network having received it from a television broadcasting station established in another Member State, without thereby infringing Community law.[44] ECJ believed,

> On the one hand, they highlight the fact that the right of a copyright owner and his assigns to require fees for any showing of a film is part of the essential function of copyright in this type of literary and artistic work. On the other hand, they demonstrate that the exploitation of copyright in films and the fees attaching thereto cannot be regulated without regard being had to the possibility of television broadcasts of those films.[45]

Here, ECJ firstly emphasized the nature of film distribution and exhibition as an exploitation of copyright law, which was a qualification listed in Article 30 of EC Treaty. Thereafter, ECJ implied the chain exhibition market confirms to the legal expectation for the fees to be charged by copyright owner of a film.[46] In another words, the chain of exhibition was regarded as the reasonable means for the copyright owner of a film to claim economic interests.

In 1996, the High Court of Shanxi Province issued a judgement, which regarded the exhibition of a film by a TV channel as a violation of the exclusive film exhibition right entrusted upon the film distributor in Shanxi.[47]

---

[44] Case C-62/79 Coditel [1980] ECR 881 §17.

[45] Ibid.

[46] "Whilst Article 59 (note: present Article 49) of the Treaty prohibits restrictions upon freedom to provide services, it does not thereby encompass limits upon the exercise of certain economic activities which have their origin in the application of national legislation for the protection of intellectual property, save where such application constitutes a means of arbitrary discrimination or a disguised restriction on trade between Member States. Such would be the case if that application enabled parties to an assignment of copyright to create artificial barriers to trade between Member States." Ibid. Please also see Goyder, 311.

[47] Case Shanxi Film Company vs. Bureau of Radio and Television of Linfen City on the 26th, April, 1996. See Legal Practices Institute of the Supreme Court of China, Edited Cases of People's Court, IP Volume, 1st Edition, Beijing 2000, 112–117. A similar case please also find in Legal Practices Institute of the Supreme Court of China, 108–112.

Although the judgements above were issued mainly on the ground of copyright law, ECJ also touched upon the freedom of service providing and competition issues but let the economic justification of this exhibition chain override all. With the concern overwhelmingly on copyright, the switching group actually is forced into the cinemas to subsidize the film lovers and the cinema exhibitors.

However, what is the damage the exhibition chain adopted by the film producer could inflict on the switching group? The cinema ticket price is normally cheaper than the selling price of DVD or other home video products, why the exhibition chain still maximize the profit of the film producers at the cost of the switching group?

The cinema exhibition of a film requires entrance fee for everyone who wants to enjoy the film in the cinema while a sold DVD can satisfy several people's interests in this film via the fair use or private use exception established by the copyright law in China as well as in EU countries.[48] If the film producer delays the offer of the DVD to the switching group and the non-cinema goers, he can theoretically successfully force every member in the switching group to see the film in the cinema while still maintains the profit of DVD sale from the non-cinema goers or those dead hard cinema lovers who want a DVD of the film which they have seen before. If the fair use or private use system in the copyright law make a DVD to be enjoyed by three or four peoples, in view of the present pricing system of a traditional cinema and DVD price of a popular film,[49] the producer actually obtains more from the tickets sold to the switching group than the profit obtained from the DVD sold to them.

However, even under the present exhibition system, the Hollywood major like MGM, saw a worldwide cinema exhibition revenues in 2003 decreased by USD 40.4 million, or 15%, to USD 220.9 million while a worldwide home video revenues in the same period an increase by USD 292.4 million, or 39%, to USD 1051.6 million. Additionally, in 2003, worldwide DVD sales of MGM increased to USD 916.1 million, or 58%, from USD 579.5 million in 2002.[50] If this trend goes on to the point that a substantial part of switching group turns into non-cinema goers who just buy DVD or other home video products, there is no reason why the producer still prefer the exhibition chain instead of doing them simultaneously. This potential danger offers a very logical incentive for the film makers to go into integrations between these three film exhibition sector or even with the communications sector as well as the film production sector, which leads the convergence in the media industry to a level never imagined of before, which is pushed by technology as well as by economic considerations. This is the underlying reason for alliances and mergers between companies which are active in sectors of the economy that used to be separate such as television and telecommunications. Operations like AOL/ Time Warner, Vivendi/Seagram/Canal+, Vivendi/Vodafone for the creation of portal

[48] Article 22, Authors' Rights Law of China; See Zhi Wei, 73–75; Article 10, the Rental Directive; Article 5, the Copyright Directive. See Pascal Kamina, 88, 111, 258, 260, and 261.

[49] The ticket price for a film is CHF 12 or CHF 18 while the price of a DVD can be ranged from CHF 19 to CHF 39 in switzerland in 2004, for instance.

[50] Form 10-K annual report issued by MGM on the 24th, February, 2004, 40, and 41.

Vizzavi or the acquisition of Dutch entertainment producer Endemol by the Spanish telecom company Telefonica clearly illustrate this trend in EU.[51]

In fact, although technology has led to the integration of film screening channels, it still has not shaken the leading position of cinema screening in the film screening market. Although the time it takes for a film to pass through each chain in the traditional screening chain is getting shorter and shorter, cinema screenings still occupy an upstream position in the film screening chain. Unless a film gives up the cinema market, the performance of the cinema market will have a decisive impact on the performance of the screening market in other chains of the film.

Moreover, in China, the potential of the cinema screening market is still very huge. Despite the significant achievements in the development of China's film industry, there is still considerable room for growth in the supply of quality films and cinema facilities in the future. On one hand, with the improvement of domestic film creation capabilities and the increase in import film quotas, coupled with the development of terminal cinema construction, the number of quality films shown in cinemas is expected to further increase. On the other hand, the screen density in China is still significantly lower than in countries like the United States. China has 29.78 screens per one million people, while the United States has 124 screens per one million people. Moreover, in terms of regional supply of cinemas, modern multiplex theaters located in prominent business districts will still experience a certain degree of supply scarcity. The development of this potential requires the efforts of the film industry's regulatory authorities and the film industry itself. At the beginning of this century, in order to solve the problem of insufficient audiences in the film screening market, cinemas across China have been piloting the "half-price on Tuesdays" policy, offering audiences a half-price discount for watching films throughout the day on Tuesdays to attract them back to the cinema. On 15 September 2012, Wang Quan'an's film "White Deer Plain" premiered and was a huge box office hit. Following the box office receipts of the four highly popular imported blockbusters "The Expendables", "Plutmetheus", "The Dark Knight Rises" and "The Amazing Spider-Man" for a whole week, it showed a strong upward trend in the market. At around 7:50 p.m. on Tuesday, September 18, 2012, the author went to the Wanda Cinema in Beijing CBD to watch the 8:05 screening of "White Deer Plain" and learned that all the tickets for this screening had been sold out. This, on the one hand, indicated the popularity of the domestic film "White Deer Plain", and on the other hand, showed that audiences are still quite fond of the "half-price on Tuesdays" movie ticket policy. The policy of "half price on Tuesdays" draws on foreign practices, demonstrating the charm of cinemas as a traditional way of making films.

The box office success of "White Deer Plain" on Tuesday, to some extent, also indicates that film ticket prices in China are relatively high to some extent. Why? Although there are multiple distribution and screening methods for Chinese films in law, such as cinemas, home audio-visual products, pay TV channels, public TV channels, and online broadcasting, as well as the distribution and screening chains formed by these methods, due to the relatively weak protection of the copyright of film and

[51] See Miguel Mendes Pereira.

television works in China, producers are not very optimistic about the profit window of cinemas in the future. This approach of achieving everything at once enables the revenue that could have been dispersed across multiple screening Windows to be fully concentrated in the cinema screening Windows. This will inevitably push up the ticket prices in the cinema screening market. The high ticket prices in cinemas have provided sufficient social soil for piracy, reducing the moral sense of guilt for purchasing pirated goods to some extent.

With the development of video websites as a form of online distribution, video websites have increasingly become an important window for film distribution and screening. In addition to professional video websites such as Youku, Tudou, Liujianfang and Ile.com, comprehensive portal websites or search service websites represented by Sohu and Baidu have also begun to take video websites as their important business areas. Meanwhile, the development of Web 2.0 also enables users to upload content for video websites by themselves, and the content of video websites is extremely rich. But at the same time, this way of providing content on video websites has also brought great problems to copyright protection. Although on the one hand, users' independent uploading of content to video websites can, in a certain sense, promote the circulation of a certain program, film, television drama or movie, thereby having a certain degree of promotional function; However, for a film, this promotional effect is achieved by disrupting the channels through which the film is broadcast on the Internet, which is extremely destructive to the film. Therefore, the film industry has always been extremely concerned about copyright issues on the Internet.

On the other hand, the issue of high ticket prices has always been a problem that the Chinese film industry must confront. One of the reasons for the high ticket prices is that rampant piracy has deprived movies of other screening channels. The problem of piracy on the Internet has increasingly become a major issue. In this sense, China needs to respond to the relationship between the Internet and copyright at least to some extent. On 10 May 2006, the 135th executive meeting of The State Council adopted the Regulations on the Protection of Information Network Dissemination Rights, which was promulgated by State Council Decree No. 468 on 18 May 2006, and came into effect on 1 July 2006 (the "Internet Dissemination Regulations" ). Article 2 of the Internet Disseminations Regulations stipulates: "The right of information network dissemination enjoyed by the right holder is protected by the Copyright Law and these Regulations." Except as otherwise provided by laws and administrative regulations, any organization or individual that provides others' works, performances or audio-visual products to the public through information networks shall obtain the permission of the right holder and pay remuneration. This regulation clarifies the boundaries of the dissemination of works through the Internet and the ownership of rights. Based on this, the Internet Disseminations Regulations returned the right to screen films via the Internet to production companies, and the Internet gradually became a screening window for films. On September 4 2007, in a case where the Intermediate People's Court of Jinhua, Zhejiang Province, made a judgment on infringement acts that occurred before the implementation of the Internet Disseminations Regulations. Although according to Article 47, Paragraph 1 of the

Copyright Law, those who reproduce, distribute, perform, screen, broadcast, compile or disseminate their works to the public through information networks without the permission of the copyright owner shall bear civil liabilities such as ceasing infringement and compensating for losses. However, due to the circumstances of the online communication market at that time, the court did not support the plaintiff's claim for high compensation. Instead, it merely ordered the defendant to pay the plaintiff a total of 20,000 yuan for economic losses and reasonable expenses incurred in stopping the infringement. Although according to Article 47, Paragraph 1 of the Copyright Law, those who reproduce, distribute, perform, screen, broadcast, compile or disseminate their works to the public through information networks without the permission of the copyright owner shall bear civil liabilities such as ceasing infringement and compensating for losses. However, due to the circumstances of the online communication market at that time, the court did not support the plaintiff's claim for high compensation. Instead, it merely ordered the defendant to pay the plaintiff a total of 20,000 yuan for economic losses and reasonable expenses incurred in stopping the infringement.[52] Furthermore, in another lawsuit filed against the same defendant for a similar cause of action, the plaintiff only received compensation of 10,000 yuan.[53] Judging from these two judgments, one of the reasons why the plaintiff's claim for the amount of compensation is difficult to be supported is that the court was cautious in defining the plaintiff's losses. After the passage of the "Regulations on the Protection of the Right of Communication through Information Network", it has stipulated considerable administrative penalties for acts of infringing copyright through the Internet. If strictly enforced, it will form a deterrent to the phenomenon of infringing film copyright through the Internet.

## 2.4 *Convergence for Film Industry*

Distribution and screening are very important links for the film industry. As for the competition law itself, in an ideal situation, the distribution and screening stages should be separated from the production stage to avoid adverse effects on the competition of the entire film market when the leading enterprises in the distribution and screening stages enter the production stage. However, this ideal situation has to confront a reality: Firstly, if there exists a global market, this global market is already dominated by Hollywood. The ideal competitive situation no longer exists. Secondly, for latecomers such as the European Union and China, integrating the issuance market and, to some extent, encouraging the integration of the issuance and setup stages has

[52] For details, please refer to the Civil Judgment on Copyright Infringement Dispute between the Plaintiff, Beijing Ciwen Film and Television Production Co., Ltd., and the Defendant, Jinhua Weite Network Information Co., Ltd. ( (2007) Jinzhong Min SAN Chu Zi No. 61).

[53] For details, please refer to the Civil Judgment No. 245 of 2007 issued by the Higher People's Court of Zhejiang Province.

also become one of the policy orientations. Finally, the heavy reliance of film production on financing makes the distribution channels that can directly face the screening stage inevitably have to be connected to the film production stage, thus making the integration of the film industry an inherent demand of the film industry.

China's Anti-Monopoly Law was promulgated in 2008. The problem China is facing is how to establish a competitive film industry and form a truly meaningful film market. After joining the World Trade Organization, given the predicament that the film industry is not yet globally competitive, horizontal and vertical integration has become an option for regulatory agencies and film industry players.

In 1993, Shanghai Yongle Co., Ltd. ("Yongle") became a truly legal film company and was established in Shanghai. Yongle is a comprehensive company integrating film production, film distribution and film screening. As the corporate restructuring of Yongle successfully drove the growth of its box office, film companies in other provinces and cities also rushed to follow suit. Meanwhile, the Ministry of Radio, Film and Television also encourages vertical mergers of companies in the fields of film and television to form group companies. In 1996, film production, film distribution and television stations in Shanghai merged to form the first vertically operated group in the film and television field. Subsequently, five group companies integrating the film and television fields were also formed in other regions.

It seems that both the European Union and China have accepted the model of the major Hollywood studios. This interesting development may be deeply rooted in the proposition of protecting cultural diversity. However, purely focusing on the scale of the film industry might also harm the domestic film industry. The European Union has an existing consolidation control system to correct this negative impact, while China's Anti-Monopoly Law still awaits the introduction of various supporting measures for implementation. Although it may seem rash to implement competition law in the film and television field and maintain the competitiveness of the domestic film and television industry at the same time without fully considering its impact on market liberalization, it is never too early to think about the thorny problem in advance before it surfaces.

## *2.5 Rating System and Film Industry*

Film is regarded as a powerful media in the society. It is also a fact that the main part of the film goers is the adolescence.[54] Therefore, a balance, which could also effect its influence economically,[55] must be carefully kept between the freedom of speech

---

[54] FOCUS 2003, 6.

[55] The British Board of Film Censors, which had imposed an initial rating of '12' on the film changed it to the newly introduced '12A' rating thereby allowing children below 12 to see the film accompanied by an adult. In its twelfth week of release, shown in 56 locations, *Spiderman* collected EUR 31,630 (£20,000) in box office receipts, compared to week 13, after the implementation of the new rating, where in 305 locations the film took considerably more—EUR 428,590 (£271,000). It

and the protection of minors.[56] Rating system, which allocates the subgroups of the film audience according to the film content, may offer an opportunity for the State to strike such a balance.

The consumers in the film market are the audiences. Among the audience, teenagers or minors are the main body. Therefore, if movies are regarded as commodities, the main target market of this commodity is teenagers. However, movie audiences include not only teenagers but also adults. Therefore, films that are harmful to children's physical and mental development but do not constitute content prohibited by law, although they cannot be shown to children, can be shown to adult audiences.

Under the premise that it can be ensured that this part of the content suitable for adults but not for children will not be shown to children, it can be shown to adult audiences. The rule for the segmentation of the film market confirmed or stipulated by this law is the classification system. The strictness of the classification system reflects the requirements of a country's laws for protecting minors. If the film classification system of a country is very strict, the range of films that are not suitable for minors to watch but suitable for adults should be wide, and the range of films that minors can watch should be correspondingly limited. If a film produced by a film production company cannot be shown to minors but only to adults, then the film loses the mainstream film market and its market return becomes a big problem. In both the member states of the European Union and the United States, there are films that can only be shown to people over 18 years old. Due to the loss of the youth market, the cost of such films cannot be recovered by cinema screening alone. Therefore, most of them are circulated in the market in the form of DVDS, and only adults can purchase or watch them in such markets. The restrictions of the cinema screening market and other screening channels make their economic gains not considerable. Therefore, the cost of such films is generally extremely low; otherwise, they would lose their commercial value in shooting. For films that target the adult market from the very beginning of their shooting, this risk of possibly losing the teenage market was originally within their expectations and therefore can be easily controlled. However, for those films that did not exclude the juvenile market at the time of production, their target audience is the mainstream market, and their shooting and production costs are correspondingly high, with the expectation of recovering the benefits. If it is eventually classified as a film that minors are not allowed to watch, its economic prospects will become dim. This kind of risk leads film production companies to conduct self-censorship of films during the shooting and production process. This kind of self-examination does not, to some extent, meet the creative requirements of the main creative personnel of the film. Moreover, such censorship does not necessarily rule out the risk that the film will be classified as an adult film when it is released and screened to the market after its successful production. Therefore, the classification system is actually also

is likely, however, that had this amendment to the 12 rating been implemented earlier the final box office cumulative would have been several million more. Ibid., 15.

[56] In Erfurt (Germany), a 19-year old boy murdered 17 people and in France where a teenager killed another teenager while replicating murder scenes taken from the feature film thriller *Scream*. See Olsberg|SPI / KEA European Affairs / KPMG, 27.

a kind of film censorship. This kind of review is based on the film screening stage, but it is reflected in the film production, distribution and screening stages, running through every link of the film industry chain. It is precisely this special kind of film censorship that this book discusses during the film screening process.

In fact, dividing legal film content into those suitable for minors and those suitable for adults is merely a simple dichotomy. Based on this simple dichotomy, most countries have further classified the group of minors. Some have divided it into three subgroups: those suitable for all children to watch, those suitable for children over 12 years old to watch, and those suitable for children over 16 years old to watch, thereby dividing the entire audience into four groups. In some countries or regions, minors are divided into two subgroups based on certain age standards, thereby dividing the entire audience into three subgroups. It should be noted here that these subgroups are not completely separate from each other but exist in a bucket form. For example, if a film is suitable for all minors to watch, then the film should also be suitable for all adults to watch; If the film is eventually classified for minors over 12 years old to watch, it is also suitable for all adults to watch. In this way, the lower the age of classification, the more people can watch the film. Without considering the audience's acceptance, its market potential will be greater. This practice of further dividing the group of minors takes into account the different mental and intellectual states of minors at different age stages, thereby better meeting the cultural needs of some minors. Therefore, the practice of further classifying the minor group on the basis of the simple dichotomy has become a common practice in the classification system.

On the premise of protecting the interests of minors, the more detailed the classification system is, the better it can meet the viewing needs of different age groups within the minor community. However, the more detailed the classification system is, the greater the difficulty of its implementation will be. Therefore, the classification is not the more detailed the better. Instead, each country and region stipulates or confirms the classification arrangements of industry organizations in the form of law based on the cultural traditions, legal traditions and public morality of its own jurisdiction. As a result, different countries and regions have formed different judgment criteria and age classification stages in terms of classification.

The legislative practice of the rating system for radio, film and television in was once tried on 25 March 1989, when the MRFT issued the "Notice on Implementing a Review and Screening Rating System for Some Films" (Guangfa Yingzi [1989] No. 201) (hereinafter referred to as the "Rating Notice"). The "Rating Notice" state: "In order to implement the important instructions in Document No. 14 of the Central Committee of the Communist Party of China in 1988 that 'a review and rating system for film and television works should be established, and clear regulations should be made on film and television works that are not suitable for primary and secondary school students to watch', and to protect the physical and mental health of the majority of primary and secondary school students, it was decided to implement a grading system for some films starting from 1 May this year." The Rating Notice stipulated that when the film review body of the MRFT—the Film Administration Bureau—reviews domestic and imported films respectively according to the standards, it should clearly define the following types of films that are "not suitable for children and teenagers to watch" (hereinafter referred to as "not suitable for children"): (1) Films with plots such as rape, theft, drug abuse, drug trafficking, prostitution, etc. (2) Any film that contains violent, murderous or fighting plots that are likely to cause a sense of terror among children and teenagers. (3) Any film that depicts sexual love and sexual behavior. (4) Any film that depicts social malformations. After the issuance of the "Grading Notice", the first film to be rated as "Not suitable for children" was "Widow's Village", produced by Zhujiang Film Studio in 1988. Although there were no scenes of "sex and sexual behavior" in this film, there were pictures that "showed social malformations", and thus it was regarded as "not suitable for children". This rating system, starting from protecting the interests of teenagers, actually holded that films could present content inappropriate for children, which was a major breakthrough in the film censorship system. However, on 17 December 2003, the SARFT issued the "Notice on Announcing the Abolition of Some Regulatory Documents on Radio, Film and Television", abolishing the rating Notice.

At the moment, China has no rating system available for the protection of the minors. Therefore, theoretically, the film must be made for everyone, including the boy who is just able to observe the things moving in front of him. In the meanwhile, since China has the obligation to import films, most of which are blockbusters from Hollywood. Thus, *Piano, Saving Private Ryan, Terminator III,* and *Spiderman* could enjoy the same audience without any restrictions as *Finding Nemo.*

It is quite unusual to let a 7 year child to decide what a director can say or show in his film. The censorship in this regard created many banned films which can only find the audience through the pirated DVDs or VCDs. With the development of technology and the explosive supply of graphic information in this world, it is hard to understand why film should be the only one chained for the content censorship, which discriminate nothing between the contents, which is illegal and prohibited by law, and the content, which is potentially harmful to the development of children. Here, the balance between freedom of speech and protection of minors must be reached via a new mechanism. In 2000, BRFT said she was drafting rating rules for the film exhibition.[57] It was reported this year that the rating rules will come out soon.[58] Although some film makers doubts whether the rule would offer more real freedom for film making,[59] it should be admitted that BRFT are beginning to withdraw the hand of total censorship from film making.

The current film censorship system actually cannot adapt to the development of the film industry and the requirements of market opening. There is no rating system, but it is necessary to regulate the content of the entire film industry to a certain extent. Therefore, all regulatory links related to the content must be carried out through

[57] Kuan Cheng.

[58] Shengxin Jiang.

[59] Jiang Wen, a famous director in China, said, "(to draft a rating system now in China is like) to decide the hair style for the one who has only two pieces of hair. It is meaningless to say which style of hair one wants to keep; you'd better let all the hair grows out beforehand." See Xi Ding.

the film review of the administrative link. At this point, the protection of minors is entirely a matter determined by the government. The government decides what films minors should watch and what they should not.

In fact, there is a complementary relationship between the legal prohibitions on film content and the rating system. In countries that implement a hierarchical system, whether it is the United States or France, the hierarchical system and the legal provisions regarding prohibited content belong to different systems. The rating system belongs to the segmented market, and the legal prohibition on content actually imposes necessary restrictions on the freedom of the form of film content. First of all, the purpose of the rating system is to protect minors. Therefore, within its framework, whether the rating decision of a film comes from an industry like the Motion Picture Association of America or a government agency like the French Ministry of Culture, to a considerable extent, it confirms the role of parental guardianship in the implementation of the rating system. In a sense, rating is a suggestion for the guardians of minors. From parents' advice to their accompaniment, it is actually a certain concretization of the way parents exercise guardianship, providing clear references for parents. Secondly, it is undeniable that the rating system also takes into account public order and good custom. For films that are not allowed to be watched by people under the age of 18, even if parents agree that minors can watch them, the law will not permit it. In a sense, this is not only a manifestation of public order and good custom, but also provides a connection point between the hierarchical permissive system and legal prohibitions. Finally, the content prohibited in films is derived from the general prohibitions of various countries. Such regulations impose restrictions on freedom of speech for various reasons.

Due to the differences in their legal traditions and historical and cultural origins, there are different regulations. For instance, in continental European countries, hate and Nazi rhetoric are legally prohibited, so of course such content cannot be contained in movies. In the United States, Nazi speech is not prohibited by law, and the freedom of speech granted by the First Amendment of its Constitution has almost a mythical status. Therefore, in the United States, the scope of what is prohibited by law is narrower than that in continental European countries. It should be noted that the hierarchical system is more related to the cultures of various countries than the restrictions on freedom of speech in their legal systems. Let's still take European countries and the United States as examples. The report published by KPMG mentioned above points out that the classification system in the United States is stricter than that in European countries. Generally speaking, due to historical and cultural origins, European countries take violence as the main factor considered when formulating classification standards. The United States, on the other hand, pays particular attention to human nudity and sexual aspects. Therefore, for the same film, it may receive different classifications in various countries. Sometimes, this difference is very large. For instance, the 1998 American film "Saving Private Ryan" was rated R by the Motion Picture Institute of America based on its realistic portrayal of war violence. However, in France, this film was rated U, meaning that anyone could watch it. Germany, also in Europe, has classified it as a film that can only be watched by audiences aged 16 and above. For another example, the 1994 film "The Shawshank Redemption" was rated

R by the Motion Picture Institute of America based on its portrayal of foul language and prison violence, while France classified it as U, meaning it was accessible to anyone. Germany, also in Europe, also rated it as a film that could be watched by audiences over the age of 12. On the other hand, European films such as Bertolucci's "Stealing Incense" in 1996 were rated as films accessible to audiences over 12 years old in Germany and as R-rated films in the United States. Another film by Bertorucci in 2003, "The Dreamer", was initially rated as NC-13 in the United States and was later edited to achieve an R rating. However, in France, "The Dreamer" was designated as a film suitable for audiences over the age of 12. The significant differences in the classification systems among different countries will have more or less an impact on the circulation of films in each country. Generally speaking, indeed, as pointed out in the KPMG report, the classification in the United States is stricter than that in Europe. This forms an interesting contrast with the relevant institutional regulations on freedom of speech. This situation has its deep-seated cultural reasons. The protection of minors' interests has always been strongly called for in the United States. Its combination with religious elements in American culture has led the United States to traditionally hold a conservative attitude towards movies, television and other contents. In a certain sense, this cultural conservative ideology has built a certain threshold for the American film market in terms of content, constituting a certain obstacle for European films to enter the American market.

It can be seen that the shielding effect of culture itself on foreign goods is stronger than that of law. The classification system precisely reflects the requirements of social culture for films in the form of legal recognition, refines the film market, and thereby strikes a balance between the development of the film industry and the need for the protection of minors. The prohibitive provisions of the law on certain contents cannot cover the functions of the classification system. Otherwise, it will either lead to too much prohibited content by law, which is not conducive to the development of the film industry, or fail to effectively protect the interests of teenagers and allow films that are not suitable for them to watch to circulate freely in the film market. Based on this, implementing a classification system among Chinese films might be a task that must be accomplished.

According to Article 20 Para. 1 Sentence 2 of the Film Industry Promotion Law, "if a film screening may cause physical or psychological discomfort to minors or other viewers, a warning should be provided." This stipulation should be in the exhibition chapter of the Film Industry Promotion Law. Interestingly, Article 20 thereof relates to the film screen licence, which embodies the legal significance of the film censorship of China. In this sense, this stipulation is of great significance that the film review institution should treat the film differently if it is not made for children. When Marvel film Wolverine was released in China after the Film Industry Promotion Law takes effect in 2017, cinemas posted the warning along with the posters. Naturally, some observers believe it be a kind of rating system with Chinese style. This interpretation seems aroused anxiety of the film regulator. After Wolverine released in 2017, not a single film was put on the screen with such a warning again. Even some volunteer warning suggestions from the influential web portal also disappeared. Apparently, it is hard to formally install some rating system in China's film regulatory regime for now.

## 2.6 *Improve the Accounting System for Film Enterprises.*

According to the annual report of Chinese film companies, cinema exhibition is an essential revenue collecting sector in the film business chain. The box office revenue of a film is normally for 90% of all the revenue this film could claim. IP protection may be an element to explain this situation, but not the only one.

Among cultural industries, the film industry is the leader. Improving the legal system of China's cultural industry, by accurately describing film companies in accounting practices, not only facilitates investors in utilizing capital markets to invest in the film industry but also holds significant importance for the enhancement of China's capital market and the healthy development of the Chinese film and television industry.

### 2.6.1 Revenue Model of Chinese Companies and Film Sales Cost Transfer

For film companies, the description of film revenue indicates the profitability of film production and distribution business, helping investors decide whether to invest in a particular film company.

Currently, China's prominent piracy issue leads to a lack of subsequent sales revenue from audiovisual copyrights (including broadcasting by TV stations, sales of audiovisual products, and online video-on-demand channels) after the film's release. Although the situation has improved somewhat, film sales revenue still primarily comes from box office earnings. Thus, each film company focuses on cinema box office during the film's release. Additionally, due to the unique nature of films as cultural consumption products and the consumption habits of Chinese audiences, box office revenue is usually realized during the strong period in the weeks following the film's release, resulting in a corresponding concentration of sales costs during this period. For films primarily released domestically, most box office revenue is generally generated within 3 to 6 weeks post-release, with the bulk of sales costs recognized during this time. For a few films with a high proportion of foreign distribution income, due to the longer overseas market release cycles, total overseas box office earnings and sales costs are typically realized within 1 to 2 years.

### 2.6.2 Limitations of the "Accounting Methods for Film Enterprises"

In view of the uniqueness of film sales revenue realization and the transfer of sales costs, on 9 December 2004 the Ministry of Finance has issued the Accounting Rules for Film Enterprises, which includes corresponding provisions: "The costs of sales for films should be entirely transferred within a period not exceeding 24 months from the date they meet the income recognition conditions (i.e., obtaining the film public screening license). If the company holds the copyright for the film, only a nominal value of one yuan should be retained and recorded as inventory." This provision reflects the current state of the film sales market for film companies in China and embodies the principle of prudence in financial processing during implementation.

However, the financial statements prepared according to this accounting treatment do not effectively reflect the core business of film enterprises. Generally speaking, under the diversified broadcasting channel situation, a film company's significant competitive advantage is not only reflected in the box office of newly released films but also in its vast library of films that have already been screened. According to China's accounting methods, films for which the film company holds copyright and has transferred sales costs are only recorded at a nominal value of one yuan in inventory; thus, the financial statements based on this principle cannot reflect the true market value of the film company's assets, failing to provide investors with accurate financial information and not showcasing its real industrial competitiveness in the capital market.

Moreover, the rapid transfer of film sales income in accounting arrangements further encourages film companies to pursue short-term box office revenue unilaterally. This leads film companies to focus more on immediate economic income when producing films, neglecting the exploration of the long-term viability of films, which is detrimental to the healthy development of the Chinese film industry.

### 2.6.3 Amending the Accounting Rules for Film Enterprises Will Facilitate Positive Incentives for Chinese Film Companies

Currently, the development of the Chinese film market is encouraging, with box office revenues experiencing rapid growth since surpassing 10 billion RMB in 2010. Measured by box office figures, the market share of domestic films in the Chinese film market is higher than that of imported films, indicating that the domestic film industry remains a formidable force in the market. In contrast to the dominance of Hollywood companies in the EU film market, this market development pattern is reassuring.

However, it should be noted that despite domestic films generating higher box office revenues than imported films, there are still certain uncertainties. For instance, from January to September 2014, a significant proportion of the top-grossing domestic films were co-productions. According to the "Closer Economic Partnership Arrangement" signed between Chinese mainland and Hong Kong, films co-produced between Hong Kong and Chinese mainland should be considered domestic films for distribution in Chinese mainland, as long as at least one-third of the crew members are from Chinese mainland, and the story and main characters are related to the mainland. Since reaching trade arrangements with Hong Kong, co-productions have accounted for a large share of box office revenues for domestic films.

Furthermore, on average, imported films (especially Hollywood blockbusters) perform better than domestic films. For example, from January to September 2014, the highest-grossing film was the American film "Transformers 4," which surpassed the box office revenue of the domestic co-production "Journey to the West: Conquering the Demons" by over 900 million RMB, while the latter's total box office revenue in Chinese mainland was just over one billion. Additionally, the total box office revenue of the top ten imported films exceeds that of the top ten domestic films (including co-productions). This indicates that there is still room for improvement in the market strength of domestic films.

Finally, the current quota system for imported films restricts the number of foreign films entering the mainland Chinese market and favors domestic films in scheduling arrangements. In response, the United States first challenged China's film import and distribution system in 2009 through rulings on publications, and later in 2012 reached a memorandum with China to increase the import of specialty films and raised its box office revenue-sharing ratio. Thus, the relaxation of import quotas and the entry of more foreign films into the Chinese market seems to be a trend. The increasingly fierce competition from foreign films may impact the market share of domestic film companies.

At the same time, in the face of increasingly fierce competition from overseas films, Chinese cinema does indeed face a shortage of high-quality films. While the film market is expanding, there are instances where box office revenue is inversely proportional to audience ratings. This situation further engenders a tendency for production companies to neglect film quality and long-term viability, damaging the reputation of domestic films among moviegoers and hindering the long-term development of the Chinese film industry.

Therefore, revising the Accounting Rules for Film Enterprises would benefit the long-term development of the film industry. The film industry, as the most promising sector of the cultural industry, plays a benchmark role in the establishment and improvement of legal systems for cultural industries. In response to the development trends of the Chinese film market, it is necessary to encourage Chinese film companies to produce high-quality and long-lasting films through institutional design and policy choices. For instance, allowing Chinese film companies to extend the duration over which film sales costs can be amortized, while also enabling these companies to evaluate and price films with copyright based on their market value, would not only promote transparency in the capital market and guide more professional investments towards the film industry, but also steer Chinese film companies towards producing higher quality and more sustainable films, thus promoting the long-term development of the Chinese film industry and helping to safeguard the overall cultural security of China.

## 3 Reference to the Accounting System of International Capital Market Film Companies

The film industry in Western countries has a long history of industrialization, and correspondingly, their accounting standards reflect the scrutiny of mature capital markets on the assets of film companies. This is beneficial for film companies to highlight their core assets and transparency.

In the United States, the film library is one of the important assets of film companies, which is recognized in the American accounting system. For example, The Walt Disney Company classifies its film library under the Studio Entertainment division, allowing it to be accurately reflected in financial statements.[60] The Studio Entertainment division produces and acquires feature films, animated films, movies released directly as audio-visual products, music recordings, and stage plays. Through the Studio Entertainment division, Disney produces and acquires films for theaters, home entertainment, and television markets, including those made and acquired for its movie and TV series library.[61] In Disney's "Intangible Assets" category, "Copyrights and Other Character Rights" make up a significant portion. In the fiscal year 2010, Disney's net "Intangible Assets" amounted to $5.081 billion, with "Copyrights and Other Character Rights" valued at $3.118 billion before depreciation. Meanwhile, the overall amortization value of "Intangible Assets" was only $360 million.[62] The balance sheet shows that Disney's total assets amount to $69.206 billion, with total equity of $37.519 billion.[63] This indicates that "Copyrights and Other Character Rights," including the rights to the films it has produced, represents a relatively high proportion of Disney's total assets and equity, accurately reflecting Disney's competitive strength and providing reliable reference for investors observing the performance of Disney's Studio Entertainment division.

Chinese film companies listed in the U.S. also accurately depict their assets and profitability. In the prospectus of Bona Film Group, the film distribution rights it acquired were reflected as $5,550,394 in the balance sheet dated December 31, 2009,[64] while the film production costs for the same period were reflected as $19,528,560, with total assets of $67,028,414 and total equity of $20,168,976.[65] According to the annual report filed with the U.S. Securities and Exchange Commission by Bona Film on June 28, 2011, as of December 31, 2010, Bona Film's film distribution rights were valued at $2,265,601, film production costs at $64,815,878, and prepaid film production costs at $484,848. The acquired intangible assets amounted to $2,293,744, with total assets of $231,236,516 and total equity of $160,072,166.[66]

[60] Disney submitted its FORM 10-K filing to the U.S. Securities and Exchange Commission for the fiscal year ending October 2, 2010, page 22.

[61] Ibid., p. 13.

[62] Ibid., p. 103.

[63] Ibid., p. 65.

[64] Prospectus of Bona Film Group Limited, filed on December 8, 2010, F 23.

[65] Ibid., p.64.

[66] Form 20-F filed by Bona Film Group Limited on June 28, 2011, F 2, F 3.

Thus, the assets formed by Bona Film Group's core business had been clearly reflected in the balance sheet. As a company whose core business is film distribution, Bona Film Group generates distribution revenue shortly after a film is released. At the same time, Bona Film Group also earns advertising revenue through product placements, pre-show ads, posters, and film promotions. Additionally, Bona Film Group generates revenue through participation in distribution and obtains sublicensing income by acquiring distribution rights for certain films.

In terms of accounting treatment, the valuation of Bona Film Group's distribution rights includes the unamortized portion of the cost of acquiring film distribution rights; the films here can either be completed films or films still in production. In some cases, Bona Film Group shares the net profits of the film with producers but does not own the film's copyrights. The amortization of the cost of acquiring film distribution rights is realized through forecasting on a per film basis. This amortization is based on the ratio of revenue generated in the current year to the management's estimate of the total revenue expected from the film through theatrical release and sublicensing. The expected final revenue for a film includes income from all markets and regions, encompassing revenue from theatrical screenings, home video sales, and licensing fees charged to television stations or pay channels. The expected final revenue for the film represents the estimated income within a period not exceeding ten years after the film's premiere, and this can be adjusted annually.

The production costs of films include the expenses of Bona Film Group for the production of movies and the acquisition of partial copyrights. The films referred to here can be either completed films or those still in production. For films that have been released or completed, the costs are capitalized and amortized based on individual film projections, similar to the treatment of distribution rights.[67]

Bona Film Group conducts annual impairment reviews of distribution rights and production costs. Such impairment reviews must also be conducted when events or changes occur that make the associated amounts of distribution rights and production costs unrecoverable. The valuation of distribution rights and production costs is reviewed on a film-by-film basis. The fair value of a film is determined based on management's estimates of future income and some form of cash flow discounting. Through the aforementioned accounting treatment, Bona Film Group presents its core business clearly as film distribution while also engaging in film production and cinema operations.

In contrast, Huayi Brothers, which was listed on China's Growth Enterprise Market during the same period, could not describe its film production business under assets and had to clarify it under "inventory." Additionally, China's accounting system does not provide a description of copyrights for films that have been produced under intangible assets, and compared to the ten-year period for the transfer of film sales costs in the U.S., the much shorter transfer period for sales costs does not reflect the reality of the extended profitability lifespan of films after diversification in the film screening chain. Therefore, before pushing film companies into the capital market, it is essential to establish an accounting system that can accurately reflect the

[67] Ibid., F 15.

assets and strength of film companies, enabling clear communication of their assets and business to investors.

In summary, the current Accounting Rules for Film Enterprises implemented in China does not adequately reflect the state of development in the Chinese film market. It requires the following adjustments to meet the intrinsic needs of the film industry in China, promote the healthy development of the film industry, and build a more friendly market environment for its growth:

First, extend the period for recognizing film sales costs to encourage film companies to explore the potential of their works and to consider the long-term viability of their products from the outset of production.

Second, for works that companies still hold copyright to, allow them to estimate their market value rather than listing them as inventory at a nominal price of one yuan. This change more accurately reflects the company's performance and competitiveness. In the context of the development of new media such as the internet, this modification is particularly important for film companies as copyright holders of their works.

As a vibrant cultural industry, film's social influence and cultural penetration should not be underestimated; thus, certain policy and legal support is necessary. As an industry, it is also unrealistic for regulatory authorities to take over the specific creative activities of film companies. In the face of fierce competition and the growing spiritual demands of the public, there is indeed a need to encourage film companies to produce high-quality works with lasting appeal. However, in addition to providing fair industry support, it is also critical to utilize existing market mechanisms to establish an internal system that encourages film companies to pursue product quality and long-term viability.

## 4 The System for the Special Fund for the Development of the National Film Industry to Be Legislated and Clarified

The Film Industry Promotion Law has been passed. However, on one hand, the relevant provisions for film promotion are vague, particularly the core principle of providing subsidies for film screenings, which has not been established in the draft law. On the other hand, there exists a special fund system for the development of the national film industry ("special fund"). This important support measure for the film industry is not currently reflected in the legal text, and there are some pitfalls in practice that urgently require reform. Although the current prosperity of the film market seems to indicate that support for the film industry is unnecessary, the booming box office does not imply the flourishing of the Chinese film industry, nor does it reflect the competitiveness of domestic films. There is a stark contrast between the actual competitiveness of Chinese domestic films and the sharply rising annual box office in China, which precisely underscores the need for legislative confirmation of this system. The absence of this system not only renders the "promotion" purpose of the Film Industry Promotion Law ineffective, wasting a valuable opportunity for the rule of unfolded law in the film sector, but also hinders the reform and balanced development of the Chinese film industry.

## *4.1 Fund of the Film Industry Promotion–Subsidy from Distribution/Exhibition Sector to Prduction Sector*

The special funds established from subsidies sourced from the film exhibition or broadcasting sector reflect an important principle of film support: the screening or broadcasting sector gives back to the film industry, driving the development of the local film industry through the growth of the film market itself. This is also a core principle of film promotion legal systems in major Western countries such as France and Germany.

According to the German Film Promotion Act (Filmförderungsgesetz, FFG), the German Federal Film Board (Filmförderungsanstalt, FFA) is specifically responsible for film promotion at the federal level in Germany, with its funding derived from a fund collected based on the revenue generated at various stages of the film income chain as stipulated by the Film Promotion Act. Previously, the law only mandated the collection of funds from cinema operating revenue and DVD sales revenue. At the same time, the German Film Board entered into agreements with public broadcasters, requiring them to invest a certain amount annually in the production of German films. In June 2010, the Film Promotion Act was reformed, expanding the scope of the fund collection to include television stations and pay-per-view video service providers, making their financial support for films a statutory obligation rather than a result of public negotiation.

In France, nearly 75% of funding sources (in terms of the government budget provided) come either from taxes and fees levied on the revenue of public or private broadcasters or from direct investments by these broadcasters in films. The remaining share comes from taxes collected on all movie tickets sold for films distributed in France. In other words, the basic principle of the French system is based on a "compulsory levy" rooted in service consumption (primarily service consumption, as reflected by taxes on movie tickets), which leads to a cycle of internal redistribution.

So, why emphasize the feedback loop from the film screening or broadcasting stage to the film industry?

On one hand, there is a conflict of interest between the production phase of the film industry and the distribution and screening phase. For distributors and exhibitors, whether the films come from Hollywood or are domestically produced makes no difference as long as they meet market demands; they are indifferent to the economic benefits. However, local filmmakers hope that domestic films will capture the largest market share. In this sense, the rise in box office revenue merely indicates the prosperity of the distribution and screening stages and does not reflect the actual competitiveness of a country's film production sector. Currently, in China's state-owned box office composition, although the proportion of domestic films (including co-productions) is slightly higher than that of imported films, this has been achieved under the protection of the import quota system and other protective measures for domestic films, and does not reflect the true competitiveness of Chinese cinema. Moreover, in recent global film festivals, the competitiveness of domestic Chinese films has evidently declined, contrasting sharply with the annual surge in China's box office revenue; in the global film trade arena, Chinese cinema hasn't made substantial breakthroughs either. Therefore, establishing a legal system where the screening or broadcasting phase provides feedback to the film industry is more necessary than ever today, as China's annual box office revenue surpasses RMB 40 billion. Compared to establishing a film support fund through separate government allocations, specialized funds represent a redistribution cycle within the film industry that does not increase the fiscal burden on external enterprises or individuals, and overall, it doesn't add to the burden of the film industry. By requiring the screening or broadcasting phases to support the film industry, the intention is to balance the interests of local production, distribution, and screening sectors, thereby promoting and supporting the domestic film industry. Given the current market realities, it is urgent and necessary for the Film Industry Promotion Law to clarify this.

On the other hand, it must be acknowledged that the global film market and international film trade are dominated by the American film industry, represented by Hollywood. At this point, the exhibition or broadcasting segment feeds back into the film industry system, which indirectly means that part of the box office revenue from American films in a country's film market is used to support the local film industry, serving as an invisible measure of protection for domestic industries. This is especially true when box office revenue from American films holds a dominant position in a country's total film box office income. In future bilateral or multilateral negotiations, China's current domestic film protection measures cannot remain unchanged. To prepare for the future, establishing a legal system for special funds based on the principle of the exhibition or broadcasting segment feeding back into the film industry will provide necessary legal leverage for China in future film trade negotiations and further promote the development of Chinese film trade on the basis of enhancing the local film industry.

## *4.2 Present Regime to Be Reorganised*

The practice of special funds in China lacks legal support, exhibiting a strong administrative character and presenting two main issues.

On one hand, the allocation of special funds lacks transparent and detailed procedural institutional support. The special funds are managed by the management committees established by the central and provincial levels according to their responsibilities. Currently considered as fiscal funds, the Ministry of Finance has detailed and clear regulations for their collection. However, existing administrative regulations and departmental rules only outline their applicable scope, lacking a selection mechanism for applicable projects and definitive selection criteria. As a result, the disbursement of special funds mainly reflects the judgment and support direction of government authorities towards the film industry, lacking independant and systematic institutional backing. Thus far, special funds mainly finance the construction of cinemas and the upgrading of related facilities, while there is no public and transparent legal system to support funding for high-quality projects concerning scripts and film production. Additionally, the channels for private producers to access special funds and premium projects are not adequately openned at all. This renders the impact of the special funds system on the film production process insignificant, unable to effectively provide industrial support as it is expected to deliver.

On the other hand, special funds carry a strong fiscal funding character, and their expenditure forms are strictly restricted. As a representation of the principle that supports the film industry through the screening process, special funds are limited to the forms of fiscal funds, specifically manifested as support from the "government treasury" to certain cinemas and films, and cannot effectively promote the development of the film industry—especially the production sector—in a manner acceptable to the film market. For instance, special funds cannot enter selected projects in the form of investments, making it impossible to integrate supportive funds for the development of the film industry, which is also detrimental to the sustainable development of the special funds themselves. In contrast, Germany's film fund system and France's National Centre for Cinema operate and manage film support funds through funding mechanisms, demonstrating significant promotional effects and integrating local film industry strengths, thereby benefiting the development of the local film industry.

The Chinese film market is undoubtedly vast, and the capital pouring into the film industry is also considerably abundant. With the annual box office of Chinese films exceeding one billion and continuing to rise, both the industry and regulatory agencies have strong confidence in the future of Chinese cinema. However, this does not change the reality that the domestic film industry still exists under trade protection conditions, and professional film capital is still in the process of cultivation. In 2016, the growth of box office revenue in China slowed, and the appeal of domestic films to audiences has also declined. In the first half of the year, the box office performance of domestic films was only slightly better than that of imported films, raising serious concerns about the market performance of domestic films. The issues caused by hot money in the film sector have also alerted industry insiders. In this context, if the principle of the film screening or broadcasting process supporting the film industry continues to be ignored during the implementation of the Film Industry Promotion Law, the effective promotion of outstanding domestic films will be limited to "declarative" provisions, and the growth of the film market may only be something as vanity, failing to provide strong support for the Chinese film industry and hindering the growth and development of professional film capital. This also adversely affects China's deeper market opening based on a strong film industry foundation, which may render the intentions of the Film Industry Promotion Law ineffective. Focusing solely on regulating the film industry cannot resolve the current issues in the film market's development and cannot advance deeper reforms and development of the Chinese film industry.

## 4.3 Possible Way Out

From the perspective of legislative logic and the actual needs and conditions of the Chinese film industry and market, based on the principle of the film screening or broadcast segment supporting the Chinese film industry, it is necessary to clearly establish a special fund system for the implementation of the Film Industry Promotion Law, including special funding for quality films, clarifying the allocation mechanism for special funds, and reforming the existing proprietary fund operation model. These are tasks that need to be completed under the Film Industry Promotion Law.

Firstly, the implementation regulations to the Film Industry Promotion Law should clarify the principle of film screening or broadcasting supporting the Chinese film industry. Therefore, it is suggested to stipulate: "The State takes necessary measures to promote the development of the film market, so as to facilitate the balanced development of the film production, distribution, and screening industries, thereby promoting the prosperity of the Chinese film industry."

Secondly, the implementation regulations to the Film Industry Promotion Law should clarify the system of film screening or broadcasting supporting the Chinese film industry. On one hand, it is necessary to encourage screening enterprises to invest in the film production industry. Hence, it is suggested that the implementation regulations stipulate: "The State encourages the operating units of the broadcasting and television industry and the Internet industry to invest in the film production industry and to establish and improve relevant institutional guarantees." On the other hand, it is important to legally establish the sources of special funds and include quality film special funds within that. Thus, it is suggested that the implementation regulations include: "Commercial film screening units must remit 5% of their box office revenue, and television stations that receive 80% financial support for their operational costs must remit 3% of their pure advertising revenue to establish a national special fund for the development of film undertakings. The specific methods for the collection and exemption of this special fund shall be jointly issued and implemented by the State Council's film management department and the finance department."

Finally, it is necessary to clarify the management and operational system of special funds in the implementation regulations of the Film Industry Promotion Law, and to implement the support for the film industry through a specific fund system. Currently, under the "treasury" support model of special funds, strict fiscal expenditure regulations prevent effective capture of the inherent demands of the film industry, and investments do not generate self-sustaining "blood supply." Its singular support method fails to integrate resources in the film industry, missing the opportunity to establish a self-sustaining development mechanism for Chinese cinema. Such a self-sustaining development mechanism will inevitably establish an effective self-regulatory mechanism that the Chinese film industry urgently needs. Therefore, it is essential to establish and reform the management and use system of special funds in law. The current special funds office has already conducted reliable and precise book of statistics on national box office revenues through the ticketing system implemented in cinemas nationwide and, based on this, the film regulatory authorities have cracked down on market violations such as box office fraud. If further progress could be made by granting the special funds office the right to select film production projects for funding based on publicly transparent rules, and by restructuring it into a fund model (special fund) for supportive investments, it might establish the self-regulatory mechanisms currently missing in the Chinese film industry through investments or rewards from the special fund. This could lead to the realization of an industry self-regulation mechanism in the film sector, establishing industry self-regulatory organizations similar to the American Film Producers Association, allowing film regulators to return to their regulatory role. This would enable regulatory oversight of the entire industry based on the self-regulation enforced by the special fund, while retaining the necessary intervention in cases of failure of the self-regulatory mechanisms. Thus, on one hand, the goal of streamlining administration is achieved, promoting further reform in the film industry, allowing the market to revert to market principles, and creating China's own film industry self-regulatory mechanism; on the other hand, it preserves the certainty and authority of the film regulatory mechanism, achieving more effective industry oversight. Therefore, it is recommended to stipulate the following in the supporting regulations:

"The State will establish a Film Promotion Fund based on the National Film Development Special Fund. The Film Promotion Fund Management Committee is responsible for the specific operations of the Film Promotion Fund according to its pre-established charter, promoting the development of the Chinese film industry. The composition of the Film Promotion Fund Committee shall be appointed by the national financial management department and the film regulatory authority, and approved by the State Council. The charter of the Film Promotion Fund shall take effect after approval by the State Council."

"The Film Promotion Fund shall establish its standards for selecting film support projects based on the provisions of Article 36 of the Film Industry Promotion Law and set up an independent evaluation committee to select its film support projects according to previously publicized procedures in a transparent, open, and fair manner."

"When selecting its film support projects, the Film Promotion Fund shall not use the form of enterprise ownership as a substantial standard for project selection."

The Film Industry Promotion Law has two pillars: one is the legislative acknowledge of regulatory measures, and the other is the legislative recognition of facilities that promote the film industry. Blind confidence based solely on current box office market performance, without establishing an effective film industry support system based on the principle of reinvesting in the film industry from screenings or broadcasts, will lead to superficiality and betray the industry's expectations, making it impossible to effectively achieve its legislative purposes. Therefore, it is urgent to establish a legal framework for special funding in the supporting regulations of the Film Industry Promotion Law to provide sufficient space for further film reform and institutional design.

# 5 Conclusion—Digital Cinema?

In China, a capital intensive industry tends to call for more strict regulation from the State. Unfortunately, film industry is the one. Regulation oriented approach is thus the most important aspect of the whole film regulatory or promotional regime in China. Parental minded approach explains the lows or highs of the film industry, if a close analysis is followed on the evolution of the legal framework of the film regulation or promotion in China. Academic observer may provide various suggestions for further reform of the film regulatory regime, for which this book has elaborate in every issue, from film rating to restriction on the remuneration to be claimed by a leading actress/actor, from switching group of the cinema goers to the national film preference...However, if the capital expenditure for film production were to be significantly lowered down to the cost for a song writing, the heavy film regulation may lose its relevance. The radical development of online drama in China may be a perfect example in this regard. Digitalisation of film production, distribution or exhibition may, indeed, at the moment, push up the cost in this three stages for a film to be formed and then exploited. In the long run, the technological breakthrough may release tremendous amount of talents into the industry and significantly reduce the production or even distribution/promotion cost of this film, which may shake the fundamentals of the current film regulatory regime in China as well as in Germany. In this sense, this book may be concluded with an exploration of the development of digitalisation in the film business.

## *5.1 Art Unfolded by Capital*

Starting from the production, copyright law has to take care of the interest of the film producers more than just to rest on the rights of artistic creators. The huge budget involving in a film production in comparison with the other forms of artistic activities forces both the copyright law and the competition law put more emphasis on the interest of the film producers. The financial requst from a film production has partly overridden the creative request from the director and other artists participating in the film production stage. Hollywood majors have consolidated their power in film industry with the help from the liberal copyright system as well as from the permissive policy in US and expanded worldwide. In terms of industry, Hollywood is leading the globalisation of film sector and will push further the liberalisation of film sector worldwide.

The most logical way for the other countries to face this situation within the world trade legal mechanism is to support the culture side of the film in the context of globalisation. However, they may have realised they cannot throw the commercials out of their mind since it is impossible in practice to divide the culture and commercial value in a film.

It is hard for French and other European countries to just follow suit of the trade liberalisation in film sector and to give up the important part of the culture movement experienced in 1968. The films made by authors played revolutionary role in the history of films.[68] Although the concept like "culture exception" has delayed the liberalisation worldwide in audiovisual sector and offered the legitimate ground for various support programs for the national film sector, they is no sign that the national film industries of EU countries and China have been better off substantially. Even US admitted the culture characteristic of films at the first, the predominant position of Hollywood in the world make them eager to hold up their power, should there be one. The mechanisms outside WTO may find an ideal way to deal with the globalisation issue in audiovisual sector. However, without the participation of US, it is doubtful whether it would really work. The culture exception argument gives the other countries just time for preparation, no more.

It is actually a chain. Film making swallows tremendous money, which could only be found in the market if no support measures available. Market requires the films favoured by the mass. Therefore, producers shall make films for the market. Maybe some support measures help the artists to give some special flavour to some films, which is however enjoyed beyond the mainstream market in most cases. No investor can sustain this luxurious hobby without economic return.

High-quality and specialized talent plays a crucial role in the investment, distribution, and screening of films. For film production, collaboration among professionals in planning, screenwriting, production, directing, and acting is essential to complete the filming. In the film distribution phase, professional film distributors need to accurately grasp market demands and feedback, thereby formulating reasonable distribution and promotion strategies and selecting suitable release dates for films. In terms of cinema construction and operation, professional cinema operators have a significant impact on various aspects such as site selection, equipment procurement and operation, film scheduling and promotion, as well as ticket pricing strategies. At present, the number of high-quality professionals in various segments of China's film industry is relatively scarce. There are numerous issues concerning the talent pool, including an unreasonable structure, a severe shortage of specialized talent, a lack of high-level professionals, a need to improve the overall quality of talent, and the urgent need to establish and refine mechanisms for talent growth and incentives. How to attract and build a professional talent team covering the entire industry chain, including investment, distribution, and cinemas, is a critical factor limiting potential entrants to the market.

China's cultural consumption demand has shown significant growth, resulting in a notable driving effect on box office revenue. The number of moviegoers increased

[68] Tanja Nadine Ertel, 44–49.

from 328 million in 2011 to 1.167 billion in 2021, with an average annual compound growth rate of 13.53%. Factors such as the growth of big-budget films, the growing numbers of moviegoers, and the application of new projection technologies had collectively driven the average ticket price up from 30.97 yuan in 2009 to a peak of 36.97 yuan in 2011. Subsequently, with the popularization of advanced projection equipment and the development of online ticketing, ticket prices stabilized and began to decrease. However, due to the impact of new ticket subsidy regulations and cinema price hikes, the average ticket price in the domestic film market has shown a sustained upward trend since 2016, reaching 40.5 yuan in 2021.

With a substantial increase in the number of moviegoers and ticket prices maintained at a high level, China's box office revenue has continued to grow. The domestic box office revenue rose from 13.115 billion yuan in 2011, and to 47.258 billion yuan in 2021, with an average annual compound growth rate of 13.68%. On the other hand, in terms of per capita indicators, both the per capita movie consumption and the per capita number of movie viewings in China have significantly increased. Overall, compared to developed countries like the United States, there is still a gap in terms of the number of moviegoers, per capita viewings, and box office revenue. However, with the ongoing development of the Chinese economy and the transformation of consumption structures, movie consumption demand is expected to maintain a positive growth trend.

## 5.2 *The Revolution Brought About by Digital Technology*

Amidst the blockbusters produced by Hollywood majors, in 1999, a film named *The Blair Witch Project*, which was shot on Super 8 video[69] with a mixture of analogue video and 16 mm film,[70] based on a production budget of USD 35,000, brought in USD 29,207,381 in its wide open weekend in the US on August 1999 and rolled in USD 140,530,114 till 7 November 1999 in the US.[71] The profit return rate reached almost 3,000,000% if the marketing expenses not included. Actually, *The Blair Witch Project* shares the same theme with the digital film *The Last Broadcast* (1998), which was produced with the total cost of USD 900. *The Last Broadcast* was exhibited via satellite download at Cannes and screened at various international film festivals with great acclaim.[72] The legend of *The Blair Witch Project* was made partly via the marketing through the Internet.[73] All these may imply another time for author's film

[69] See Movie Reviews: The Blair Witch Project, downloaded on the 18th, May, 2004 from http://www.imdb.com/title/tt0185937/news.

[70] Wheeler Winston Dixon.

[71] See its business data on http://www.imdb.com/title/tt0185937/business downloaded on the 18th, May, 2004.

[72] Wheeler Winston Dixon.

[73] Ibid. See also Blair Witch Filmmakers Credit the Internet, Blair Witch Changing Movies' Power Structure? Downloaded from http://www.imdb.com/title/tt0185937/news on the 18th, May, 2004.

may come in the near future with the aid of the digital camera and the passions from the amateurs. If to shoot a film is a hobby which costs no more than to paint a picture, what is the point to keep the film producers' power authorised by copyright law and competition law at the price of the autonomy as enjoyed by the authors in the other culture areas? Instead of films, digital film uses data, which can be transferred freely without substantial cost. Then, what is the economic ground for the existence of the distributors and the huge budget for promotion? Even if the work made by a director is a failure, what does it matter? It is just a common hobby, in which capital cannot voice its will as freely as it does in traditional film sector.

On the other hand, digital technology has also made many special effects possible. For instance, in the 2001 film "The English Marquess and the French Lady" released by the French film master Homer, antique oil paintings were embedded into the film using computer technology, enabling the film to achieve an unexpected effect through this ingenious special effect. In the distribution and screening stages, the production and circulation costs of film copies have been greatly reduced through data technology. Digital technology has also greatly enriched the display platforms for films, and the competition among various platforms has become increasingly fierce. The Internet also has a huge impact on the film industry. Cinema will change. The film, in which a drama is on, will live forever.

## 5.3 *The Establishment of Digital Film Standards and Their Impact on the Film Industry*

In 2002, seven Hollywood giants initiated the establishment of the "Digital Cinema Initiative" (DCI), aiming to determine the technical indicators of digital films. Metro-goldwyn-mayer withdrew in 2005. These identified technical indicators were announced in July 2005 and were immediately recognized by the "Society of Motion Picture and Television Engineers" in the United States, which established them as standards. Such standards include compression formats with a resolution of 20481080, the so-called 2k, and JPEG 2000, so that digital cinemas can provide audiences with a higher level of audio-visual enjoyment with the help of new technologies. When the screen span exceeds 15 m, its resolution must reach 40962160, that is, 4k. At present, the International Organization for Standardization is considering designating the technical standards formulated by the Digital Cinema Initiative as international standards that can be independently determined as applicable. The determination of these standards is conducive to the promotion of digital cinema technology worldwide.

If the cost of making a film as a hobby does not exceed the cost of painting a picture, what reason is there to still maintain the highly regarded status of producers in copyright law and competition law and demand that the autonomy enjoyed by authors in other art media give way to it? Unlike traditional film, digital films use digital technology, can be transmitted effortlessly and cost very little at the same time. So, in the traditional sense, what economic justification does the distributor and the large budget invested for promoting the film have? Even if the film created by the director is a complete mess, so what? It was just an ordinary hobby, in which capital might no longer be able to control the elements as it did in traditional films.

In 2001, a five-minute digital film titled Qing Na (similar to the English pronunciation of China) was produced in China and costs RMB 2 million.[74] Zhu Wen, a writer of China, shoot a film, *Seafood,* in 2000 with a production cost nearly RMB 1 million, which was awarded in the 58th Venice Film Festival in 2001.[75] "Art is from amateur." claimed Zhu Wen.[76] This offers best notation for the implications of digital films to the film industry. Via digital camera, film goes into individual creation instead of collective investment, which may wipe off the influence of industry on film making and make the film independent as an artistic work from the media like cinema, TV, internet. Capital has to find its place in the media while arts are released to the individuals. Then, the issue of competition in film industry turns into a general issue to be solved by the media competition law. The concern for culture pluralism becomes unnecessary. The Case Coditel decided by ECJ will be outdated since a film is really like a book or a novel. Private production by authors, private use via internet and DVDs may be the features of the future film. Film company will become the publishing house for the film, instead of the one to produce it. Cinema going may be like today's concert for the classical music or pop songs, which stirs public passion for a short while since people obtain the individual entertainment for the films via DVD, internet or TV most time. Maybe then the quarrel between Hollywood and the film industries in other countries will not be so dramatic.

However, there is also another trend. Filmmakers have invested heavily in building so-called digital cinemas. In August 2003, there were a total of 144 digital cinemas worldwide [MEDIA Salles, European Cinema Year Book, 2003 advance edition]. Among them, the European Union carefully built 16 digital cinemas. However, China has built 34 digital cinemas across the country, second only to the 40 digital cinemas in the United States. But is there really any difference between a digital cinema and a high-definition TV except for the size of the projection screen? Before the birth of digital films, film remained the best mode for film projection with its unparalleled picture quality. If traditional films lose their superiority in terms of picture quality compared to digital films, who can deny that high-definition television is more suitable for the projection of digital films in terms of visual effects? While Europe is still observing, China has already been actively operating in the trend. Which way is wiser? It's very difficult to judge. Although people can have dinner at home, restaurants remain popular dining places. Digital films might free filmmakers from their high budgets. However, a digital cinema may still function as a public place providing services—for which even highly personal digital film viewers cannot resist.

---

[74] Yizhong Li.

[75] Yellow Pavilion Film, The Film Events of China in 2001, dated 27, 12 2001, and downloaded form Cinekino of www.163.com on 5 November 2003.

[76] Yizhong Li.

It is undeniable that the savings in film production and distribution costs brought about by digital technology are only one aspect of its impact on the film industry. In addition to the adoption of digital technology in traditional film production, digital technology also offers the possibility of conducting higher-level audio-visual creation. “Avatar” and the 3D wave it led illustrate this point. Meanwhile, the emergence of a large number of digital films has also put forward requirements for equipment renewal and technical training in the projection industry. The standardization of digital technology has further strengthened it. Therefore, if the costs of film production, distribution and screening are considered as a whole, digital technology may not have significantly reduced the cost of films. On the contrary, the pursuit of audio-visual effects driven by digital technology has instead increased the cost of film shooting and screening, thereby offsetting, if not exceeding, the cost savings of films in other aspects brought about by digital technology. In this way, the threshold for competition in the film industry remains high. Digital Cinema Advocacy is a company jointly established by Hollywood giants in the United States. The standards it designates cover the main technical parameters of digital cinemas and are actually adhered to by the industry. Adhering to these standards means incurring significant cost expenditures in the processes of film production, distribution and screening. The former dominant players in the film market continue to dominate the application of digital technology in the film industry, which fully demonstrates the gap between the possibilities brought about by technological development and the actual market conditions.

Take the European Union as an example. The 2K and 4K projection standards led by the Digital cinema advocacy mean significant investment in film projection facilities. As mentioned earlier, the film screening industry in Europe is also characterized by fragmentation and is relatively small in scale. This puts it at a disadvantage when facing the promotion of digital technology. The financial crisis that broke out in 2008 also had an impact on the European film industry, making the digital predicament of the European film industry more prominent. In the short term, apart from screening 3D films, digital cinemas do not bring profits to European film projectors. In the long term, as digital projectors have a shorter lifespan and more frequent update cycles than traditional 35mm projectors, they increase the equipment update costs of digital cinemas, thereby exerting pressure on the long-term profits of film projectors.

It is worth mentioning the booming 3D film wave in the film industry recently. Although the screening of 3D movies also means a relatively high screening cost, the audience has a strong interest in them. Meanwhile, there is no unified standard for 3D movies at present. Therefore, film projectors can easily achieve a rapid cost recovery from the high ticket prices charged to audiences after installing 3D digital film projection equipment. Moreover, for the content of concerts and sports events, distributors will not have too many requirements for the screening of these contents through 3D cinemas, and 3D digital cinemas will also have some backup content sources. All these are sufficient to ensure that the profits of 3D digital cinemas are still encouraging at present.

## *5.4 The Impact of Digital Technology on the Film Screening Market and Its Legal Significance*

The development of digital technology in the film industry has also made the protection and utilization of film heritage a problem. Under the trend of digital transformation of films, it is necessary to update the mandatory film archiving requirements through legal measures in line with the development of digital technology, so as to cover films produced in all forms. To this end, standards need to be established, specifying the criteria for submitting archived digital films and their retention. If it is stipulated that digital films must be archived, then film archives and other institutions specializing in archiving films need to store and retain the digital materials containing digital films for a long time. For this reason, film archives and other institutions that archive films need to conduct research on them, update the relevant equipment and train the relevant talents. All of this means incurring considerable cost expenditures. Meanwhile, film archives and other institutions that archive films also need to be equipped with relevant digital film projection equipment in order to utilize the film heritage in digital form. All of this requires the government to provide financial support and establish relevant standards for film projection equipment that utilizes digital forms of film heritage.

In the process of transforming traditional cinemas into digital cinemas, a unique financing model is relied on. Its typical financing business model was established by the six Hollywood giants that advocated and determined digital cinema technology through digital cinema: the "Virtual Print Fee" (VPF) model. Under the VPF model, film distributors generally sign long-term contracts with so-called integrators. Integrators provide financing to purchase digital film equipment and collect capital contributions from film distributors to cover part or all of the expenses incurred by providing financing on behalf of film projectors for the purchase of digital film equipment. In this way, when digital film distributors first screened digital films in cinemas through the VPF protocol, they enabled the integrators to recover their investment by paying "virtual copy fees" to the integrators. At present, digital cinemas mainly rely on the VPF model to obtain commercial financing. All the Hollywood giants have distributed digital films by signing VPFS, and other digital film distributors have now begun to follow suit. Obviously, this model will not provide financing for those independent and small cinemas or art cinemas, and these cinemas have a very weak ability to obtain the necessary financial support to update their projection equipment. If left unchecked, the decline of independent small cinemas or art cinemas will have an extremely adverse impact on the development and prosperity of a country's film industry, the cultivation of film talents, and the creation of film culture. Therefore, during the transition stage from traditional cinemas to digital cinemas, government intervention is truly necessary.

China has drawn up an ambitious blueprint for promoting digital cinemas nationwide. But at the same time, China still insists that the BFA needs to approve the production of digital films.[77] An ambitious blueprint for the future of the film industry is equipped with outdated regulatory concepts. Do Chinese filmmakers need to rethink this? Perhaps it is needed, and it is a very urgent need.

Meanwhile, the development of digital cinemas has also had a huge impact on the shooting and production of Chinese films. Digital films are developing rapidly. If before "Avatar" was introduced to the Chinese market, digital films mainly reflected in the cost savings during the distribution and screening stages, the box office miracle of "Avatar" has promoted the digitalization of Chinese film production. This has led to the increasing application of digital technology in the production of domestic films, enhancing their visual impact. Some films have attempted to use 3D digital shooting and digital production technologies and have achieved good market performance. For example: In 2010, as a commercial film positioned as a disaster movie, the IMAX version of "The Great Earthquake of Tangshan" performed strongly at the box office, with an average box office of over 1 million yuan per screen.[78]

Based on the outstanding performance of digital films in the film market and the fact that digital cinemas have become an important means for the upgrading of film markets in various countries around the world, the National Film Special Fund Office issued the "Notice on Subsidizing the Installation of 2K and 1.3 Digital Projection Equipment in Cinemas" at the end of December 2009, encouraging cinemas to install digital screens and super-large screens. Since then, the digitalization of cinemas has developed rapidly, and digital cinemas have basically formed a digital projection market application system of different grades such as 2K, 1.3K and 0.8K.[79]

The digital development trend of cinemas has further promoted the digital development of film shooting and production. In terms of shooting, film and digital shooting coexist at present, but the proportion of films shot digitally is constantly increasing, and the quality has also reached a new level. In 2011, films including "The Thirteen Orphans of Nanjing" were shot with digital technology or mixed with film. Correspondingly, the application of 4K film production technology has accelerated, and 4K digital camera systems have been launched and their application has been expedited.

The above explanation indicates that the development of digital cinemas in China has also promoted the development of film production and manufacturing, and injected vitality into the development of China's film industry. Cinemas will change. The movies that present us with good shows will live forever.

---

[77] Article 5 of the Interim Provisions on the Administration of Digital Films issued by the SARFT on 7 August 2002.

[78] Development Research Center of the State Administration of Radio, Film and Television: "Report on the Development of China's Radio, Film and Television (2011)", p. 96, Social Sciences Academic Press, 2011.

[79] Ibid.

# Bibliography


Bakker, G. (2003, February). *Decline and Fall of the European Film Industry: Sunk Costs, Market Size and Market Structure, 1890–1927*. Retrieved from May 10, 2004, from http://www2.warwick.ac.uk/fac/soc/economics/news/2002/summer2002/papers/bakkerabstract.pdf

BBC MMII. (2003). Hollywood, Inc., Documentary Series Produced and Directed by Philip Day.

Bernier, I. (2003). *Local Content Requirements for Film, Radio, and Television as a Means of Protecting Cultural Diversity: Theory and Reality*. Retrieved from May 3, 2004, from www.mcc.gouv.qc.ca/international/diversite-culturelle/eng/pdf/update031112section1.pdf

Beviglia Zampetti, A. (2003). *WTO Rules in the Audio-Visual Sector*. Hamburgisches Welt-Wirtschafts-Archiv (HWWA), Hamburg Institute of International Economics. Retrieved from May 3, 2004, from http://www.hwwa.de/

Cheng, K. (2003). *Bureau of Film is Drafting Film Law*. Retrieved from November 5, 2003, from www.yzwb.com.cn/shzb/20000713/GB/shzb%5E235%5E4%5Esh13b003.htm

Cocq, E., & Messerlin, P. (2003). *The French Audiovisual Policy: Impact and Compatibility with Trade Negotiations*. Hamburgisches Welt-Wirtschafts-Archiv (HWWA), Hamburg Institute of International Economics. Retrieved from May 3, 2004, from http://www.hwwa.de/

Cowen, T. (2001, Summer/Fall). Why Hollywood Rules the World (and Should We Care?) in Correspondence, an International View of Culture and Society (Issue No. 8). Retrieved from May 3, 2004, from http://www.cfr.org/pdf/correspondence/CORRSum01.pdf

Ding. G. (1996). *Producing More Excellent Works to Prosper the Film Industry*, in China Film Yearbook 1996, Beijing: China Film Press, 1997 edition, (p. 8).

Ding, X. (2003, July 4). *Two Pieces of Hair, Which Style?* Nanfang Dushi Bao.

Dixon, W. W. (2001). Twenty-Five Reasons Why It's All Over. In J. Lewis (Ed.), *The End of Cinema, As We Know It* (p. 356).

Dörfler, H. (1999). Bilanzierung bei Eigen- und Auftragsproduktionen sowie bei der Filmförderung. In J. Becker & M. Schwarz (Hrsg.), *Aktuelle Rechtsprobleme der Filmproduktion und Filmlizenz* (p. 7).

Doyle, G., & Hibberd, M. (2003). *Competition, Cultural Variety and Global Governance: The Case of the UK Audiovisual System*. Retrieved from May 3, 2004, from http://www.hwwa.de/

Elaesser, T. (2001). The Blockbuster. In J. Lewis (Ed.), *The End of Cinema, as We Know It* (p. 11).

Ertel, T. N. (1999). *Globalisierung der Filmwirtschaft*.

Fan, L. (2003, May). Film Reform and the Magic of Cinema Circuits. *China's Culture Newspaper*. Retrieved from November 23, 2003, from http://www.filmsea.com/focus/200401070028.htm

Fei, W. (2002, August 1). The Commission for Economics and Trade Is Busying of Assessing and Amending the Draft Anti-Monopoly Law. *People's Daily*.

Frau-Meigs, D. (2002). *"Cultural Exception", National Policies and Globalisation: Imperatives in Democratisation and Promotion of Contemporary Culture*. Retrieved from May 3, 2004, from www.audiovisualcat.net/publicationsing/Q14france.pdf


© Social Sciences Academic Press 2026

J. Wu, *Legal Mechanisms for Film Financing and Support in China*,
https://doi.org/10.1007/978-981-95-0922-5

Graber, C. B. (2003). *Handel und Kultur im Audiovisionsrecht der WTO.*

Graber, C. B. (2004). *Audiovisual Policy: The Stumbling Block of Trade Liberalisation?* Retrieved from November 18, 2003, from www.unilu.ch/rf/4949.htm

Goyder, D. G. (1998). *EC Competition Law* (3rd ed.). Oxford University Press, Oxford 1999.

Guo, Y. (2002, April 27). Difficult to Say Good-Bye to Monopoly—Disclosure of the Game Rules of China's Film Industry. *Caijing Magazine*

Gyory, M. (2002). Filmproduktion und -verleihen in Europa: Die Bestimmung Des Herstellungslandes. In *Kooperation mit und im Auftrag von der Europäischen Audiovisuellen Informationsstelle.* Retrieved from April 30, 2004, from http://www.obs.coe.int/online_publication/reports/natfilm.html

Hancock, D. (1998). Global film production. In Working document for Venice Conference held by EURO-MEI (pp. 29–30). Retrieved from May 3, 2004, from www.obs.coe.int/oea_publ/eurocine/global_filmproduction.pdf.en

Herold, A. *European Public Film Support Within the WTO Framework.* IRIS Plus (Issue 2003–6). Retrieved from May 3, 2004, from www.obs.coe.int/oea_publ/iris/iris_plus/iplus6_2003.pdf.en

Hong Kong Film Industry Association (2009). *The Overall Situation of the Hong Kong Film Market in 2009*, January 2, 2010.

Jiang, S. (2004, April 26). Age of 16 Will Be A Standard, The Rating Rules Is In Draft. *Wenhui Bao.*

Jiang, W. (2004). *Draft of Film Development Law to Take Shape in May.* Retrieved from April 20, 2004, from http://news.sohu.com/2004/03/22/93/news219529333.shtml

Konvitz, J. S. (2004, May). Independent Wealth. *Los Angeles Lawyer* (Vol. 27).

Legal Practices Institute of the Supreme Court of China. (2000). *Edited Cases of People's Court* (IP Volume, 1st ed.).

Lewis, J. (2001). The end of cinema as we know it and I feel. Pluto Press: London. New York University Press, New York

Li, H. (2003, August 9). *A Gradually Industrialized China's Film—The Roadmap of a Blockbuster, South Weekly.* Retrieved from May 3, 2004, from http://medianet.qianlong.com/7692/2003/08/09/33@1530482.htm

Liu, Y. Mengjia, L. *Research on the Financing Legal Issues of China's Film Industry——From the Perspective of the Article Fortieth of Film Industry Promotion Act of People's Republic of China,* in Journal of Beijing Union University (Humanities and Social Sciences) Vol. 56, p. 106.

Li, Y. (2003, October 17). *The Situation and Opportunities of the Development of China's Digital Audiovisual Industry.* The Network of Media Academic Studies.

Li, Z. To Be or Not To Be—Reform of China's Film Industry. *China's Newsweek.* Retrieved from February 5, 2004, from http://www.filmsea.com/focus/200401070030.htm

Liu, J. (2002). Negotiation for Access to WTO and Our Commitment to Film Market. In Z. Q. Zhang & Y. Yang (Eds.), *China's Film and WTO* (p. 3).

Lowe, P. (2004). Media Concentration & Convergence: Competition in Communications Speech as delivered on the 13th, January, 2004 on Oxford Media Convention 2004. Retrieved from May 1, 2004, from http://europa.eu.int/comm/competition/speeches/text/sp2004_002_en.pdf

Lü, X. (2002). The Important Topic for Film Reform—Some Thoughts for the Change of Government's Function. In Z. Q. Zhang & Y. Yang (Eds.), *China's Film and WTO* (p. 231).

Macnab, G. (2013). *J. Arthur Rank and the British film industry.* Routledge.

Martel, F. (2001, Summer/Fall). *France's Film Subsidy System, in Correspondence, an International View of Culture and Society* (Issue No. 8). Retrieved from May 3, 2004, from http://www.cfr.org/pdf/correspondence/CORRSum01.pdf

Maule, C. Rhetoric and Reality—The Debate over Trade and Culture, the 21st, January, 2002 draft. Retrieved from May 3, 2004, from http://www.carleton.ca/economics/cep/cep02-02.pdf

Meng, L. (2001). *The Combination of Principle and Flexibility,* in Film Art, Issue 4, 2001, pp. 9–10.

Olsberg|SPI, KEA European Affairs, & KPMG. (2003, May). *Empirical Study on the Practice of the Rating of Films Distributed in Cinemas Television DVD and Videocassettes in the EU and*

*EEA Member States, on Behalf of the European Commission.* Retrieved from April 30, 2003, from http://europa.eu.int/comm/avpolicy/stat/studpdf/rating_final_report.pdf
Orbach, B. Y., & Einav, L. (2007). Uniform prices for differentiated goods: The case of the movie-theater industry. *International Review of Law and Economics, 27*(2), 129–153
Kamina, P. (2016). *Film copyright in the European Union* (Vol. 33). Cambridge University Press.
Pereira, M. M. (2002, April 23). *EU Competition Law, Convergence, and the Media Industry.* Speech for Law Society of England and Wales, London. Retrieved from November 23, 2003, from http://europa.eu.int/comm/competition/speeches/text/sp2002_016_en.pdf
Reber, N. (2002). *Film Copyright, Contracts and Profit Participation.* Wiley VCH Verlag.
Rehbinder, M. (2002). *Urheberrecht* (12th ed.). Beck Juristische Verlag, München.
Ren, Z. (2002). Preparing a Breakthrough When Facing the Challenge. In Z. Q. Zhang & Y. Yang (Eds.), *China's Film and WTO* (p. 79).
Senti, R. (2001). *WTO Die Neue Welthandelsordnung nach der Uruguay- runde* (3. Auflage).
Shen, S. (2002, June 17). Dream Industry Crashes Monopoly. *Economy Observer.*
Shen, Y. (2005). The Beginning and End of the Creation of the New Chinese Film Industry (1949-1957), in Contemporary Film, No. 4.
Shibazhang, X. *The Situation of HK's Film.* Retrieved from October 29, 2003, from http://www.filmsea.com.cn/focus/200301030044.htm
Tang, R. (2008). *'The reform of the film system in the 30 years of reform and opening up and its impact on Chinese cinema'*, in Film Bureau of the State Administration of Radio, Film and Television, China Film Art Research Centre, Film Channel Programme Centre (eds.), Reform and Opening Up and 30 Years of Chinese Cinema, China FilmPress, pp. 474–75
Tang R. (2009). *A Study on the Reform of China's Film System in the 30 Years Since Reform and Opening Up [J].* Modern Communication-Journal of Communication University of China, (02): 5-9
Tang, R. (2010). *Financial Innovation and Film Growth*, in Cui Baoguo, ed. Media Blue Book: 2010: Report on the Development of China's Media Industry, Social Science Literature Press, pp. 299–311.
Toubiana, S. (2001, Summer/Fall). Paradoxical French Cinema, in Correspondence, an International View of Culture and Society (Issue No. 8). Retrieved from May 3, 2004, from http://www.cfr.org/pdf/correspondence/CORRSum01.pdf
Unternährer, R. (2003). *Kinofilmverwertung in der Schweiz.* Schulthess Verlag, Zürich.
Vogel, H. L.(2011). *Entertainment Industry Economics, A Guide for Financial Analysis*, 8th Ed., New York: Cambridge University Press 2011.
Weber, R. H. (1995). *Medienkonzentration und Meinungspluralismus.* Schulthess Verlag, Zürich.
Weber, R. H., Unternährer, R., & Zulauf, R. (2003). *Schweizerisches Filmrecht.* Schulthess Verlag, Zürich.
Wei, Z. (1998). *Copyright Law of China.*
Westcott, T. *Public Funding for the Film and Audiovisual Sector in November 2003.* Retrieved from April 23, 2004, from http://www.obs.coe.int
Ying, H. (2002). *General Situation of the National Film Industry in China.* Retrieved from November 12, 2003, from http://www.chuanmei.net
Yu, L. (2006). *Studies in the Professional History of Chinese Cinema: Film Production, Distribution and Projection*, China Film Press, Beijing.
Yin, H. (2002~2003). *Chinese Film Industry Memo (Part I) [J].* Film Art, 2004, (02): 4–8
Zhai, X. (2002, January 1). A Opened Door for Private Capital. *Xinwen Wanbao Newspaper.*
Zhan, Q. The Multinationals are Operating with Monopoly? Relevant Enterprises Defending Themselves. *Beijing Youth Newspaper*, the Issue of the 28th, May, 2004
Zhang, X. (2002). *History of the Banned Films in China after 1990.* Retrieved from December 23rd, 2002, from www.tom.com
ZHI, W. (1998). *Copyright Law of China*, Peking University Press, Beijing.
Zhu, Y. D. (2003). *Chinese Cinema During the Era of Reform.*

Zhu, Y. (2002). *Challenge in the Reality*. In Z. Q. Zhang & Y. Yang (Eds.), *China's Film and WTO* (p. 19).

MIX
Papier aus verantwortungsvollen Quellen
Paper from responsible sources
FSC® C105338

If you have any concerns about our products,
you can contact us on
**ProductSafety@springernature.com**

In case Publisher is established outside the EU,
the EU authorized representative is:
**Springer Nature Customer Service Center GmbH**
**Europaplatz 3, 69115 Heidelberg, Germany**

Printed by Libri Plureos GmbH
in Hamburg, Germany